A SOVIET HERETIC: ESSAYS BY
Yevgeny Zamyatin

Yevgeny Zamyatin

A SOVIET HERETIC: ESSAYS BY
Yevgeny Zamyatin
EDITED AND TRANSLATED BY MIRRA GINSBURG

The University of Chicago Press   Chicago & London

Евгений Замятин

Standard Book Number: 226–97865–6
Library of Congress Catalog Card Number: 71–94104

The University of Chicago Press, Chicago 60637
The University of Chicago Press, Ltd., London

What we need in literature today are vast philosophic horizons;
. . . we need the most ultimate, the most fearsome, the most
fearless "Why?" and "What next?"

"On Literature, Revolution, Entropy,
and Other Matters"

In art the surest way to destroy is to canonize one given form
and one philosophy.

"The New Russian Prose"

CONTENTS

3. The Writer's Craft

4. Eight Writers and One Painter

5. Two Letters

ILLUSTRATIONS

Portraits by Yury Annenkov

INTRODUCTION:
ZAMYATIN THE CRITIC

Until recently Yevgeny Ivanovich Zamyatin was known in the West primarily as the author of *We,* an anti-Utopian novel that first appeared in English translation in 1924 but has yet to be published in the Soviet Union, where it was written in 1920 and 1921. With the publication of *The Dragon* (New York, 1966), a collection of fifteen stories translated by Mirra Ginsburg, Zamyatin's accomplishments as a master stylist and narrator became accessible to the American reading public. The present collection of essays in translation reveals hitherto unexplored but intrinsically important areas of Zamyatin's creative art: those of critic, essayist, memoirist, and lecturer.

A schoolteacher's son, Zamyatin was born on February 1, 1884, in the small provincial town of Lebedyan, which overlooked the River Don some two hundred miles south of Moscow and was known for its swindlers, gypsies, horsefairs, and robust Russian speech. Despite the local color, Zamyatin found life in the provinces gray and monotonous—a theme that recurred throughout his early fiction. In 1902 he enrolled at the Saint Petersburg Polytechnic Institute and was immediately caught up in the capital's ferment. He joined the Bolshevik party, took part in the Revolution of 1905, was imprisoned and exiled, but returned illegally to continue his studies at the institute. He graduated as a naval engineer in 1908, and was retained by the institute.

Although the next three years were devoted to shipbuilding, he did find time to write and publish his first two stories, "Alone" (1908) and "The Girl" (1910), which deservedly passed without notice. In 1911 the forced inactivity of renewed exile enabled him to begin writing *A Provincial Tale* (published in 1913), his first major work, which brought him immediate literary fame. Reprieved in the general amnesty of political prisoners on the tercentenary of the Romanov dynasty in 1913, Zamyatin again took up shipbuilding and in March 1916 was commissioned to supervise the construction of Russian icebreakers in England. A year and a half later, he returned to Petersburg in time to witness the October Revolution and thereafter devoted all his energies to writing and to related literary activities. In addition to holding various administrative positions on the executive councils of literary groups such as the Union of Practitioners of Imaginative Literature, the All-Russian Union of Writers, the House of the Arts, and the House of Writers, Zamyatin lectured on the craft of fiction in the literary studios of the House of the Arts and the World Literature Publishing House. His editorial activities included work on three journals—*Dom iskusstv* [House of the arts, 1921], *Sovremenny zapad* [Contemporary West, 1922–24], and *Russky sovremennik* [Russian contemporary, 1924]—as well as the coeditorship, with Korney Chukovsky, of World Literature's English section. During this post-revolutionary period Zamyatin was widely recognized as one of the leading figures in Russian literature; some Soviet critics considered him to be on a par with Gorky and Bely in stature and influence. Continued attacks on Zamyatin throughout the twenties by Communist critics who had no taste for his "pernicious" ideology culminated in a defamatory campaign which ostracized him from Soviet literature in the autumn of 1929. The ostensible, although somewhat belated reason for the attack on Zamyatin had been the publication of his novel *We* in the Russian émigré journal *Volya Rossii* [The will of Russia] in Prague during the spring of 1927. In fact, both Zamyatin and his fellow victim Pilnyak were simply the scapegoats in the government's drive to divest the All-Russian Union of Writers of its apolitical stance and to press all writers into the service of socialist reconstruction. Through Gorky's intercession, Zamyatin obtained permission to go abroad, and in November 1931 he and his wife left the Soviet Union, never to return. His years in exile were spent in Paris, where he remained aloof from Russian émigré circles. He died on March 10, 1937.

Traditionally some of Russia's most astute and articulate critics have themselves been writers. Zamyatin is a case in point. The style and imagery of his critical essays are often equal to those of his highly polished prose fiction, while his ironic wit is given even freer—and more direct—rein. The reader of Zamyatin's essays sees and hears the writer who in his fiction has deliberately concealed himself behind an objective narrative or a fictional narrator. In this respect, the essays provide an important key to understanding Zamyatin the writer.

Zamyatin was a highly conscious craftsman. His finely honed "Backstage" is perhaps the best single summary of his ideas on the writer's creative process. In addition to providing a valuable insight into the writer's psychology at the moment of creation and the specific catalysts which precipitated certain works, Zamyatin skillfully elaborates his conception of prose rhythm (based on logical, not syllabic stress), of visual leitmotivs, of integrating images, and of the very important process of rewriting and polishing the finished product. His emphasis on the role of the writer's unconscious was decried as "false and pernicious bourgeois ideology" by Soviet critics and was subjected to violent criticism in 1931 during the extensive discussions of creative method in writing, which took place in Leningrad and Moscow literary organizations. His lectures on the craft of fiction, "The Psychology of Creative Work," "Theme and Plot," and "Language" contain many pregnant ideas whose intrinsic significance rivals their elucidation of Zamyatin's intent and goals in his own fiction. The lecture "Contemporary Russian Literature," which was delivered at the People's University of Lebedyan on September 8, 1918, stands apart from the others in that it combines a formalistic analysis of style with a historical application of Hegel's dialectical process. The resultant definition of the Neorealistic movement in Russian fiction (which Zamyatin elsewhere calls *Synthetism*) represents his major contribution in the area of literary history and even today remains basic to any consideration of early twentieth-century Russian prose fiction.

Zamyatin's reminiscences, which were usually occasioned by the death of a literary acquaintance, are characterized by a subdued eulogistic tone and a highly personal approach. The essays on Kustodiev and Gorky convey great warmth and affection. The reminiscences about Blok, Kustodiev, Bely, and Gorky, with their direct, personal approach and lucid, unconstrained style, high-light a few salient characteristics and incidents, infusing our image of these men with the fresh breath of life. Rather different in character is Zamyatin's brief and controversial appreciation of Anatole France. Himself an ironist of note, Zamyatin was very much attracted by France's irony, skepticism, and relativism; and, true to his predilection for polarity, he extravagantly juxtaposed France and Leo Tolstoy (with his absolutism and faith) as the two contrasting peaks of French and Russian cultures. It is significant that Anatole France symbolized to Zamyatin that peculiar European quality of satiric irony which he felt to be lacking in Russian literature and hoped to contribute with his own works. In this respect, the obituary on France is more closely related to Zamyatin's programmatic essays than to his reminiscences.

A third type of essay evolved in connection with his activities for the World Literature Publishing House, for which he edited fifteen volumes, including works by H. G. Wells, Jack London, G. B. Shaw, O. Henry, Upton Sinclair, and Romain Rolland. His introductory essays were, by and large, intended for the general Russian reader unfamiliar with modern European literature—hence their rather limited scope. Nonetheless, they frequently were revealing of Zamyatin's own artistic inclinations and criteria. His excellent introduction to a collection of O. Henry's stories included an astute formalistic analysis of style and structure in the manner of his lectures on the craft of fiction and revealed his growing interest in plot dynamism, which became apparent in his own ironic short stories of the twenties. But undoubtedly his slender brochure on H. G. Wells, which was published in 1922 after he had written half a dozen different introductions to separate volumes of Wells, marked the zenith of his achievement in this vein. Displaying a far-ranging grasp of Wells's entire literary output and of the utopian literary tradition in general, Zamyatin succeeded in creating one of the best critical summations of Wells's novels, both fantastic and realistic. Many prominent features such as the combination of fantasy with a scientific base, the recurrent appeal to the humanistic tradition, the use of the future to mirror social ills of the present, the hatred of philistin-ism, the vision of our world from a new "aeroplanar" perpective —all these and more, found fertile ground in Zamyatin's critical essays as well as in his dystopia *We.*

Zamyatin's most stimulating writing, however, is to be found in his finely wrought programmatic essays and polemical criticisms of contemporary Russian literature. Giving full rein to clever irony and penetrating wit, Zamyatin skillfully derides all that is trite while encouraging the original. His romantic philosophy, which he continued propounding in the face of increasing hostility, remains especially relevant today in a world of growing pressures for conformity. Zamyatin began his career as a critic in 1914 with three reviews in V. S. Mirolyubov's *Yezhemesyachnuy zhurnal* [Monthly journal]. Although of no great intrinsic value, these reviews eloquently reveal his inclination for a polished style and extended comparisons, which create an artistic unity far superior to those of the standard review. His first significant polemical essay, ostensibly a review of the Scythian group's second literary miscellany, was appropriately entitled "Scythians?" and appeared in 1918 under the pseudonym Mikhail Platonov. Himself a member of the group, Zamyatin challenged the statement of its leader, the literary critic and historian R. Ivanov-Razumnik, that the spiritual revolutionary "works for the near or distant future." Unequivocally rejecting the middle-of-the-road conjunction "or," Zamyatin argued that the true Scythian works "*only* for the distant future, never for the near future, and never for the present. Hence to him there is but one way—Golgotha—and no other; and but one conceivable victory—to be crucified—and no other." In Zamyatin's view, the true revolutionary devoted his life to an endless seeking that promised no attainment, for to realize an idea meant to philistinize it. In short, he had to be an uncompromising heretic who stood isolated from the mass of the philistines and, by rejecting the present in the name of the distant future, ensured man's never ending progress in the face of ubiquitous philistinism. Zamyatin also expressed his faith in brotherly love, in a humanism that would establish universal peace among men (hence the warmth of his appreciation of Wellsian humanism).

"Scythians?" proved to be of paramount importance in Zamyatin's work, for it formed the philosophic nucleus not only of all future essays, but of his philosophic chef d'oeuvre as well—the novel *We*. In "Tomorrow" Zamyatin reaffirmed the heretic's role in effecting the cruel but wise law of never ending dissatisfaction, onto which he grafted the Hegelian dialectic of thesis (yesterday), antithesis (today), and synthesis (tomorrow). He also asserted his faith in the written word as the sole means worthy of man in seeking to achieve human progress, an idea which found new form in Zamyatin's championing of satire as the antidote to philistinism in his lecture delivered at the celebration of the fortieth anniversary of Fyodor Sologub's literary activity (hence the eulogistic tone, which is more reminiscent of Zamyatin's necrologies than of his critical articles). The essay "I Am Afraid," in which Zamyatin attacked the growth of conformity spawned by nimble authors who slavishly followed changing political winds, provided Soviet critics and literary historians with several pithy quotations which they delighted in pointing to as examples of Zamyatin's aberrant "bourgeois individualism." They were especially incensed by such statements as: "The Proletcult art is at present a step backward to the 1860s"; "Real literature can be created only by madmen, hermits, heretics, dreamers, rebels, and skeptics, not by diligent and trustworthy functionaries"; and Zamyatin's closing sentence, "I am afraid that the only future possible to Russian literature is its past." Similar ideas are developed in "Paradise," where Zamyatin ridicules the "majestic, monumental, and all-encompassing unanimity" of the proletarian poets, which results in gray, monophonic banality, and in "The Day and the Age," where a distinction is made between the topical literature and nimble authors, which lives only for today, and the truly contemporary literature that lives for an entire age.

A notable portion of Zamyatin's essays of the twenties was devoted to the development of his conceptions of the energy-entropy dichotomy on a sociophilosophical level and of Synthetism in contemporary Russian literature. While writing his fascinating biography of the founding father of modern thermodynamic theory, Julius Robert von Mayer,[1] Zamyatin was undoubtedly struck by the analogy between Mayer's thermodynamic concept of entropy ("the tendency of the universe's energy toward rest—toward death") and his own conception of human society as reflected in *The Islanders* (1918) and "The North" (1922, written in 1918), where the universal tendency toward philistinism and spiritual death corresponded to entropy,

[1] This biography was not included in the present volume both because of its length and because it bears only tangentially on the main subject of this collection—literature.—EDITOR

while solar energy (Mayer's energy source corresponded to Zamyatin's symbolism) stimulated the ardent passions, spiritual or corporeal, which disrupted the tendency toward a lukewarm philistine equilibrium. The philosophic conception of energy and entropy became the central thesis in *We,* where the heroine I-330 states that "There are two powers in the world—entropy and energy. One leads to blissful rest, to a happy equilibrium; the other—to the destruction of equilibrium; to a tormentingly endless movement." In October 1923, probably under the stimulus of an unusual essay on solar energy published in the *Atlantic Monthly* (May 1923) by the British physicist and physiologist Frank C. Eve, Zamyatin summarized all his basic philosophical thinking in a brilliant essay entitled "On Literature, Revolution, Entropy, and Other Matters." Eve, in analyzing the basic motive power of life itself in physical terms of an energy flow to a lower potential, essentially removed the distinction between organic and inorganic chemistry. Entranced by the scientific extension of physical (thermodynamic) concepts to biology (life itself), Zamyatin went a step further and extended the concepts of energy and entropy to the social sciences and philosophy. Conversely, he extended sociophilosophic concepts, such as revolution, to the physical and biological sciences.

> Revolution is everywhere, in everything. It is infinite. There is no final revolution, no final number. The social revolution is only one of an infinite number of numbers: the law of revolution is not a social law, but an immeasuraby greater one. It is a cosmic, universal law—like the laws of the conservation of energy and of the dissipation of energy (entropy). Someday, an exact formula for the law of revolution will be established. And in this formula, nations, classes, stars—and books—will be expressed as numerical quantities.

But the essence of Zamyatin's philosophy, although cast in a new scientific form, had not changed appreciably from that expressed five years earlier in his essay on the Scythians.

Synthetism, a legacy of the Hegelian dialectic which Zamyatin used synonymously with Neorealism, received its greatest elaboration in his essay on the art and graphics of Yury Annenkov. Equally applicable to Zamyatin's own literary work, Synthetism in literature signified a compressed style, the union of fantasy and reality, Impressionism, and a significant philosophic synthesis that looked to the future, for true Realism consists in the distortion of "objective" reality. The same concepts underlay Zamyatin's extensive survey of contemporary fiction ("The New Russian Prose"), in which he rejected the proletarian return to pre-revolutionary analytical Realism in favor of formal experimentation and artistic synthesis. His final review of Russian literature of the 1920s, included in "Moscow-Petersburg," lacks the polemical verve of his earlier essays due to its retrospective character and foreign audience (it was written in France), but its calm tone in no way minimizes the sensitive perception of Zamyatin the critic and historian.

The legacy of Zamyatin the critic is no less significant than that of Zamyatin the writer. The American reader is fortunate in gaining access to nearly all of Zamyatin's important critical works, for he can now judge for himself the extent of Zamyatin's contribution to Russian literature.

ALEX M. SHANE

University of California at Davis

EDITOR'S PREFACE

Yevgeny Zamyatin the critic and teacher was probably as influential in Soviet literature of the 1920s as Zamyatin the writer of fiction.

A consummate craftsman, he was enormously concerned with the problems of craft. But he was also a thoroughly "engaged" writer, equally involved with the problem of the artist in society —a problem, as he saw it, both political and philosophic. He had an extraordinary sense of time, of the constant flow and flux of history. And it was perhaps his refusal to accept the absolute— as well as the romantic humanist values he refused to abandon —that brought him into sharpest conflict with the absolutist regime.

These informal essays, many of them written in the heat of battle, reflect a time when conflict of ideas was still possible in Communist Russia, even if dissent was becoming increasingly dangerous.

Always lucid, always witty, original, courageous, merciless to cant and warmly generous, the essays are a portrait of an epoch and a portrait of a man and an artist. Yet because the conflict of the period was so fundamental, because it still persists, in Russia and elsewhere, and because Zamyatin's thought always rose above the specifics of the moment, the essays retain a great deal of their freshness and validity today.

I owe a great debt of gratitude to Professor Alex M. Shane, author of an excellent study, *The Life and Works of Evgenij Zamjatin,* for his gracious consent to write an introduction to the present volume and his unstinting help in its preparation. He generously supplied me with bibliographic data and the texts of a number of essays which are not easily available (particularly "Scythians?" "Paradise" and *"Gryadushchaya Rossiya,"* signed by the pseudonym of Mikhail Platonov). For this, both the reader and I owe him thanks.

Warm thanks are also due to Yury Annenkov and the Inter-Language Literary Associates for permission to use the magnificent portraits which illustrate this volume.

I am grateful to Possev Verlag, publishers of *Grani,* for permission to translate the essays "Contemporary Russian Literature" and "The Psychology of Creative Works."

I also wish to thank Roman Goul, editor of *Novy zhurnal,* for permission to translate "Moscow-Petersburg," "Theme and Plot," and "On Language."

The largest number of essays included here appeared in the collection *Litsa,* published in 1955 by the Chekhov Publishing House in New York. I am grateful to the National Board of Young Men's Christian Associations, present owners of legal rights to books published by the Chekhov Publishing House, for permission to use them.

I am especially grateful to the National Translation Center of Austin, Texas, for the grant which made it possible for me to do the extensive research required in the preparation of this volume.

And, finally, warm thanks are due to Gunther Stuhlmann, my agent and friend, for his unfailing encouragement and good advice.

ЕВГЕНИЙ ЗАМЯТИН

AUTOBIOGRAPHY

And so you insist on my autobiography. But you will have to content yourself with a purely external view, with perhaps a fleeting glance into darkened windows: I rarely invite anyone to come inside. And from the outside you will not see much.

You will see a very lonely child, without companions of his own age, on the sofa, on his stomach, over a book, or under the piano, on which his mother is playing Chopin. Two steps away from Chopin, and you are in the midst of provincial life: windows with geraniums, a piglet tied to a stake, in the middle of the street, and hens bathing in the dust. If you want geography, it's this: Lebedyan, the most Russian of towns, in Tambov Province—a town about which Tolstoy and Turgenev wrote. Time: end of the 1880s, early 1890s. After that, Voronezh, *gimnaziya,* boarding school, boredom, mad dogs at Bolshaya Dvoryanskaya. One of them nipped my leg. I was very fond at that time of experimenting with myself, and I decided to wait and see—would I, or would I not go mad? But the main thing was curiosity—what would I feel when the incubation period (two weeks after the bite) was over and I started going mad? I felt a great deal but did not develop rabies. Therefore I declared to the school authorities that I was rabid and was promptly shipped off to Moscow for inoculations.

At school I received marks of Excellent on compositions but

In the early 1920s much stress was laid in Soviet Russia on the biographies of writers, and numerous autobiographical sketches, written in response to questionnaires, were published in periodicals, collections, and as prefaces to volumes of the given author's works.—Editor was not always on easy terms with mathematics. This was perhaps why (out of stubbornness) I chose the most mathematical of professions, naval engineering, which I studied at the Saint Petersburg Polytechnic Institute. Thirteen years ago in May (snow fell on the flowers that May) I finished my qualifying projects in engineering and my first story. The story was published then and there in the old *Obrazovaniye* [Education]. Well, then, this meant that I could write stories and get them published. Hence, for the next three years, I wrote—about icebreakers, about motorships, about "Theoretical Investigations into the Functioning of Dredges." This had to be: I was retained as an instructor in the Department of Naval Architecture of the Shipbuilding Faculty (I am still teaching there today).

If I have any place in Russian literature, I owe it entirely to the Saint Petersburg Department of Secret Police: in 1911 they exiled me from Petersburg, and for the next two years I led an extremely isolated life in Lakhta. There, in the white winter silence and the green silence of summer, I wrote *A Provincial Tale*. After which the late Izmailov[1] decided in print that I was a shaggy provincial in high boots, with a thick cane—and was astonished to find me altogether different.

I had become altogether different, however, only after two years in England during the war. In England I built ships, looked at ruined castles, listened to the thud of bombs dropped by German zeppelins, and wrote *The Islanders*. I regret that I did not see the February Revolution and know only the October Revolution (I returned to Petersburg, past German submarines, in a ship with lights out, wearing a life belt all the time, just in time for October. This is the same as never having been in love and waking up one morning already married for ten years or so.

Today I do not write much—probably because I am becoming ever more demanding of myself. Three new volumes of my works (*At the World's End, The Islanders,* and *Tales for Grown-up Children*) have lain for the past three years at the Grzhebin Publishing House and are only now going into type. The fourth volume will be my novel *We*—my most jesting and most serious work.

But perhaps the most interesting and most serious stories have not been written by me, but have happened to me.

1922

[1] A. A. Izmailov (1873–1921), critic and journalist.

AUTOBIOGRAPHY

At the very center of the map there is a tiny circle—Lebedyan, which Tolstoy and Turgenev wrote about. I was born in Lebedyan, in 1884. I grew up under the piano—my mother was a fine musician. I began to read at the age of four. My childhood was spent almost without friends. My friends were books. I still remember how I shivered over Dostoevsky's *Netochka Nezvanova* and Turgenev's "First Love." These were my elders and, perhaps, a bit terrifying. Gogol was a friend.

I finished school in Voronezh (1902) with a gold medal; the medal soon found itself in a pawnbroker's shop in Saint Petersburg. After high school, I attended the Saint Petersburg Polytechnic Institute (Shipbuilding Faculty). I spent the winters in Petersburg, the summers doing practical work in factories and on ships. The best of my journeys in those years was the one from Odessa to Alexandria (with stops at Constantinople, Smyrna, Salonika, Beirut, Jaffa, Jerusalem, and Port Said). I was in Odessa during the mutiny on the battleship *Potemkin,* and in Helsingfors during the Sveaborg uprising.

All that seems like a whirlwind today: demonstrations on Nevsky Prospekt, cossacks, student and workers' circles, love, huge mass meetings at the universities and the institutes. I was a Bolshevik then (today I am not) and was active in the Vyborg district. At one time my room was a clandestine printing shop. I fought the Kadets[1] in the Student Council of Class Representatives. The outcome of all this was, of course, a solitary cell in the prison on Shpalernaya.

[1] Constitutional Democrats.

5

I graduated from the Polytechnic in 1908 and was retained as a member of the faculty in the Department of Naval Architecture. That year I also wrote and published my first story in *Obrazovaniye* The three subsequent years were devoted entirely to engineering and articles in technical journals. I began to write seriously in 1911 (*A Provincial Tale*—published in *Zavety* [Behests]).

In early 1916 I went to England to build Russian icebreakers. One of our largest icebreakers, the *Lenin* (formerly the *Alexander Nevsky*), is my work.

When the English newspapers broke out with huge headlines, ABDICATION OF TSAR! and REVOLUTION IN RUSSIA, I could no longer bear to remain in England. In September 1917, I returned to Russia. Here I have given up technical work, and now I have only two occupations, literature and teaching at the Polytechnic Institute.

Thus far, I have been in solitary confinement only twice, in 1905–6 and in 1922; both times on Shpalernaya and both times, by a strange coincidence, in the same gallery. I have been exiled three times, in 1906, in 1911, and in 1922. I have been tried only once, in the Saint Petersburg District Court, for my novella *At the World's End.*

1924

AUTOBIOGRAPHY

Several isolated moments from my earliest childhood, like holes cut in a dark, dense curtain.

Our dining room, an oilcloth covered table, and on the table a dish with something strange, white, gleaming, and—a miracle— the white stuff disappears as I look, who knows where. In the dish is a piece of the still unknown universe that exists outside the room. In the dish is some snow which someone has brought in to show me. And that marvelous snow is with me to this day.

The same dining room. I am in someone's arms before the window. Outside the window, through the trees, the red sphere of the sun. Everything is darkening, and I feel that this is the end—and the most frightening thing of all is that my mother has not yet returned from somewhere. Later I learned that the someone was my grandmother, and that I was indeed within a hairsbreadth of death at that moment. I was about a year and a half old.

Later. I am two or three. For the first time, many people, a multitude, a crowd. We are in Zadonsk: my parents have come there in a charabanc and brought me with them. A church, blue smoke, chanting, lights, an epileptic woman barking like a dog, a lump in my throat. Now it is over, everybody is pushing, I am carried outside by the crowd like a bit of flotsam, and suddenly I am alone in the crowd. My father and my mother are gone, they will never come back, I am alone forever. I sit on a gravestone in the sun, crying bitterly. For a whole hour I live in the world alone.

Voronezh. A river, a very strange box of a bathhouse, and in

7

this box (I remembered this later, when I saw polar bears in the zoo) a huge, pink, fat, bulging female body plashes about—my mother's aunt. I feel curious and a little awed: for the first time I understand that this is a woman.

I wait by the window, looking out upon an empty street, with hens bathing in the the dust. At last, our carriage appears, bringing father home from the *gimnaziya*. He sits on an absurdly elevated seat, his cane between his knees. I wait for dinner with a fast-beating heart. At dinner I solemnly unfold the newspaper and read aloud the huge letters: "Son of the Fatherland." I have been initiated into this mysterious thing, letters. I am about four.

Summer. A sudden smell of medicines. My mother and my aunt hastily shut the windows and close the balcony door. I look, with my nose pressed to the glass door: they are *bringing them!* The driver is dressed in a white robe; the wagon is covered with white cloth; under the cloth are people, bent, arms and legs writhing—cholera patients. The cholera infirmary is on our block, next door to us. My heart is hammering, I know the meaning of death. I am five or six.

And finally: an airy, glasslike August morning. Distant, transparent pealing of bells from the monastery. I walk past the front garden before our house and know without looking: the window is open, and my mother, grandmother, and sister are looking at me. I am wearing for the first time long "street" trousers and the uniform jacket of the *gimnaziya* student, with a schoolbag over my shoulder. The water carrier Izmashka jogs along the street with his barrel and glances at me several times. I feel proud. I am a big boy—over eight.

All of this among the Tambov fields, in Lebedyan, famed for its cardsharpers, gypsies, horse fairs, and the most vivid Russian speech. The years are 1884–1893.

After that—school, as gray as the cloth of our uniforms. And sometimes, in the grayness—a marvelous red flag raised on the fire tower, symbolizing, not the social revolution, but twenty degrees of frost.[1] But in the dull, regular routine of school life, it also meant a welcome one-day revolution.

The Diogenes lamp of skepticism was lit for me at the age of

---

[1] I.e., on the Réaumur scale—equivalent to twenty-one degrees below zero Fahrenheit.

twelve. It was lit by a strapping second-grader. The shiner—blue, violet, and red—burned under my left eye for two whole weeks. I prayed for a miracle, I prayed for it to disappear. The miracle did not take place. I began to wonder.

A great deal of solitude, many books, and very early—Dostoyevsky. I still remember the shivers and the flaming cheeks as I read *Netochka Nezvanova*. For a long time, Dostoyevsky remained an elder, awesome. But Gogol was my friend (and, much later, Anatole France).

From 1896 the *gimnaziya* in Voronezh. My specialty, which everyone knew about, was Russian compositions. Another, known to no one, was a series of experiments—to "harden" myself.

I recall the spring when I was in the seventh grade. I was bitten by a mad dog. I found a textbook somewhere and read that the first symptoms of rabies usually appear after two weeks. And I decided to wait and see—Will I go mad or not?—to test both myself and fate. Those two weeks I kept a diary, the only diary I ever kept in my life. After two weeks, I did not go mad. I went to the office and reported that I had been bitten, and was immediately sent to Moscow for Pasteur injections. My experiment ended well. Some ten years later, during the white Petersburg nights, when I went mad with love, I carried out another experiment on myself, more serious, but hardly more intelligent.

In 1902 I discarded the gray school uniform. My gold medal was soon pawned for twenty-five rubles in a Petersburg pawnshop and remained there.

I remember the last day, the office of the inspector. Spectacles up on his forehead, he pulled up his trousers (his trousers were always slipping down) and handed me a pamphlet. I read the author's inscription: "To my alma mater, about which I can remember nothing good. P. E. Shchegolev." And the inspector sententiously drawled through his nose: "Fine, isn't it? He also finished with a gold medal, and what does he write? Of course, he ended up in prison. My advice to you is: Don't write. Don't follow this path." His admonition had no effect.

Petersburg in the early 1900s—the Petersburg of Komissarzhevskaya, Leonid Andreyev, Witte, Plehve—trotters with blue netting over their backs, rattling double-decker horsecars, students with swords and uniforms and students in blue Russian shirts. I am a Polytechnic student, of the Russian-shirt category. On a white winter Sunday, the Nevsky Prospekt is black with slow crowds, waiting for something. The Nevsky is dominated by the Duma tower, and everyone's eyes are glued to it. And when the signal comes—the stroke of one—dark figures streaming in all directions, fragments of the Marseillaise, red flags, Cossacks, janitors, police. The first demonstration (the first for me). 1903. And the nearer to 1905, the more feverish the unrest, the noisier our meetings.

In the summer—practical work in factories, Russia, jolly third-class railway carriages resounding with banter, Sevastopol, Nizhni Novgorod, plants on the Kama River, Odessa with its port and its tramps.

The summer of 1905—unusually blue, kaleidoscopic, filled to the brim with people and events. Work on the steamship *Rossiya,* plying between Odessa and Alexandria. Constantinople, mosques, dervishes, bazaars, the white marble embankment of Smyrna, Bedouins in Beirut, the white tide in Jaffa, black-green Athos, plague-ridden Port Said, tawny-white Africa, Alexandria with its English policemen, sellers of stuffed alligators, the famous Tartouche. Astonishing Jerusalem, altogether special and apart from everything, where I lived for a week with the family of an Arab I knew.

And on return to Odessa, the epic mutiny on the battleship *Potemkin.* With the machinist of the *Rossiya*—submerged, awash in the crowd, drunk with it—I wandered all day and all night through the port, amid shots, fires, rioting.

In those years, being a Bolshevik meant following the line of greatest resistance, and I was a Bolshevik at that time. In the fall of 1905 there were strikes, and the dark Nevsky Prospekt was pierced by a searchlight from the admiralty building. October 17. Meetings in the universities.

One evening in December, a friend, Nikolay B., a worker with protruding ears, came to my room in Lomansky Lane. He had with him a paper bag, of the kind that Philippov rolls were sold in. It contained pyroxylin. "I'll leave it here, the police are on my heels." "All right, leave it." I can still see that bag—on the windowsill, at the left, next to the bag of sugar and the sausage.

The next day at the "revolutionary headquarters" of the Vyborg district, at the very moment when plans and pistols of various types were spread out on the table—the police. There were about thirty of us in the mousetrap. And back in my room, on the windowsill, at the left—the bag that had once contained Philippov rolls, and under the bed—leaflets.

When after being arrested and beaten up we were divided into groups, I found myself near the window with four others. Under the street light outside I caught sight of familiar faces. Snatching a convenient moment, I threw out a note through the transom to remove everything compromising from my room and the rooms of my four comrades. This was done. But I did not know it until much later. Meanwhile, for several months in my solitary cell on Shpalernaya, I had dream after dream about the Philippov bag on my windowsill, at the left.

In my solitary cell I was in love, studied stenography and English, and wrote poems (that was inevitable). In the spring of 1906 I was released and exiled to my native region.

I could not long endure the quiet of Lebedyan, its churchbells, its little front gardens. That very summer I went back illegally to Petersburg, and from there to Helsingfors. Beneath my windows, rocks and sea. In the evenings, when faces could barely be made out, there were meetings on the gray granite. And at night we could not see each other's faces, and the black warm rock seemed soft because *she* was near me, and the rays of the Sveaborg searchlights moved lightly and delicately.

One day at the bathhouse a naked friend introduced me to a naked, potbellied little man. The potbellied little man turned out to be the famous captain of the Red Guards, Kok. A few days later, the Red Guards were in action. Dark spots of the Kronstadt fleet just visible on the horizon, rising spray from shells exploding in the water, the booming of the Sveaborg guns, first strong, then slowly dying out. And, disguised, clean-shaven, with a pince-nez astride my nose, I returned to Petersburg.

A parliament in the country. Little states within the state— higher educational institutions, with their own parliaments, the Councils of Class Representatives. The struggle of various parties, electioneering, posters, pamphlets, speeches, balloting urns. I was a member, at one time chairman, of a Council of Class Representatives.

Then came a summons to report at the police precinct. At the precinct, a green sheet of paper, concerning the search for "the university student Yevgeny Zamyatin," subject to deportation from Petersburg. I honestly declared that I had never attended a university,[2] and that there was evidently an error in the document. I remember the police officer's nose, hooked like a question mark. "Hm—we'll have to make inquiries." I moved to another district. Six months later, a second summons: "university student," question mark, inquiries. And so, for five years, until 1911, when the error in the green sheet was finally corrected, and I was duly expelled from Petersburg.

In 1908 I had graduated from the Shipbuilding School of the Polytechnic Institute and was retained at the Department of Naval Architecture (where I began to teach the subject in 1911). On my desk, together with the blueprints for a turret-deck ship, were the pages of my first story. I sent it to *Obrazovaniye,* a journal edited by Ostrogorsky; the literary department was headed by Artsybashev. In the fall of 1908, the story was published in the magazine. Today, when I meet people who have read this story, I feel as embarrassed as I do when meeting an aunt of mine, whose dress I once wetted in public at the age of two.

For three years after graduation—ships, naval architecture, the slide rule, blueprints, construction, specialized articles in shipping journals—*Teplokhod* [The diesel ship], *Russkoye sudokhodstvo* [Russian shipping], and in *Izvestia Politekhnicheskogo Instituta* [News of the Polytechnic Institute]. Numerous journeys in Russia in connection with my work: down the Volga to Tsaritsyn, Astrakhan, the Kama River, the Donets region, the Caspian Sea, Archangel, Murmansk, the Caucasus, and Crimea.

During the same years, among blueprints and figures—several stories. But I did not offer them for publication; I still felt that they were "not quite it." "It" was found in 1911. It was a year of extraordinary white nights, a great deal of white, and a great deal of black. It was also the year of my deportation, of severe illness, of nerves frayed to the breaking point. I lived first in an empty *dacha* in Sestroretsk, then, in winter, in Lakhta. There,

[2] Zamyatin attended a polytechnic institute.

amidst snow, solitude, quiet, I wrote *A Provincial Tale*. After that came close contact with the *Zavety* group—with Remizov, Prishvin, Ivanov-Razumnik.

In 1913 (the third centennial of the Romanov dynasty), I was granted the right of residence in Petersburg. This time the doctors sent me away. I went to Nikolayev, where I built several dredges and wrote several stories, including the novella *At the World's End*. When it was published in *Zavety*, the issue was confiscated by the censors, and both the editors and the author were tried in court. The trial took place a short time before the February revolution; we were acquitted.

The winter of 1915–16 was again windswept and stormy. It ended with a challenge to a duel in January, and my departure for England in March.

My only previous visit to the West had been to Germany. Berlin had impressed me as a condensed, 80-percent version of Petersburg. In England it was quite different: everything was as new and strange as Alexandria and Jerusalem had been some years before.

In England it was at first all iron, machines, blueprints. I built icebreakers in Glasgow, Newcastle, Sunderland, South Shields (among them, one of our largest icebreakers, the *Lenin*). The Germans showered us with bombs from zeppelins and airplanes. I was writing *The Islanders*.

When the newspapers broke out with huge headlines, REVOLUTION IN RUSSIA, ABDICATION OF THE RUSSIAN TSAR, I could no longer bear to remain in England. In September of 1917, on an antiquated little British ship (expendable—it would be no great loss if the Germans should sink it), I returned to Russia. The journey to Bergen took a long time, about fifty hours, with lights out, life belts on at all times, lifeboats ready.

The merry, eerie winter of 1917–18, when everything broke from its moorings and floated off somewhere into the unknown. Shiplike houses, gunshots, searches, night watches, tenants' clubs. Later, streets without streetcars, long queues of people with sacks, miles and miles of walking daily, potbellied "bourgeois" stoves, herring, oats ground in the coffee mill. And, along with the oats, all sorts of world-shaking plans: publication of all the classics of all periods and all countries, a united organization of all artists in every field, the staging of the entire history of the world in a series of plays. This was no time for blueprints; practical technology dried up and fell away from me like a yellowed leaf (all that remained of it was my teaching at the Polytechnic Institute). And, at the same time, I gave a course on the newest Russian literature at the Hertzen Pedagogical Institute (1920–21), and a course on the technique of literary prose at the studio of the House of the Arts. I was a member of the editorial board of the World Literature Publishing House, the Committee of the Writers' House, the Council of the House of the Arts, the Section on Historical Plays; I was active in several publishing houses (Grzhebin's, Alkonost, Petropolis, Mysl); I helped to edit the journals, *Dom iskusstv* [House of the arts], *Sovremenny zapad* [Contemporary West], *Russky sovremennik* [Russian contemporary]. I wrote relatively little during those years. Among my longer works, I wrote the novel *We,* which appeared in English in 1925, and later in translations into other languages; the novel has not yet been published in Russian.

In 1925 I turned to the theater, with the plays *The Flea* and *The Society of Honorary Bell Ringers. The Flea* was first produced at the Moscow Art Theater on February 2, 1925; *The Society of Honorary Bell Ringers,* in the former Mikhailovsky Theater in Leningrad, in November of 1925. A new play, the tragedy *Attila,* was finished in 1928. In *Attila* I came to the verge of poetry. Now I am returning to the novel and to short stories.

I think that had I not come back to Russia in 1917, had I not lived all these years with Russia, I would not have been able to write. I have seen much: in Petersburg, in Moscow, in the small towns of Tambov Province, in villages in Vologda and Pskov Provinces, in third-class railway carriages and freight cars.

And so the circle closes. I still do not know, do not see what curves my life will follow in the future.

1929

ЕВГЕНИЙ

ЗАМЯТИН

SIRIN

In springtime, the hurdy-gurdy starts its mournful wailing in the yards, a wretched, frozen bird jumps up onto the box to pick out tickets with your fortune, someone shakes his rags, tinkles his bells, and starts a jolly song. But it is sad to hear this song, and frightening to look down into the well of the courtyard; it's all you can do not to shut the window. And when they spread their little rug, and the inevitable rubber boy leaps onto it and starts walking with his head between his legs, you cannot bear it any longer—you are both sorry for the child and repelled by his antics—and you slam the window.

You feel as sorry for Andrey Bely when you read his novel *Petersburg* as you do for the poor rubber boy.[1] It's no easy task to twist yourself into a pretzel, head between legs, and carry on in that position for three hundred pages without a respite. A difficult profession—it makes your heart bleed to think of it!

The wretched rubber boy was made to don a clown's costume and pushed out front by heartless people to face the audience. And he begins to send up his witticisms to the gallery:

"Your excellencies, your highnesses, your honors . . ." "Nevsky Prospekt, like every other avenue, is a public avenue, that is to say, an avenue for the circulation of the public (and not air, for example)." "Apollon Apollonovich was of very respectable descent: his ancestor was Adam. . . ."

The rubber boy says "not air, for example" or "his ancestor

[1] Zamyatin's estimate of Bely was radically revised in subsequent years (see "Contemporary Russian Literature" and the essay on Bely in this volume).

was Adam" and is the first to roar with laughter. But to the public, to those with softer hearts, it isn't funny at all.

Ah, so it isn't funny? Well, in that case the rubber boy will astound you with his art, his antics, his unnatural contortions—he'll stick his head between his legs, if need be, but astound you he will.

"In a certain important place there occurred an appearance of extreme importance; the appearance occurred, that is to say, it was." "Likhutin rushed headlong into the hallway (I mean, simply into the hall)."

Or take the chapter headings: "And, Having Seen, Expanded," "Of Two Poorly Dressed Little Students," "And His Face Was Shiny," and so on and on.

And, of course, the novel abounds in contortions—"miracleries," "flamings," "Septemberly night," "Octoberly day."

"Septemberly" and "Octoberly"—try and get anyone to say such things of his own free will! No one will do it, not for anything —his conscience will speak up: it's too offensive. But Andrey Bely . . .

Yet, look we must: Andrey Bely also plays the part of the bird atop the hurdy-gurdy, the one that picks out tickets with your fortune, or misfortune. Andrey Bely prophesies every kind of disaster for Russia: "There will be a leap over history; there will be a great upheaval; the earth will crack; the very mountains will tumble from the great quake, and the plains will everywhere rise up in humps . . ." "I await thee, Kulikovo Field![2] On that day the last sun will shine over my native land."

A cruel destiny pursues our rubber boy: when he twists himself into pretzels to amuse you, you pity him; when he prognosticates in a sepulchral voice, you want to laugh.

And this destiny of his is all the more cruel because he is not untalented. If Bely were without talent, what the devil, there would be no reason to feel sorry. But even in his *Petersburg* you see a keen eye and valuable ideas: he wants to grasp all of the Russian revolution, from the very top down to the lowliest policeman. Take, for instance, Senator Ableukhov (for all the

---

[2] Kulikovo Field on the Don River, the scene of a great battle in the fourteenth century, in which the Russians defeated the Tartars of the Golden Horde.

world, a picture of Pobedonostsev,[3] of blessed memory). What a portrait! Protruding ears, face of an aged infant; bookcases with innumerable shelves, each marked with a letter; favorite reading, planimetry; fear of open space. Well done, you feel in the presence of a true spark of God. And all the more pity that Bely uses this spark to light lanterns in a second-rate raree-show.

Reading Blok after Andrey Bely is like coming out of a smoke-filled show booth into the clear, still night. Blok is bright and frosty, but in the cold distance flash the inconstant, tender stars. And it is toward them, the unattainable, that Blok directs his steps—toward the Fair Lady, who does not exist, who is a dream, the road toward whom means suffering. *The Rose and the Cross,* Blok's play in the first issue of *Sirin,* is about knights, castles, minstrels, and tournaments, and yet the play is ours, it is close to us, it is Russian. It calls us to suffering, it says that there is no joy nobler than suffering for the sake of love for man. And what could be more Russian? Whatever else we may or may not know, we know how to suffer.

And here are Remizov's tales—also Russian, and also full of suffering: about the sun, God's tear; about the angel of doom and the angel guardian of pain. Remizov is deeply, truly Russian not only in the essence but also in the form of his tales. But these tales do not contain all of Remizov, all of his power; they are not his *Sisters in the Cross* and not "The Irrepressible Tambourin."

Fyodor Sologub's poems in the first collection are very simple, unwontedly simple. Simplicity does not sit well with Sologub. It's like dressing up Mephistopheles as a respectable German burgher, with a pipe in his mouth and a mug of beer in his hand. Not bad, but not Mephistopheles. No.

In Bryusov's poems, in the second issue, there is a different simplicity—contrived, artful. Bryusov is true to himself. Some of his poems are wonderfully good ("Persian Quatrains"); others, where Bryusov, following in Balmont's steps, descends to the savages, are something else again. The road to the savages is dangerous: Balmont has come down along this road to his famous "Huitzilopochtli."

---

[3] K. P. Pobedonostsev (1827–1907), reactionary statesman, procurator of the holy synod in Russia during the last decades of the nineteenth century and the early years of the twentieth.

One righteous man, they say, can save ten drowning sinners. But in *Sirin* the sins of the unrepentant Andrey Bely are so great both in kind and in number (350 pages out of 500!) that they drag both issues down to the bottom.

1914

SCYTHIANS?

> *There is no target against which the Scythian will fear to draw his bow*
>
> Preface to *Skify,* book 1

A solitary, savage horseman—a Scythian—gallops across the green steppe, hair streaming in the wind. Where is he galloping? Nowhere. What for? For no reason. He gallops simply because he is a Scythian, because he has become one with his horse, because he is a centaur, and the dearest things to him are freedom, solitude, his horse, the wide expanse of the steppe.

The Scythian is an eternal nomad. Today he is here, tomorrow, there. Being attached to one place is unbearable to him. And if in his wild gallop he should chance upon a fenced town, the will give it a wide detour. The very odor of a dwelling, of settled existence, of cabbage soup, is intolerable to the Scythian. He is alive only in the wild, free gallop, only in the open steppe.

This is how we see the Scythian. And therefore we rejoiced in the appearance of the *Skify* anthologies. Here, we thought, we'll surely find unlabeled men, here we shall breathe the air of love for true, eternally untamed freedom. After all, we have been promised from the first page that "There is no target against which the Scythian will fear to draw his bow."

But pages turned, and days. *Znamya truda* [The banner of labor] has blossomed forth, the second book of *Skify* has come out. And it is bitter to see the Scythian bow bound to service,

Zamyatin published this article under the pen name of Mikhail Platonov.

21

the centaurs in stables, freemen marching to the sounds of a band. The Scythians have settled down. Too soon, there was a target against which they "feared to draw their bow."

The *spiritual* revolutionary, the genuine freeman and Scythian, is envisaged by Ivanov-Razumnik[1] thus: he "works for the near or distant future," he knows that "the way of the revolution is verily a way of the cross." We can almost agree with this definition, but how often "almost" makes a world of difference. The true Scythian does not know of any straddling "or." He works *only* for the distant future, never for the near future, and never for the present. Hence to him there is one way—Golgotha—and no other, and one conceivable victory—to be crucified—and no other.

Christ on Golgotha, between two thieves, bleeding to death drop by drop, is the victor—because he has been crucified, because, in practical terms, he has been vanquished. But Christ victorious in practical terms is the grand inquisitor. And worse, Christ victorious in practical terms is a paunchy priest in a silk-lined purple robe, who dispenses benedictions with his right hand and collects donations with the left. The Fair Lady, in legal marriage, is simply Mrs. So-and-So, with hair curlers at night and a migraine in the morning. And Marx, come down to earth, is simply a Krylenko.[2]

Such is the irony and such is the wisdom of fate. Wisdom, because this ironic law holds the pledge of eternal movement forward. The realization, materialization, practical victory of an idea immediately gives it a philistine hue. And the true Scythian will smell from a mile away the odor of dwellings, the odor of cabbage soup, the odor of the priest in his purple cassock, the odor of Krylenko—and will hasten away from the dwellings, into the steppe, to freedom.

This is the tragedy and the bitter, racking happiness of the

[1] R. V. Ivanov-Razumnik (1878–1946), critic and sociologist; after the revolution of October 1917, a member of the Left Socialist-Revolutionaries; leader of the Scythians, a literary group that included Blok and Bely; and editor of *Skify*. Subsequently, he spent many years in prison and penal exile during the Stalin regime.

[2] N. V. Krylenko (1885–1940), leading Bolshevik, Commissar of War in the first Bolshevik government. In 1918 he became public prosecutor in revolutionary tribunals.

true Scythian: he can never rest on laurels, he will never be with the practical victors, with those who rejoice and sing "Glory be." The lot of the true Scythian is the thorns of the vanquished. His faith is heresy. His destiny is the destiny of Ahasuerus. His work is not for the near but for the distant future. And this work has at all times, under the laws of all the monarchies and republics, including the Soviet republic, been rewarded only by a lodging at government expense—prison.

"The victorious October Revolution," as it is referred to in official sources, in *Pravda* and *Znamya truda,* has not escaped the general law on becoming victorious: it has turned philistine.

What the priest in the purple cassock hates most of all is the heretic who does not recognize his exclusive right to bind and to permit. What Mrs. So-and-So with her hair curlers hates most of all is the Fair Lady who does not recognize her sole right to the prerogatives of love. And what every philistine hates most of all is the rebel who dares to think differently from him. Hatred of freedom is the surest symptom of this deadly disease, philistinism.

Shave all heads down to the skin; dress everybody in the regulation uniform; convert all heretical lands to your own faith by artillery fire. This was how the Osmanlis converted the giaours to the true faith; this was how the Teutonic Knights saved heathens from eternal flames—by the sword and by temporal flames; this was how dissenters, sectarians, and socialists were cured of their errors in Russia. And is it not the same today? Konstantin Pobedonostsev is dead—long live Konstantin Pobedonostsev![3]

But this is not the Scythians' cry. Their cry is an eternal "Down with—!" And if a Scythian is found in the camp of the victors, harnessed to the triumphal chariot, then he is not he, he is not a Scythian and has no right to this free name.

Fortunately, it is not so easy to shave a Scythian's head. The prickly heretic stubble will persist for a long time, and—even when he is already in the stable—the centaur will continue for a long time, by old habit, to neigh at the wrong times. And perhaps this is why, despite the praiseworthy efforts of the chief

[3] Pobedonostsev, identified in a footnote to the preceding essay, was notorious for his persecution of nonconformists. Zamyatin's reference also contains the elements of a pun, since Pobedonostsev's name is derived from *pobeda,* "victory."

overseer in the taming of the Scythians, Ivanov-Razumnik, we find images in *Skify* most devastating to the revolution of the victors.

Perhaps the strongest, truly Scythian words were spoken by Sergey Yesenin in his poem *"Otchar"*: "There is no deadly freedom in this world."

Exactly. What is deadly is not freedom, but the violation of freedom. But for those who have openly allied themselves with the victors, to speak of such things is tantamount to speaking of rope in a house where a man has hanged himself. The trouble with children! They're always blurting out something improper in the presence of elders. And aren't these hints in "Marfa Posadnitsa," by the same infant, patently improper?

It's not a monk conversing with the Lord in his retreat—
It is the Moscow Tsar calling out to the Antichrist:
O Beelzebub, my heart, I'm deep in trouble,
Novgorod the free won't kiss my boot! . . .
And the Tsar speaks thus to his beloved wife:
There will be a great feast with rivers of red brew!
I have sent matchmakers to the discourteous clans,
There is a bed awaiting them in the dark ravine!

The subjugation of the heretical Novgorods and other "discourteous" clans with the aid of the knife—is it permissible to speak of this today and to recall, in addition, that this was the specialty of our glorious Tsar Ivan Vasilievich? The trouble with children!

However, it is not much better with adults. Even Kluyev, who occupies the place once held by the court poet Derzhavin,[4] imprudently dreams out loud of a time when

No sword, no iron hail will break
The corn city's walls,
They'll not profane the fiery face
Of golden freedom.

In the first issue of *Skify* we read these ruby red lines, watered with the heart's blood, by Bely, who always glitters with such icy brilliance:

---

[4] G. R. Derzhavin (1743–1816), poet patronized for a time by Catherine the Great.

All boundaries of emotion and of truth
   have been erased.
In worlds, in years, in hours—
Nothing but bodies, bodies, bodies prone . . .
And idle ashes . . .
We march into the future, rank on rank!
Slaves—emotionless, without souls—
We'll cover the future, as the past,
Only with piles of carcasses.

But this is about the Krylenkos, who have covered Russia with
a pile of carcasses, who are dreaming of socialist-Napoleonic
wars in Europe—throughtout the world, throughout the universe! But let us not jest incautiously: Bely is trustworthy, and
did not *intend* to speak about the Krylenkos.

Ivanov-Razumnik shaved his head more carefully than other
Scythians, but even his stubble stands up and pricks the wrong
people, rather than those he would like to prick.

In his article "Two Russias" Ivanov-Razumnik wrote: "And
when their bitter hate ceases to be impotent and becomes a force,
when it is given vent in actions in the name of 'law,' and 'order,'
'in the name of Christ' . . . Just let them gather strength and wait
it out until the right moment—they will spill rivers of blood in the
name of suppressing revolutionary lawlessness." What Ivanov-
Razumnik had in mind when he prophesied this was, of course,
a Russian Thiers, shooting down communards on a hypothetical
Russian Père Lachaise. But by the whim of that mocker, fate,
the prophecy of Ivanov-Razumnik is being fulfilled chiefly by
Russian communards—in the name of their own Christ, whom
they had brought down to earth. Perhaps a Thiers will also come,
but what is permissible to Thiers is not permissible to Caesar's
wife.

It is good to be a profound expert on Russian literature, like
Ivanov-Razumnik: not everyone can dip into the well of the
classics and bring up such a present-day image as the fool
Yekimovna from *The Moor of Peter the Great*.[5] From the avalanche of Western culture that rushed into old Russia through
the window on Europe hacked out by Peter the Great, the
fool Yekimovna assimilated only "monsieur-mam'selle-assembly-

---

[5] Prose work by Pushkin.

pardon." Inevitably, irresistibly, like iron to Magnet Mountain, this image is drawn and clings to our victors. From the French Revolution, from Hertzen, from Marx, they have learned by rote nothing more than "assembly and pardon," mouthing the words in the accents of Nizhny Novgorod. And this is why there is so much vaudevillian grotesquery in their deeds and in the written monuments they are leaving as a heritage to curious posterity.

Saul, converted to the true believer Paul, should stay Paul, if only for the sake of style. And it is not becoming for Paul to utter such heresies as "Can absolutism, whoever may wield it, be compatible with freedom?" ("Two Russias" by Ivanov-Razumnik).

However, we shall refrain from comments dangerous to Paul, if only to avoid emulating the bad example of Ivanov-Razumnik, who unhesitatingly declares in the same article in the hearing of "all—all—all," that Remizov is untrustworthy, Remizov is a White Guard, Remizov is outside the law.

But how, indeed, did it happen that Remizov, with his "Tale of the Ruin of the Russian Land," is now part of the triumphal march of those who sing the glory of the victors? And what is he there for?

The explanation is this. Whenever the Roman emperors marched into Rome after a victory over the barbarians, the king of the barbarians was led in the procession behind one of the chariots, and a special crier called out the wealth and power of this king for the greater glory of the victorious emperor. And it was to the same end that Ivanov-Razumnik brought Remizov into the triumphal procession—for the greater glory of the victors. And therefore, after smashing Remizov in the face, Ivanov-Razumnik proclaims: "The 'Tale of the Ruin of the Russian Land' is one of the most powerful, most remarkable works written in our day."

We quite agree with Ivanov-Razumnik's judgment: Remizov's "Tale" is a work of great power. But the power lies not in Remizov's usual artistry, but in the shattering sincerity of the work. Remizov's other works can be admired from this side, from that, from a plank thrown over them: far below, under the plank, the beautiful, clumsy wheels of the mill are turning, the water hums and glitters like a rainbow. But the "Tale" cannot be admired from the outside: it draws you in, hand and foot, it whirls and wrings you, so that you reach the last page crushed and ground to bits.

"My homeland, my humbled mother. I kiss thy wounds, thy parched lips, thy heart, breaking with pain and bitterness, thy slashed, bleeding eyes. I shall not leave thee in thy misfortune, free and captive, free and shackled, holy and sinful, bright and dark. I shall preserve my Russian soul, with faith in thy martyred truth."

What grieving love pulses in every word—love for Russia, always and whatever she may be: holy and sinful, bright and dark! And what a bookish, what a chemical heart one must have not to see that this love and this grief are the soul of Remizov's "Tale," and that the wrath and the "bitter hate" rise from this love as smoke from fire.

The smoke has blinded Ivanov-Razumnik, he has discerned nothing but the smoke. And out of this smoke he has created an image unknown to us, a dark, distorted image of Remizov—the hater of freedom Remizov—the philistine.

Remizov grieves for his humbled mother. And is it not, indeed, degrading when a Prussian general can throw into the face of the Russian revolution such words as "But where is your freedom?" Is it not a humiliation when, a day after shouting warlike slogans, the Russian revolution meekly and "immediately" sues the Prussian general for peace? Remizov grieves for his humbled mother.

"O my doomed homeland, the royal purple has fallen from thy shoulders. Thou art humbled and trampled."

And the member of the revolutionary tribunal, Ivanov-Razumnik, reads the heart of the defendant Remizov: "When Remizov weeps that the royal purple has fallen from her shoulders, we can see that he is grieving not only over the purple of his homeland, but also over the purple of the tsar."

Everything is permitted in the name of speedy action by the revolutionary court, and Ivanov-Razumnik judges Remizov for the words of the Babylonian elders in his "Prayer for Georgiy the Brave." "The sovereign is gone from the city, every man preys on his neighbor; would that the tsar return speedily," said the

Alexey Remizov

elders. And the member of the revolutionary tribunal affixes his
seal to the verdict: "When we hear this, we know Remizov is
fond kin and ally of the Babylonian elders."

To the revolutionary tribunal, the most important thing is that
Remizov did not prostrate himself before the victors but dared
to discern in them (in *them!*) the marks of philistinism. With all
of his ten volumes, Remizov scourged the philistinism of old
Russia, but he must not dare to lash out at the philistinism of
the new. Remizov's eyes are like Gogol's; he is always quick to
see the black. Of what concern is this to the revolutionary tribunal? Its verdict is predetermined, and, indeed, how could it
be otherwise? After all, it is in Remizov's "Tale" that we read:

> We are weary of men's idleness, of their bragging, of fly-
> ing, empty words. . . . Greedily, with apish hoots and yowls,
> they are tearing to pieces the funeral cake baked once upon
> a time by Russia, who now lies dead. Tearing and gulping
> and choking. And with bloodshot eyes gnawing the table
> as a hungry horse gnaws his crib. And rushing to gobble
> up all there is before the guests arrive.

This is something that Remizov will not be forgiven for. What
the priest in the purple cassock hates most of all is the heretical,
disobedient word. What the priest in the purple cassock hates
most of all is the true Scythian, of whom the Scythian preface
says: "Is not the Scythian always ready for rebellion?" The true
Scythian always is.

In Remizov's "Tale," permeated through and through with
love and grief, Ivanov-Razumnik saw only smoke—bitter hatred.
And is it any wonder, when—as we see—the only thing that
Ivanov-Razumnik remembers of the whole gospel, of the whole
sermon of love, are the words: "I came not to send peace, but a
sword." Throughout his "Two Russias," the suddenly warlike
Ivanov-Razumnik rattles the sword for the glory of the noble
victors, who are so brave with those who are weaker, and so . . .
prudent with those who are stronger. And energetically searches
for the sound of the sword in Kluyev and Yesenin—the objects
of his commendation—even where it does not exist.

To the fundamental, the best, the greatest qualities of the
Russian soul, to the Russian nobility of spirit, the Russian ten-

derness and love for the lowliest human being, the least blade of grass—to all this Ivanov-Razumnik is blind. Yet it is precisely these best qualities of the Russian soul that underlie the unquenchable Russian longing for peace, for all mankind. Love of the sickle and hate of the sword are the qualities that are most truly Russian, most truly of the people. And this is why the strophes born of these stand out so movingly in the "made-to-order" revolutionary poems of Yesenin and Kluyev.

Here are the magnificent closing lines of Yesenin's "Singing Call":

> People, my brothers,
> Where are you? Answer me!
> I do not need you, fearless,
> Bloodthirsty knight.
> I do not want your victory,
> I need no tribute!
> We are all apple trees and cherry trees
> In a blue orchard. . . .
> We did not come into the world to destroy,
> We came to love and to believe.

But what the victors and Ivanov-Razumnik need are precisely the "bloodthirsty knight" and the "tribute," and this is why Ivanov-Razumnik finds that "Singing Call" has a *victorious* ring. And, of course, what Ivanov-Razumnik will quote is not the above lines, but something "arrogantly Berlinian," such as:

> My Russian field,
> And you, its sons,
> Who have caught
> The sun and the moon
> On your paling.

Or:

> Russia, Russia, Russia—
> Messiah of the coming day!

Truly remarkable is Ivanov-Razumnik's adventure with Kluyev's "Song of the Sun-Bearer": he not only tolerated this tasteless "Ode to Felice"[6] in the pages of *Skify*, but even praised it without blinking an eye.

[6] "Ode to Felice" by Derzhavin (1782), dedicated to Catherine the Great.

China and Europe, North and South
Shall gather in the chamber in a round dance of friends,
In order to unite the Zenith with the Abyss . . .
We have won three acorn suns—
Equality and Freedom, and the crown of Brotherhood—
A living pasture for ardent hearts . . .
The workbench—Nazareth, the anvil—Nimrod.

And after that, of course, it is "Arise, ye. . . ."[7] How near this
is to Minsky's famous "Workers of the world, unite" and to
Sologub's "arrogant Berlin," but how far from our Kluyev—the
Kluyev we have known and loved. The capitalized words alone—
a tasteless custom introduced, if I am not mistaken, by Andreyev,
and the first symptom of creative impotence—would be enough
to damn this doggerel. And Kluyev's "Song of the Sun-Bearer"
abounds in such goodies: World, Zenith, Wisdom, Labor, Equality, Song—and Mystery—and that fly-specked old standby, Love
—and the Abyss, which has long become as shallow as a puddle.

However, Kluyev's failure is understandable: he is, after all,
but a novice in internationalism. In his "Conversational Tune"
(*Besedny naigrysh*), the same Kluyev wrote with high patriotism
about the Germans:

The old man called a Hundred Tribes in One
Has heard a ringing, as of waters.
He looked out from his bed at dawn
And saw the enemy hosts.
The old man said, "This filthy scum,
Like lice on betony, can only be
Steamed out in the bath with scalding steam."

In his cycle "Hut Songs," on the other hand, Kluyev threw
away the Swords and Abysses that had been thrust into his hands.
And immediately the inspiration is no longer official, but genuine. These songs are not tinsel, but pure gold, which will last
for centuries without a spot of rust. And here you do not know
what to choose, what is better: everything is splendid and alive
in Kluyev's hut: the stove bed, the tom cat, the bellied pot, "the
house goblin pattering behind the stove," the "mother stove"
itself, the loaf on the table, "muttering to the knife, 'I am ready
to be sacrificed.' " After the "Hut Songs," it is still more dis-

[7] The opening words of "The International."

tressing to see Kluyev as the author of odes. The little gray ones may run after the victors like a flock of roosters—God himself has meant them to. But not the Kluyevs: this is not for them.

Defeat, martyrdom on the earthly plane—and victory on a higher plane, the plane of ideas. Victory on earth—and inevitable defeat on the other, higher plane. No third alternative exists for the true Scythian, for the spiritual revolutionary, for the romantic. Eternal reaching out, but never attainment. The eternal wandering of Ahasuerus. The eternal quest for the Fair Lady— who does not exist.

And Ivanov-Razumnik knows this, but he is afraid to see the truth. And indeed, just think of it: what if our revolution enters history not with "the fiery face of golden freedom," but with the face of Remizov's master workman Semyon Mitrofanovich, who forced his apprentice to kiss his heel? True, a fire is sweeping toward us today, and it may erase Semyon Mitrofanovich's face from the revolution. But Semyon Mitrofanovich does everything he can to save himself from the destroying and cleansing flames. And he may save himself, too, he may emerge victorious on earth once more—and so perish, turn philistine still more irrevocably.

The lot of the true Scythian is hard to bear. And therefore the weak close their eyes and swim with the current. And there are "hosts, and hosts, and hosts" of them, as Blok exclaims in his poem "The Scythians" (*Znamya truda*, no. 137). But are they Scythians? No, they are not. There will be true Scythians, true revolutionaries and freemen under every regime, for they have "a cause—eternal rebellion—under any regime, any external order" (from the introduction to *Skify*, no. 1). Yes, under *any* regime. But there will never be "hosts" of them. The divine curse of every true Scythian is to be "a stranger in his own land, not in a strange land" (from "Tale of the Ruin of the Russian Land").

And Ivanov-Razumnik knows all this—he has told us so himself, and told it well, in his article on "Poets and the Revolution" (*Skify,* no. 2):

> The revolution has come, and who was the first to bow down before it? And should the counterrevolution come,

who will be first to run, like a "cocky rooster," after its droshky, carrying the mayor and Khlestakov, under the protection of Derzhimorda?[8] . . . The great who live in the great will not bow, will not follow. But how many are they?

No, there are not many of them. And there can never be "hosts, and hosts, and hosts." And if they can be counted in hosts, they are not stubborn, freedom-loving Scythians. Free Scythians will not bow to anything. Free Scythians will not run after the victors, after rude force, behind "the mayor and Khlestakov, under the protection of Derzhimorda," whatever the color of the mayor's cockade.

1918

[8] The reference is to Gogol's *Inspector General.*

CONTEMPORARY
RUSSIAN LITERATURE

You come to a mountain. You ascend it. You see the mountain very well: a stone, a shrub, a caterpillar crawling on the shrub. You see everything. And yet, when you are on the mountain, you cannot judge its size or trace its contours. It is only from afar, when you have gone a dozen versts away, when the shrub and the caterpillar and all the details of the mountainside are long out of sight, that you will see the mountain itself.

The grandiose events of recent years—the World War, the Russian Revolution—are much like the mountain. For the time being, we see only the shrub, the caterpillar, the stone; we'll see the mountain only when we are ten years away from it. And only then can genuine literature about the war and the revolution begin to appear. The attempts of our writers to speak about this today are wasted labor (one-sided in one way or another). The contemporary inevitably finds himself in the position of the petty officer's wife who cursed Napoleon in 1812 for no other reason but that her excellent cow had been hit by a stray bullet during the Battle of Borodino.

This is why, when I discuss the newest Russian literature with you, I shall not touch upon the very latest writers—I shall bypass attempts at an immediate response to the roar of the storm outside the walls. Such attempts will become part of the history of the revolution, but not the history of literature.

In order to approach what I call the newest Russian literature,

This was a public lecture delivered at the People's University in Lebedyan, one of the many adult education schools which sprang up in Russia after the revolution.

34

permit me to begin with Adam. The period I wish to discuss with you begins with Chekhov and ends with the prerevolutionary epoch. During the revolution literature has not created anything—or if it has, we do not know of it.

As you will see, the period I have in mind represents a complete logical cycle; moreover, it is bounded by similar landmarks—the landmarks of tendentious literature.

You surely remember the biblical legend about the appearance of the first man. In the beginning, his body was created. Then came the spirit, the antithesis of the body. And, finally, when the two opposites united, there was man.

The social organism develops along the same lines. For example, capitalism means the parliamentary democratic freedom of the individual, free economic competition, but it also means the economic subjugation of one class by another. The opposite of capitalism is the socialist order: state limitation of the individual, state regulation of the economy, but also economic emancipation. The next stage of development, perhaps in the distant future, will be a social order under which there will be no need for the coercive power of the state. You have probably read about this course of development, which is called *dialectic*. We shall try to trace its path in the development of recent Russian literature.

At the end of the nineteenth and the beginning of the twentieth centuries, the rulers of Russian literature were the Realists—Gorky, Kuprin, Chekhov, Bunin, and later, Artsybashev, Chirikov, Teleshov and others, whose works were published in *Znaniye*[1] and *Zemlya*.[2] In the works of these writers everything is corporeal, earthly, everything is based on daily life. Gorky's small town, Okurov, may well be found not only on earth, but also on the map. Kuprin's Lieutenant Romashev ("The Duel") may well, under another name, have served in the same regiment with Kuprin. Chekhov's servant girl, Varka, from his magnificent story "Dying to Sleep," rocked her master's baby all night and, finally unable to stay awake any longer, smothered the child.

---

[1] *Znaniye* [Knowledge], a series of literary anthologies published in Petersburg (1904–13) under the guidance of Maxim Gorky. Their contents were usually revolutionary in outlook and realistic in style.

[2] *Zemlya* [Land], a series of literary anthologies published in Moscow (1908–17), stressed individual freedom from the yoke of society, eternal values, naturalism in style.

This was a true incident; Dostoyevsky also recorded it in his *Writer's Diary.*

Of course, you will understand: I am not trying to say that everything described in the books of the writers of this period really happened. But all of it could have happened. The writers of that time were excellent mirrors, turned toward the earth. And their art consisted of reflecting in a tiny splinter of a mirror—a book or a story— the truest and most vivid piece of the earth.

The most genuine, most typical, and most important artists of this group are Chekhov and Bunin. Gorky, one of the major figures of the group, has, in essence, become a Realist only in recent years. Life as it is, in its true reality, is given only in his latest stories—in "Yeralash." Before this, he produced idealized and romanticized tramps—attractive, perhaps, but unalive, unreal. At that time he belonged to the tendentious period.

Chekhov was the first to raise the slogan of pure literature, pure unapplied art. "I am not a liberal, not a gradualist, not a conservative, not a hermit, not an indifferentist. I want to be a free artist. I am equally without special preference for gendarmes, butchers, scientists, writers, youth. To me, form and label are nothing but superstition, prejudice. My holy of holies is the human body, health, intelligence, talent, inspiration, love."

The Realists, at least the older ones, have a religion and a god. This religion is the earth, and this god is man. There is a remarkable coincidence in the statements of Gorky and Chekhov. "Man —that is truth. This holds all the beginnings and all the ends. Everything is in man, and everything is for man. Only man exists" (Gorky). "Man must know himself to be higher than lions and tigers, higher than anything existing in nature, even higher than that which is incomprehensible and seems to be spirit. We are the highest beings, and if we truly realized the full powers of human genius, we would become as gods" (Chekhov).

In Chekhov's work the art of portraying life, of portraying the earth, attained its highest point. After that, it seemed that there was nowhere else to go. But after that, art did the same thing that technology was doing at about the same time. The technology of railway communication attained a high level of efficiency: trains began to travel 150 to 200 versts an hour. But mankind was not content. It rose from the earth and began to fly in airplanes through the air. The early airplanes may have been clumsy, they may have tumbled to the ground—no matter, it was a revolution in means of transportation, it was a step forward.

At the beginning of the twentieth century, Russian literature resolutely cut itself off from earth: the Symbolists made their appearance. You will recall what I said earlier about the dialectic method of development, and the crude example of Adam. First the body—the earth, daily life—developed as far as it could go. Now the spirit began to develop—a principle antithetical, revolutionary in relation to the corporeal, to earth.

The beginnings of this were already apparent in Chekhov. Then came Andreyev. The Symbolists—Fyodor Sologub, Andrey Bely, Gippius, Blok, Bryusov, Balmont, Andreyev, Chulkov, Vyacheslav Ivanov, Minsky, Voloshin—are definitely hostile to the earth, to daily life. "What daily life? There is no such thing. All the plots have been raveled and unraveled. There is but a single, eternal tragedy—Love and Death—and it alone clothes itself in a variety of vestments." "To be with people—what an intolerable burden!"

Sologub, in his novel *Deathly Charms* and in many of his other works, always has two images side by side: Aldonsa and Dulcinea. Aldonsa, a ruddy, buxom female, is the crude earth the writer hates. Dulcinea, beautiful and delicate, is the air, the dream in which Sologub lives and which does not exist on earth. Alexander Blok's poems—entire volumes of them—speak of one thing—the Unknown One, the Fair Lady, the Snow Maid. And she is, in essence, the same as Sologub's Dulcinea. Blok seeks his Fair Lady everywhere on earth. For a moment it seems he has found her. But he raises the veil—and it is not she, it is not the Fair Lady. Blok's Fair Lady is not to be found on earth. And, of course, Sologub and Blok are not speaking only of the woman Dulcinea or the woman who is the Fair Lady. The disappointments in Dulcinea, the impossibility of finding the Fair Lady, are a symbolic reflection of the fate of every achievement, every ideal on earth. Those who have seen high mountains know: from a distance, the mountain is crowned with pink and golden clouds of ineffable beauty; once you climb up to the very top, into the very clouds—you find blurred mist, and nothing else.

And so the Symbolists do not find answers to their questions or solutions of their tragedy on earth and seek them in the upper spheres. Hence their religiosity. But, naturally, their god is no longer man, but a higher being. To some, this god has a "plus sign"—Ormuzd, Christ. To others, He has a "minus sign"—Ahriman, Devil, Lucifer (Sologub, Voloshin). Here you have mysticism. And a bridge to romanticism.

I have said of the Realist writers that in their works everything was on earth, or could be. The Symbolists chose as their subject that which is not on earth, that which cannot be found on earth. I have said of the Realist writers that they have a mirror in their hands; it can be said of the Symbolists that they have an X-ray apparatus. Those who have been in hospitals in wartime have seen how a wounded man is set before a stretched square of linen and the X-ray apparatus is turned on; the miraculous rays pass through the body, and a human skeleton appears on the linen, with a dark spot somewhere between the ribs—a bullet. This was how the Symbolists looked through corporeal life in their works and saw the skeleton of life, a symbol of life and at the same time also a symbol of death. Those whose eyes are so constructed that they always see the skeleton are not happy people. Consequently, we do not find in the Symbolist writers the cheerfulness and humor of a Gorky, Chekhov, or Kuprin. We do not find in them that active denial of life in the name of the struggle against it, in the name of building a better life on earth. The Symbolists do not believe in happiness of earth.

That which the Symbolists chose as their subject was much more difficult to depict than some simple provincial town of Okurov, or Lieutenant Romashev, or the nursemaid Varka who can barely sit up for lack of sleep as she rocks the baby. This difficulty of their subjects and the difficulty in depicting them compelled the Symbolists to search for new methods or portrayal, forced them to work much more over the exterior—the form of a piece—than the Realists had to do. You know very well from your own experience the complex emotions that music arouses in us, emotions it is not always possible to convey in words. Such was the complexity of the emotions the Symbolists had to write about, and they had no other method of conveying the emotions aroused by music than by means of verbal music. They began to use words like music, they began to tune words as a musical instrument is tuned.

This refinement of literary form and the perfecting of the writer's craft is the enormous, the basic contribution of the Symbolists. We can find traces of the same methods in earlier writers—in Pushkin, Lermontov, Tyutchev. But the earlier writers utilized these methods accidentally, spontaneously. The Symbolists conquered chance, they created a science of verbal music.

Now I wish to return to what I called the dialectic path of development. Take a certain phenomenon: it develops to its utmost limits, makes use of all its potentialities, creates the highest thing it can, and stops.

Then comes the antithetical, hostile force; it also unfolds to the very end, so that it can no longer go on, and stops.

And now, out of these two hostile phenomena, a third one is born, making use of the results achieved by the first two, reconciling them. And society, or the art, is given an opportunity to move forward, always forward, always toward the new.

The Symbolists made their contribution to the development of literature and gave way, in the second decade of the twentieth century, to the Neorealists, who received as their heritage features both of the former Realists, and of the Symbolists.

Among the writers who belong to this literary trend are Andrey Bely, whose feet are still somewhere on the platform of Symbolism, but whose head is already in the realm of Neorealism; Fyodor Sologub, in some of his works; Alexey Remizov, Ivan Novikov, Sergeyev-Tsensky, Mikhail Prishvin, Alexey Tolstoy, Shmelyov, Trenyov. I also belong to this trend, and therefore it will be both easier and more difficult for me to speak about it.

Among the Neorealists are Kluyev, Yesenin, Akhmatova, Gumilyov, Mandelshtam, Gorodetsky, and Zenkevich.

Since it is the newest literary trend, still young, still far from having exhausted all its potentialities, and already recognized by the critics, I shall deal with Neorealism in greater detail.

As you will recall, I said about the Symbolists that they wielded an X-ray apparatus—their eyes were constructed in such a way that through the material body of life they saw its skeleton. Now imagine a scientist who has just discovered those X-rays and is so powerfully affected by this discovery that for many years, whenever he looks at a person, he sees the skeleton and is unable to see the muscles, the body, the color of the face. (Or else, think of a first-year medical student who has just begun to work in the anatomical theater, dissecting cadavers. For months he will be seeing severed arms and legs everywhere, with the skin removed, with a network of blue veins, and will be pursued by the smell of the anatomical theater. But afterwards, he will grow so accustomed to it that he will come home from the anatomical theater and dine with the best of appetite.) In time, the scientist too will grow accustomed to his discovery, and, when he looks at a woman, he will see not only the skeleton, but perhaps also the golden hair and blue eyes which adorn it.

The same thing has happened to the Neorealist writers. They grew up under the influence of the Symbolists. They were nourished by the sweet bitterness of Gippius and Blok. But this bitterness did not spoil them for the earth and the body, as it had spoiled the Symbolists. To them, this bitterness was only a preventive inoculation.

You will remember the example of the clouds around the summit of a high mountain. The Realist writers accepted the clouds as they saw them: rosy and golden, or black and heavy with storm. The Symbolists had the courage to climb to the summit and discover that there was nothing pink or golden there, nothing but slush and fog. The Neorealists were on the mountaintop together with the Symbolists and saw that clouds are fog. But having come down from the mountain, they had the courage to say: "It may be fog, but it's good fun all the same."

And so in the works of the Neorealists we find once more an active denial of life—in the name of the struggle for a better life. We hear laughter, we see humor—as in Gogol, Gorky, Chekhov. Each of the Neorealists laughs differently, but each one laughs. Take the schoolteacher Peredonov in Sologub's novel, *The Petty Demon:* to spite his landlady he furiously spits at the walls and smudges them whenever he is alone in the room. This is annihilating laughter. Remizov's Ionych, in the story "Undeadly Life," is drunk; some urchins have stolen his trousers; huddled in a luggage basket, he relives his entire life. This is the laughter of a man who knows how to laugh out of intolerable pain, and through this pain. Or take Prishvin's recent story in which a merchant tells about his journey from Petersburg: "Well, now, everything's fine, thank the Lord. The ticket's in my hand. For ten rubles a soldier knocked the window out in the railway car. I climbed in. Everything as it should be, thank the good Lord." This is the laughter of a man who has not yet lost his joy in living. Or take another writer: officers in their club in a god-forsaken little town get drunk and sing, "The priest had a dog. . . ." This is sinister, nightmare laughter.[3]

Humor and laughter are the hallmark of a vital, healthy man who has the strength and the courage to live. They express the joy in living felt by the old Realists and by the Neorealists, and they distinguish the Neorealists from the Symbolists. In the Symbolists you find only a smile, a contemptuous smile at the contemptible earth. But you never hear them laugh.

When you laugh at your enemy, it is a sign that he no longer frightens you, that you feel stronger than he, and this is already a mark of victory. We hear laughter in the works of the Neorealists, and this tells us that they have somehow overcome, subjugated the eternal enemy, life. It tells us that we are in the presence of a healthier and stronger literary generation than the Symbolists. The Realists lived in life. The Symbolists had the courage to withdraw from life. The Neorealists had the courage to return to life.

But they have returned, perhaps, too knowing, too wise. And therefore most of them have no religion. There are two ways of conquering the tragedy of life: religion or irony. The Neorealists chose the latter. They believe neither in God nor in man.

On returning to life the Neorealists began to depict it differently from the Realists. And to convey this difference to you, I shall first cite an example.

Have you ever had occasion to examine a tiny piece of your own skin under a microscope? If you ever do, you will probably be startled at first: instead of your pink, delicate, smooth skin,

---

[3] The reference is to Zamyatin's own novella, *At the World's End*. The song is an endlessly repeating ditty about a priest who had a dog, who loved the dog, who killed the dog when it stole some meat, who buried the dog and wrote on the gravestone that there was a priest who had a dog, etc.

you will see clefts, enormous bumps, pits; from the pits something rises, as thick as a young lime tree—a hair; next to it is a huge boulder—a speck of dust.

What you see will bear little resemblance to the usual appearance of skin; it will seem incredible, like a nightmare. Now ask yourselves: which is more real—this smooth, pink skin, or that one, with the bumps and clefts? After some thought, you will have to say: the real thing is that incredible skin we see under a microscope.

You understand now that what appears at first glance incredible and shocking reveals the true nature, the reality of a thing far more accurately than the credible. No wonder Dostoyevsky—I believe it was in his novel *The Possessed*—said that "real truth is always incredible."

And so, the Realists depicted the apparent reality, visible to the naked eye. The Neorealists deal most frequently with the other, true reality that is concealed under the surface of life just as the true structure of the human skin is concealed from the unaided eye.

This is why the picture of the world and of people in the works of the Neorealists often strikes you with its exaggerations, its grotesque and fantastic qualities. Take the same Peredonov, mentioned earlier, who spits at the walls of his room. This action is, perhaps, implausible, but it conveys Peredonov's petty viciousness better than pages of realistic description. Wherever he looks, Peredonov sees something nasty, unclean, grayish—perhaps a clump of dust, perhaps a devil's cub. This gray little vision hounds him and lies in wait for him everywhere. Peredonov always feels it behind him and crosses himself to exorcise it. In reality there could be no such thing, it is incredible, but the author has created it to convey the state of mind of a man who lives in the atmosphere of constant gossip, spying, eavesdropping, and malicious rumors that prevailed in the small town. And the device accomplishes its purpose.

Or take another example, from Andrey Bely's novel, *Petersburg*. One of the principal characters in the novel is the chief procurator of the holy synod, Pebedonostsev, of evil memory. In the novel he is called Apollon Apollonovich; he owns a carriage of a special, geometric shape—a perfect cube—and his room is also cubelike, geometric. In reality, of course, Pobedonostsev had a perfectly ordinary carriage and an ordinary room. Yet, by stressing this implausible cubelike form, the author gives us a true and forever memorable impression of Pobedonostsev's extraordinary bureaucratic exactitude, precision, and pedantry.

Or take a third writer.[4] To convey the sly duplicity of the lawyer Semyon Semyonych Blinkin, he writes: "Semyon Semyonych blinked all the time, blink, blink. But it wasn't only the eyes. All of him blinked. He'd walk along the street and limp on his left foot—his whole body, his whole being blinking." Here again the author makes use of the device of exaggeration. Of course, the lawyer did not blink his whole body, but the impression as the lawyer walked limping down the street was exactly this—all of him was blinking. And in conveying this impression the author immediately suggests a cunning, secretive character without saying a word about Blinkin's duplicity.

In the last fragment I cited, the author never says "like," "as if," or "as though," but says directly, "all of him blinked. He'd walk along the street . . . his whole being blinking."

The old Realist would inevitably have put it cautiously, "Semyon Semyonych seemed to be blinking with his whole body." The Neorealist submits completely to the impression; he fully *believes* that Semyon Semyonych blinked with his entire being. To the Neorealist, this is no longer seeming; it is not "as though," it is reality. And the author infects the reader with this belief in the impression. The image becomes bolder, more daring, more vivid. This manner of writing is called impressionism, from the French *impression,* and is highly characteristic of the Neorealists.

Let me cite a few examples. Here are three lines from a poem:

> His distant mother, ill in bed,
> And bowed over her, with growing sadness,
> Silence, her nurse.

The Realist would not have said "Silence, her nurse." The Neorealist completely believes in his impression of silence as a nurse, and fixes this impression in a bold and vivid image.

Or another example, from Sergeyev-Tsensky's *Forest Swamp:* "The forest creature wandered about, putting up curtains of river mist over the distance, bringing this distance closer, all around."

The impression of twilight, when the distance is increasingly veiled in mist, when the horizon becomes ever narrower and the world surrounds one as with walls, is conveyed in the words, "bringing this distance closer, all around." No "it seemed," no "as if," and this makes the picture all the more convincing and compels the reader to accept a seemingly implausible image.

Now recall what I have said earlier about the Symbolist manner of depicting life. The Symbolists' characters were Someone in Gray, Man with a capital "M." Or take Sologub, much of whose writing is in the spirit of the Symbolists. In his novel *Deathly Charms* we find some strange, vague "silent boys" in Professor Trirodov's school. Or Blok's Fair Lady, the Unknown One, the Snow Maid. Everywhere a deliberate vagueness, blurred images, deliberately indefinite places of action, deliberate veiling of the characters in mist.

In the works of the Neorealists, the action takes place in Petersburg; or in the Burkov house on Tavricheskaya Street (Remizov's *Sisters in the Cross*); or in the town of Alatyr, or the town of Krutogorsk. The characters are: the high school teacher Peredonov (Sologub); Senator Apollon Apollonovich (Bely); the official Marekulin (Remizov), and so on.

In contrast to the characters of the Symbolists, the Neorealists' characters are exaggeratedly sculptural, in the round; the colors are exaggeratedly garish. Here are some examples, taken at random.

In Gorodetsky's poem "Yaga" there is a description of three brothers:

> The first, black-eyed, his cheeks a ruddy dawn,
> The second, blue-eyed, hair the black of night,
> The third all yellow and red—all straw and bunting.

Or, in Akhmatova's poem—"A sky more vivid than blue faïence."

The life of big cities is like the life of factories. It robs people of individuality, makes them the same, machinelike. Hence, wishing to draw the most vivid characters possible, many of the Neorealists turned from the big city to the deep province, to the village, to remote, godforsaken regions. The entire action of Sologub's *The Petty Demon* takes place in the provincial hinterland. Most of the extraordinary occurrences, marvels, and anecdotes in which Remizov's heroes are involved happen in the province. Alexey Tolstoy has chosen as his specialty the crude, primitive landowners of the Russian steppe regions. Bunin devoted volume after volume to the village. In Kluyev's poems, we find the hermitages of Olonetsk, Old Believers, hermits, pilgrims, the Russia of village huts and cornfields.

Here the Neorealists find not only genre, not only a way of life, but a way of life concentrated, condensed by centuries to a strong essence, ninety proof.

In short, the material of the Neorealists is the same as that of the Realists: life, earth, rock, everything that has weight and dimensions. But, while they use this material, the Neorealists do primarily what the Symbolists sought to do; they create generalizations and symbols.

In *The Life of Man,* Leonid Andreyev designates his characters as Man, Man's Wife, Man's Friends, Man's Enemies, in order to compel the reader to reflect on human existence generally.

Now take the Neorealist Remizov. Here is the Burkov house, in his *Sisters in the Cross.* The official Marakulin looks down from his window into the yard, where the cat Murka is rolling and writhing, dying: someone has fed her pellets of bread with ground glass. Murka screams and rolls, and the whole world turns black for Marakulin. He would willingly see everything obliterated—this house, that street light—if only the cat Murka would stop crying. The author speaks of Marakulin and Murka. But he writes in such a way that the reader's mind immediately turns to all of Russia, fed on ground glass and writhing in agony, to the whole world, dying from the fruits of the old culture.

And this is yet another characteristic of the Neorealists: they lead the reader to generalizations, to symbols, while depicting entirely realistic specific facts.

And now about the language, the verbal art of the Neorealists.

By the time the Neorealists appeared, life had become more complex, faster, more feverish. It had become Americanized. This is especially true of the big cities, the cultural centers for which writers primarily produce their works. In response to this new way of life, the Neorealists have learned to write more compactly, briefly, tersely than the Realists. They have learned to say in ten lines what used to be said in a whole page. They have learned to compress the contents of a novel into the framework of a novella or a short story. Their teacher in this respect was Chekhov, who produced astonishing models of compactness. I shall deal with brevity briefly. It will suffice to recall the three lines from Gorodetsky's poem "Yaga," quoted earlier.

For the sake of the same economy and greater vividness in depicting the movement of life, the Neorealists avoid descriptions of place or characters. The Neorealists do not describe, they show, so that their works could more aptly be described by the term *showings,* rather than *narratives* or *stories.*

For example, take two characters—Ivan Ivanych, tall, already old and gray, and Marya Petrovna, short and small. The old-school Realist would begin: Ivan Ivanych was so and so, and Marya Petrovna, such and such.

The Neorealist will convey the appearance of his heroes by some action: "Ivan Ivanych was putting on his coat. He grunted, his joints creaked, his hands would not obey him. He asked Marya Petrovna to help him. And to make it possible for her to reach, Ivan Ivanych had to bend, as usual." There is no description of the characters' appearance, but it is clearly visible between the lines. The same was true in the characterization of Semyon Semyonovich Blinkin. There was not a word about the cunning that was the essence of Blinkin's character, only action, and the action immediately presented all of Blinkin, briefly and vividly.

I have said earlier that, in their search for vivid, colorful ways of life the Neorealists turned to the backwoods, to the village. This left a special imprint on the language of many of them. The language of the Neorealists was enriched by purely folk expressions and turns of phrase, as well as by localisms hitherto unknown in Russian literature. The greatest contribution in this respect was made by Remizov. Among the Neorealist poets who worked a great deal over their store of words, I would mention Gorodetsky, Alexey Tolstoy, Kluyev and Yesenin.

When we discussed the Symbolists, I mentioned that, because of the special difficulty of their themes, they had to develop the technique of word usage to perfection and, among other means, to utilize the music of the word. The Neorealists inherited this inventiveness from the Symbolists. We shall certainly find verbal music in the poetry of the Neorealists. But even more interesting is the fact that the same verbal music, the special tuning of words, their careful and deliberate choice for the sake of the desired impression, will be found also in the novels and stories of some of the Neorealists.

The technique of the musical construction of words is too complex to be discussed here; I shall merely provide a few examples to clarify my meaning.

In Bely's novel, *Petersburg,* one of the principal characters, a certain Alexander Ivanych, lives in an attic. One night he is delirious, and in his delirium he imagines that the statue of Peter the Great, the Bronze Horseman, is coming up the stairs to visit him. The author describes this approximately as follows: "The rails creaked. Peter's spurs clattered on the wood. Red circles turned more and more rapidly in Alexander Ivanych's skull. And Alexander Ivanych saw—spurs, and Peter's frock coat, and his terrible hands." You constantly hear in this passage the sound of *r* —ra, re, ur, er, ro. The author has deliberately chosen a series of rumbling, clattering words, which convey with particular force the impression of a bronze statue marching up the wooden stairs.

Or from another author:[5] "Around Saint Michael's day the snow began to fall. The white flakes tumbled down, and everything grew still. The barking of dogs rolled quietly in the air like a white bun. The white-cowled hermit pines prayed silently for all mankind." Here you see a repetition of the sounds of *fl, l*—to create the impression of flakes, of falling, whirling flakes of snow.

I have spoken about Realists, Symbolists, and Neorealists, who represent the most recent trend in Russian literature. To sum it up briefly: the development of literature has followed a dialectic path. First, one phenomenon developed, then its opposite, and finally, a combination of two antithetical phenomena.

In the works of the Realists, we find the earth—that which happens, could happen, on earth. They are the mirror of the earth. Their religion is earthly; they believe in the divinity of man.

In contrast to the Realists, who depicted the body of life, its everyday events, the Symbolists created broad, generalizing symbols of life, which I have likened to the skeleton of life. Their

5 Zamyatin himself.

methods of portrayal were also skeletal, incorporeal. The difficulty of their themes compelled the Symbolists to develop a high degree of verbal technique. They are characterized also by religious mysticism.

Out of the combination of these two antithetical trends, Realism and Symbolism, emerged Neorealism, an antireligious trend. To the Neorealists, the tragedy of life is its irony. They have returned to the depiction of life, flesh, everyday facts. But while they make use of the same material as the Realists, the facts of daily life, the Neorealist writers use it chiefly to depict those aspects of life that the Symbolists were concerned with. The characteristic features of the Neorealists are the seeming improbability of characters and events, which reveals true reality; representation of images and moods by means of one particularly salient impression—in other words, use of the method of Impressionism; clarity and sharp, often exaggerated, vividness of colors; use of the village, the backwoods, as the scene of action; broad, abstract generalizations—achieved by depiction of everyday trifles; terseness of language; "showing" rather than "telling about"; use of folk and local speech; use of verbal music.

My survey of the latest trends in literature would be incomplete without mention of the so-called Futurists, from the Latin *futurum*. Futurism is an even more recent trend than Neorealism. It is undoubtedly an offshoot of the Symbolist movement. From the Symbolists, the Futurists have borrowed the idea that the word—taken separately, by itself, and not only the word, but even the individual sound, the individual consonant or vowel, evokes certain associations. This idea is well founded, and its effective application by the Symbolists produced rich results. But the Futurists have carried it to an extreme, to absurdity. Their argument has been that, if words and sounds evoke images by themselves, there is no need to trouble about binding the words by any unity of meaning, there is no need for logical connection. In other words, there is no need for content; the words will speak for themselves and produce an impression. The works based on this theory, which are no more than simple collections of musical words and sounds, might have been appropriate for people if they were devoid of the faculty of thought and equipped only with ears—and, I would say, ears somewhat longer than ordinary human ones.

The lengths to which the Futurists went in their predilection for extremes can be illustrated by the following example. At a certain Futurist evening, a poet came out upon the stage and pronounced the title of his poem, "A Poem of Silence." Whereupon he stood for several minutes with folded hands, without a sound. Then he turned and walked out. So much for the poem. Later on, the Futurists abandoned their extremes to some extent and began to produce work that is more comprehensible. In addition to the stress on sound, the Futurists are distinguished by three other characteristics: intensified use of the device of brief, momentary impressions, which I described earlier as impressionism; search for extraordinary words and topics at any cost; and, finally, choice of subjects primarily from big city life, with its feverish movement and flicker.

If the Futurists succeed in freeing themselves still further from their childhood diseases and concentrate their attention on one of their characteristics—preoccupation with city life—then perhaps the same dialectical process will produce, out of a combination of Neorealism and Futurism, a new and viable literary movement. For the time being, the Futurists are a mere literary curiosity.

The most outstanding Futurist is the serious and talented poet, Mayakovsky, who represents Futurism at its best. In his poems you will find all the typical features of Futurism—impressionism carried to its utmost limits, unusual imagery, and stress on verbal music.

Now for a few concluding words. I do not insist that I have been absolutely correct in dividing writers according to trends or in characterizing each of these trends. We still have no firmly established judgments with regard to our newest literature. The critics are still debating. I have merely offered my opinions. If they differ from others, well, I prefer being wrong in my own way to being right in someone else's.

I recall an Indian story. Several blind men were asked to feel an elephant and describe him. One felt the tail and said that an elephant is like a rope; a second felt the leg and said that an elephant is like a pillar, but soft; a third felt the trunk and said that an elephant is like a sausage. This is the fate of most literary critics: literature is too vast a phenomenon to be encompassed all at once.

Perhaps I have not succeeded in conveying to you a picture of the whole elephant; I am not the judge of that. But if I have not done so, the fault is not mine. It is the fault of Russian literature, its complexity, its breadth, its rich flowering.

8 September 1918

TOMORROW

Every today is at the same time both a cradle and a shroud: a shroud for yesterday, a cradle for tomorrow. Today, yesterday, and tomorrow are equally near to one another, and equally far. They are generations, they are grandfathers, fathers, and grandsons. And the grandsons invariably love and hate the fathers; the fathers invariable hate and love the grandfathers.

Today is doomed to die—because yesterday died, and because tomorrow will be born. Such is the wise and cruel law. Cruel, because it condemns to eternal dissatisfaction those who already today see the distant peaks of tomorrow; wise, because eternal dissatisfaction is the only pledge of eternal movement forward, eternal creation. He who has found his ideal today is, like Lot's wife, already turned into a pillar of salt, has already sunk into the earth and does not move ahead. The world is kept alive only by heretics: the heretic Christ, the heretic Copernicus, the heretic Tolstoy. Our symbol of faith is heresy: tomorrow is inevitably heresy to today, which has turned into a pillar of salt, and to yesterday, which has scattered to dust. Today denies yesterday, but is a denial of denial tomorrow. This is the constant dialectic path which in a grandiose parabola sweeps the world into infinity. Yesterday, thesis; today, the antithesis; and tomorrow, the synthesis.

Yesterday there was a tsar, and there were slaves; today there is no tsar, but the slaves remain; tomorrow there will be only tsars. We march in the name of tomorrow's free man—the royal man. We have lived through the epoch of suppression of the masses; we are living in an epoch of suppression of the individual

51

in the name of the masses; tomorrow will bring the liberation of the individual—in the name of man. Wars, imperialist and civil, have turned man into material for warfare, into a number, a cipher. Man is forgotten, for the sake of the sabbath. We want to recall something else to mind: that the sabbath is for man.

The only weapon worthy of man—of tomorrow's man—is the word. With the word, the Russian intelligentsia, Russian literature, have fought for decades for the great human tomorrow. And today it is time to raise this weapon once again. Man is dying. The proud *Homo erectus* is dropping to all fours, is growing fangs and fur; the beast takes ascendancy in man. The brutal Middle Ages are returning, the value of human life is falling precipitously, a new wave of European pogroms is rolling on. It is impossible to be silent any longer. It is time to cry out: man is brother to man!

We call the Russian intelligentsia to the defense of man, and of human values. We appeal, not to those who reject today in the name of a return to yesterday, not to those who are hopelessly deafened by today; we appeal to those who see the distant tomorrow—and judge today in the name of tomorrow, in the name of man.

1919–20

I AM AFRAID

I am afraid that we preserve too fondly too much of what we have inherited from the palaces. Take these gilded chairs—yes, surely, they must be preserved: they are so graceful, they embrace so tenderly any rear end deposited in them. And it may, perhaps, be true that court poets resemble the exquisite gilded chairs in their grace and tenderness. But is it not a mistake to preserve the institution of court poets with as much solicitude as we preserve the gilded chairs? After all, only the palaces remain; the court is no longer here.

I am afraid that we are too kind, and that the French Revolution was more ruthless in destroying everything connected with the court. On the eleventh day of Messidor, in 1794, Payan, chairman of the Commission on Public Education, issued a decree, which stated, among other things:

> We have a multitude of nimble authors, who keep a constant eye on the latest trend; they know the fashion and color of the given season; they know when it is time to don the red cap, and when to discard it. . . . As a result, they merely corrupt and degrade art. True genius creates thoughtfully and embodies its ideas in bronze, but mediocrity, hiding under the aegis of freedom, snatches a fleeting triumph in its name and plucks the flowers of ephemeral success.

With this contemptuous decree, the French Revolution guillotined the masquerading court poets. But we offer the writings of these "nimble authors, who know when to don the red cap, and

Vladimir Mayakovsky

when to discard it," when to sing hail to the tsar, and when to
the hammer and sickle—we offer them to the people as a literature worthy of the revolution. And the literary centaurs rush,
kicking and crushing one another, in a race for the splendid prize
—the monopoly on the scribbling of odes, the monopoly on the
knightly pursuit of slinging mud at the intelligentsia. I am afraid
Payan was right—this merely corrupts and degrades art. And
I am afraid that, if this continues, the entire recent period in
Russian literature will become known in history as the age of
the nimble school, for those who are not nimble have been silent
now for the past two years.

And what was contributed to literature by those who were
not silent?

The nimblest of all were the Futurists. Without a moment's
pause, they proclaimed themselves the court school. And for a
year we heard nothing but their yellow, green, and raspberry red
triumphant cries. However, the combination of the red sanscu-
lotte cap with the yellow blouse and yesterday's still visible blue
flower on the cheek proved too blasphemously glaring even for
the least demanding. The Futurists were politely shown the door
by those in whose name these self-appointed heralds galloped.
Futurism disappeared. And as before, a single beacon rises amid
the tin-flat Futurist sea—Mayakovsky. Because he is not one of
the nimble. He sang the revolution when others, sitting in Petersburg, were firing their long-range verses at Berlin. But even this
magnificent beacon is still burning with the old reserves of his
"I" and "Simple as Lowing." In the "Heroes and Victims of the
Revolution," in "Doughnuts" and the poem about the peasant
woman and Wrangel, it is no longer the same Mayakovsky, the
Edison, the pioneer whose every step was hacked out in the
jungle. From the jungle he has come out upon the well-trodden
highway; he has dedicated himself to perfecting official themes
and rhythms. But, then, why not? Edison, too, perfected Bell's
invention.

The "horsism" of the Moscow Imaginists is too obviously
weighed down by the cast-iron shadow of Mayakovsky. No matter how they exert themselves to smell bad and to shout, they
will not outsmell and outshout Mayakovsky. The Imaginist
America, alas, has been discovered long before. Back in the era
of Serafino, one who considered himself the greatest of poets

wrote: "Were I not fearful of disturbing the air of your modesty with a golden cloud of honors, I could not have refrained from decking the windows of the edifice of fame with the bright vestments with which the hands of praise adorn the backs of names that are the portion of superior beings" (Letter from Pietro Aretino to the Duchess of Urbino). "The hands of praise," "the backs of names"—isn't this Imaginism? An excellent and pungent means—the image—has become an end in itself; the cart pulls the horse.

The proletarian writers and poets are diligently trying to be aviators astride a locomotive. The locomotive huffs and puffs sincerely and assiduously, but it does not look as if it can rise aloft. With small exceptions (such as Mikhail Volkov of the Moscow "Smithy"), all the practitioners of proletarian culture have the most revolutionary content and the most reactionary form. The Proletcult art is, thus far, a step back, to the 1860s. And I am afraid that the airplanes from among the nimble will always outstrip the honest locomotives and, "hiding under the aegis of freedom," will snatch a fleeting triumph in its name.

Fortunately, the masses have a keener nose than they are given credit for. And therefore, the triumph of the nimble is only momentary. Thus, the fleeting triumph of the Futurists, and the equally fleeting triumph of Kluyev, after his patriotic verses about the base Wilhelm and his enthusiasm over the "rebuff in decrees" and the machine gun (a ravishing rhyme: *machinegunning* and *honey!*). And even this brief measure of success was apparently denied to Gorodetsky: at the evening in the Duma hall he had a cool reception, and his own evening at the House of the Arts was attended by fewer than ten people.

And the nonnimble are silent. Blok's "Twelve" struck two years ago—and after the last, twelfth stroke, Blok fell silent. Barely noticed, the "Scythians" rushed, long ago, down the dark, trolleyless streets. Last year's *Zapiski mechtateley* [Notes of dreamers],[1] published by Alkonost are but a dim, solitary glimmer in the dark yesterday. And in them, we hear Andrey Bely complaining:

> The conditions under which we live are tearing us to pieces.
> The writer often collapses under the burden of work that

[1] Series of anthologies of the Symbolist group, published by the Alkonost publishing house in 1919–22.

is alien to him. For months, he has no opportunity to concentrate and finish an uncompleted phrase. Frequently of late the author has asked himself whether anyone needs him—that is, whether anyone needs *Petersburg* or *The Silver Dove*. Perhaps he is needed only as a teacher of "poetic science"? If so, he would immediately put down his pen and try to find a job as a street cleaner, rather than violate his soul by surrogates of literary activity.

Yes, this is one of the reasons for the silence of true literature. The writer who cannot be nimble must trudge to an office with a briefcase if he wants to stay alive. In our day, Gogol would be running with a briefcase to the Theater Section; Turgenev would undoubtedly be translating Balzac and Flaubert for World Literature; Hertzen would lecture to the sailors of the Baltic fleet; and Chekhov would be working for the Commissariat of Public Health. Otherwise—to live as a student did five years ago on his forty rubles—Gogol would have to write four *Inspector Generals* a month, Turgenev would have to turn out three *Fathers and Sons* every two months, and Chekhov would have to produce a hundred stories every month. This sounds like a preposterous joke, but unfortunately it is not a joke; these are realistic figures. The work of a literary artist, who "embodies his ideas in bronze" with pain and joy, and the work of a prolific windbag—the work of Chekhov and that of Breshko-Breshkovsky—are today appraised in the same way: by the yard, by the sheet. And the writer faces the choice: either he becomes a Breshko-Breshkovsky or he is silent. To the genuine writer or poet the choice is clear.

But even this is not the main thing. Russian writers are accustomed to going hungry. The main reason for their silence is not lack of bread or lack of paper; the reason is far weightier, far tougher, far more ironclad. It is that true literature can exist only where it is created, not by diligent and trustworthy officials, but by madmen, hermits, heretics, dreamers, rebels and skeptics. But when a writer must be sensible and rigidly orthodox, when he must make himself useful today, when he cannot lash out at everyone, like Swift, or smile at everything, like Anatole France, there can be no bronze literature, there can be only a paper literature, a newspaper literature, which is read today, and used for wrapping soap tomorrow.

Those who are trying to build a new culture in our extraordinary time often turn their eyes to the distant past—to the stadium, the theater, the games of the Athenian demos. The retrospection is correct. But it must not be forgotten that the Athenian *agora,* the Athenian people, knew how to listen to more than odes; it had no fear of the harsh scourge of Aristophanes either. And we—how far we are from Aristophanes when even the utterly innocuous *Toiler of Wordstreams* by Gorky is withdrawn from the repertory to shield that foolish infant, the Russian demos, from temptation!

I am afraid that we shall have no genuine literature until we cease to regard the Russian demos as a child whose innocence must be protected. I am afraid that we shall have no genuine literature until we cure ourselves of this new brand of Catholicism, which is as fearful as the old of every heretical word. And if this sickness is incurable, then I am afraid that the only future possible to Russian literature is its past.

1921

PARADISE

Much has been said by many about the imperfection of the universe, the creation of old Ialdabaoth. But, I believe, it never occurred to anyone that the focal tastelessness of the universe lies in its astonishing lack of monism: water and fire, mountains and abysses, saints and sinners. What absolute simplicity, what happiness, unclouded by any thought, there would have been if he had from the very first created a single firewater, if he had from the very first spared man the savage state of freedom! In polyphony there is always a danger of cacophony. After all, he knew this when he established paradise: there you have only monophony, only rejoicing, only light, only a unanimous Te Deum.

We are unquestionably living in a cosmic era—an era of creation of a new heaven and a new earth. And naturally we will not repeat Ialdabaoth's mistake. There shall be no more polyphony or dissonances. There shall be only majestic, monumental, all-encompassing unanimity. Otherwise, what kind of a realization of the ancient, beautiful dream of paradise will it be? What sort of paradise will it be, indeed, if the thrones and dominions thunder forth Te Deums, and the powers and principalities sing Miserere?

And so, it is clearly on this granite foundation of monophony that the new Russian literature and the new poetry are being created. The cunning bringer of dissonance, the teacher of doubt, Satan, has been forever banished from the shining mansions. All we hear now are the voices of angels, and the rejoicing of kettledrums and bells, of hail and glory and hosanna.

This essay was signed with the pseudonym Mikhail Platonov.

Prop up the sky with your skyscraper shoulders,
Shouting hosanna with your concrete lips!
> Obradovich, in *Kuznitsa* [The smithy], no. 5–6 (1920)

Henceforth, on land, in seas and deserts—
Glory!
Oh, how infinitely great
The worker's brain!
Sing hail to it!
> Dorogoychenko, in *Kuznitsa*, no. 5–6 (1920)

O Moscow! Glory, glory, glory!
> Obradovich, in *Kuznitsa*, no. 5–6 (1920)

Hail to thee, fire-visaged!
Hail to the workers' and peasants' land!
> K. Baryshevsky, in *Plamya* [Flame], no. 11 (1920)

Bands, storm louder!
Trumpets, thunder with all your might!
> Smirenskye, in *Plamya*, no. 11 (1920)

Now we shall sing hail to the Hammer
And the World Soviet of People's Commissars.
> (Kirillov, in *Raduga* [Rainbow] no. 1 (1920)

Glory to the future builders!
> (O. Leonidov, in *Khudozhestvennoye slovo*
> [Artistic word], no. 1 (1920)

Aren't we singing the new hymns
In unison and harmony?
> V. Bryusov, *Khudozhestvennoye slovo*, no. 2 (1920)

Arsky's "Hymn," Vasiliev's "Hymn," Vadimov's "Hymn," Barvshevsky's "Cantata"—hymns are the natural, logical, basic form of paradisiac poetry.

True, not every member of the choir sings with equal passion: some sing from the heart, others merely *ex officio angelorum*. But this is easily explained by the fact that some of the many-eyed and six-winged have moved to the new, monophonic universe from the old, polyphonic one. Yet they, too, carefully avoid dissonances, and therefore V. Bryusov's question is obviously superfluous.

Besides, in a monophonic universe there is generally no room for questions. Doesn't the very curve of the question mark—?—

suggest the Great Serpent, tempting the blessed inhabitants of the ancient paradise with doubts?

To the citizens of the ancient paradise there was no question, no dissonance even in the divine institution of hell. On the contrary, Saint Bernard of Clairvaux taught that the torments of the sinners make the bliss of the righteous and the angels still more dazzling and perfect. And this is why there is so much logic in the lines, "We are in a boiling Gulf Stream of blood. Skeletons floating by. Rot! We shall reach our goal" (Dorogoychenko, in *Kuznitsa,* no. 5–6 [1920]). This is why the Te Deums are intertwined so logically with extremely Krupp-like themes.

> Fall in love with bullets and with burning, thousand-year-old revenge!
> Hurrah for the laughter of cannon!
> > Dorogoychenko, in *Kuznitsa,* No. 5–6 (1920)

> Lightning and thunder
> Serve me in the ecstasies of revenge.
> > Studentsov, in *Plamya,* no. 7 (1920)

> The bloody draught of vengeance
> Spilled out in a scarlet arc!
> > Alexandrovsky, in *Gryadushcheye*
> > [The future], no. 12–13 (1920)

> Not singly and not by twos
> Drag the poisonous scum to the wall!
> > Dorogoychenko, in *Kuznitsa,* no. 5–6 (1920)

And so on and on, with sweet "machine-gun trills," "the roar of cannon throats," fragments of lead, bloodied scraps of garments, smashed skulls. In the ancient paradise, the extermination of Satan's angels was carried out more aesthetically: the only weapon was Michael's graceful fiery sword. But what can you do?—life is becoming ever more complex, weapons are more complex, and so is the task of establishing monophony. To fulfill this task, to rhyme with angelic ease such words as "blood" and "rot" demands superhuman qualities. Hence we are, of course, "Red Eagles," "Giants," "Titans," "Colossi," "Mighty, ever-wakeful Colossi." And the same etiquette prevails as had once prevailed in relation to Ialdabaoth and High Personages on earth: We, Ours, All-Blessed, All-Merciful. But today it isn't only "We" and "I." Today we have also Labor, Life, Strength, Will, Sleep, Laziness, Merriment, Love, Proud Reason, Achievement, Evil, Blood, Joy, Youth, Knowledge, Rot, the Future in a Fiery Cradle, Everydays, Yesterday, Tomorrow, the Ninth Wave. Self-veneration has reached such extremes that everything relating to the Self is Written in Capitals: even Sleep and Laziness.

Naturally, one must not compare the Titans with the Pushkins and the Bloks: the latter belong to the old, lilliputian universe. Titans can be compared only to one another. The Petersburg *Gryadushcheye* and *Plamya,* the Pskov *Severnye zori* [Northern dawns] play in the chorus of Titans the role (perhaps the comparison is too mundane) of the left section of the church choir, consisting, by established custom, of the little goat-bearded deacon and his sons, who sing just anyhow, in the plain old-fashioned way. They are helped by amateurs from among the people—the Moscow *Tvorchestvo* [Creation] and the Poltava *Raduga.* And, finally, there is the right section of the choir, where the singing is in real earnest, with proper voice parts—*Kuznitsa, Gorn* [Forge], *Khudozhestvennoye slovo.*

Only one voice stands out in the left choir—that of Ivan Yeroshin. He has a good teacher, Klyuev, and not the Klyuev of "The Copper Whale," but the Klyuev of the "Hut Songs." The rest are little deacons.

The amateurs—how can art be demanded from them? So long as they are zealous, so long as they are pious.

And who can say that this is not duly pious? Lilies, we are told,

> Have turned as red as blood,
> Feeling both rapture and love
> As they watch the heroism of the proletarian.
>
> D. Tumanny, in Tvorchestvo

Or:

> O valiant knight without reproach or fear!
> O heart-pure fighter for the poor!
>
> M. Zorev, in Tvorchestvo

And who will say that there is no zeal in the rhapodist's eulogy on the taking of Kazan by Raskolnikov[1]:

---

[1] An incident in the Civil War.

The river banks moaned
When Raskolnikov came from the river at night,
Smashing all locks
On the enemy guns.

This is by S. Gorodetsky, who modestly joined the crowd of amateurs in *Severnye zori.*

The newborn Muscovites of the *Gorn* and *Kuznitsa* are treading in the dangerous paths of the angels who loved the beautiful earthly daughters of Seth: they love Bely, Mayakovsky, Yesenin. And they feel that they must justify themselves: "It is, after all, quite natural that bourgeois literature, with its long experience and worldwide scope, possesses arms of the latest design" (V. Alexandrovsky, in an article in *Kuznitsa,* no. 4 [1920]). They are obliged to listen to calls urging them on to the "lyrical realism of civic themes" (Aksyonov, in *Khudozhestvennoye slovo,* no. 2 [1920]). But love of the beautiful is incurable, and there is danger that some of the Muscovites (Alexandrovsky, Gerasimov, Kazin, Rodov, Obradovich) will forget the grammar of paradise, which recognizes only exclamation points, and become true poets, knowing our earthly love and our human restlessness and pain. The greatest misgivings in this respect are inspired by Alexandrovsky, who contributed an excellent poem, "Mother," to *Gorn,* no. 5.

Now, as we well know, when the denizens of paradise descend from the abodes of ineffable glory into our sinful valley and speak in the language of prose, they carry in their hands the scrolls of the law and hold edifying converse.

Edifying converse fills the greater part of the fiction of the new universe, especially of the Petersburg one. Sadofiev tells us about a certain Senya who, for the sake of the Proletcult Studio, had even spurned earthly love; but, needless to say, his virtue was rewarded: " 'My dearest, my love . . . I was twice at your concerts . . . and I realized. . . . You are right, forgive me,' cried the flaming lines of her letter" ("Found," in *Gryadushcheye,* no. 12–13 [1920]). M. Belinsky wrings tears from the eyes of the reader with his story about the dying Vladimir, the "bright-eyed skeleton": " 'The Reds have taken Odessa! I am well!' cried Vladimir. And tears burst from his eyes and mingled with the

Boris Pilnyak

happy tears of his wife, who had hastened to his bed" ("White Terror," in *Plamya* [1920]).

And here is a sermon on the topic, "Long Live the United Labor School!" And a sermon on the topic, "The Duty of a Revolutionary—Stronger than Love, Stronger than Death." And a sermon on the topic "The Old God, Served by the Minions of Darkness, Ignorance and Superstition, Does Not Exist." And a sermon on Whitsuntide. And a sermon on Good Friday. And a sermon . . .

Even at the risk of perishing from association with the angels of Satan, the poets of the new universe (Muscovites) are nevertheless learning to use "weapons of the latest design." The prose writers, on the other hand, firmly remember the wise words of F. Kalinin:[2] "Even in the tiniest doses, bourgeois art is extremely noxious and demoralizing" (*Gryadushcheye,* no. 4 [1920]). And they beware of this deadly poison and choose the wooden plow rather than the tractor, the good, old, creaky coach of the 1860s rather than the automobile. They all merge into a single monophonic grayness, like stately ranks, companies, and battalions dressed in uniforms. And, indeed, how else? After all, rejecting banality means standing out from the orderly ranks, violating the law of universal equality. Originality is unquestionably criminal.

Nevertheless, there are still a few criminals. And the foremost of these is Kiy; once read, he cannot be forgotten like the rest. Take the rhythm of his prose—what's Andrey Bely compared to him! And the style—what's Count Rostopchin![3]

"The poor abroad came out and overthrew the ancient thrones and crowns, lending wings to our struggle, but the calls to world unity were drowned out by the voices of the flabby leaders, social liars, and cowards." And "Islands came in sight, golden shores, where the bright good sun shone for everyone, beckoned everyone to brotherhood and equality." And "The greenery around spread like a carpet, glimmered brightly with aromatic little flowers, with velvet little butterflies" ("Truths and Fictions," in *Gryadushcheye,* no. 3 [1920]).

And it is not only little butterflies that are obedient to Kiy's

[2] F. I. Kalinin (1882–1920), Soviet critic, member of the Central Committee of Proletcult.

[3] Count F. V. Rostopchin (1765–1826), Russian statesman, general, and writer.

talent; he is also capable of profound psychological analysis: "Zorev hated the defensive policy with his whole heart, and burned with internationalism. Therefore Plekhanovism was to him a kind of gangrene on the body of social democracy" ("Loyalty and Treason," a story, in *Gryadushcheye*, no. 4 [1920]). Are any further quotes necessary? And is it any wonder that Kiy is at the same time also an *arbiter elegantiarum?*—that he is at the same time the most competent critic in Petersburg in the realm of fine literature (*Gryadushcheye, Pravda*)?

Another transgressor against banality is Mikhail Volkov. His stories, "The Rooster" (in *Kuznitsa*), "Clever Marinka" (in *Severnye zori*), "On the Volga" (in *Gryadushcheye*) also stand out of the gray ranks. He has many fresh, unexpected images and a well stylized peasant language, marred only occasionally by exaggerations. But he is constantly aware of the angelic wings behind his back and remembers that he must—must! must!—speak edifyingly. And it is still unclear how he will end up—with edification and closed ranks, or with diabolic, disobedient art.

The third and gravest offender is Pilnyak. He is a man, a descendant of the banished Adam, who has insidiously and unlawfully stolen back into paradise. He is a man who will suffocate in the highly distilled air of paradise: he needs the earthly air, sinful, full of smoke, fog, the smell of women's hair, the close breath of Maytime cherry blossom, the pungent exhalations of the earth in spring. And even if he writes in the epigraph to his story "At the Door" (in *Khudozhestvennoye slovo*, no. 1 [1920]) that "this story is one link in the chain of stories about the Beautiful Face of the Revolution," you see clearly that this is not an icon dauber but an artist; and these are not radiant images drawn in obedience to paradisiac regulations, but human faces and bestial snouts. This is flesh and blood, and the rebellious floods of spring. It is Russia, the mother, and, whatever she may be, he loves her.

A man—in paradise! Without wings, without a halo, and without a Te Deum! This, of course, is not permissible. And, of course, they bethought themselves in the second issue of *Khudozhestvennoye slovo*, and wrote about Pilnyak: "The weak side of the young writer is his lack of a definite philosophy. . . . Pilnyak should either make an open break with Russia, or join the ranks of the revolutionary fighters" (Garmody). And, as far as we know, that negligent apostle with the keys to paradise, Valery Bryusov,[4] had no end of vexation at the hands of those who guard the purity of paradise. To let a man barge into paradise, just like that, and in boots? Unthinkable!

But this, of course, is a mere accident. Otherwise everything is perfect in paradise—angels and angels, wings, visages, little butterflies, Te Deum . . .

And the archangel Michael had already raised his sword at Satan, but the Lord stopped his zealous archangel: "What should we do without him?"

And the teacher of eternal questing, eternal rebellion, Satan, replied: "Yes, without me time and space would freeze into crystalline perfection. . . . It is I who trouble the waters. I trouble all things. I am the spirit of life. . . . If it had not been for me, man would still be a needless gardener, pretending to cultivate a weedless garden that grew right because it couldn't grow wrong. . . . Think of it. . . . Perfect flowers! Perfect fruits! Perfect animals! Good Lord! How bored man would have been! How bored!"

But this, properly speaking, has nothing to do with the case: it is the dialogue between God and Satan, from the latest novel of H. G. Wells, *The Undying Fire.*

1921

[4] Valery Bryusov (1873–1924), formerly a leading Symbolist, joined the Communist party in 1920 and became for a time the arbiter of revolutionary purity in literature.

GRYADUSHCHAYA ROSSIYA

I have on my desk two issues of *Gryadushchaya Rossiya* [The future Russia], a genuine "thick" journal, containing a genuine new Russian novel. What a historic event—"a newly published Russian novel"! We have novels in manuscript, I know, in the RSFSR as well. But in our country, where the most popular writer, recognized as a master by the government itself, is Demyan Bedny,[1] it is not fashionable to publish novels. And here we have a printed novel, *The Road to Calvary*, by A. N. Tolstoy. This novel, or rather, half of it (the two issues of *Gryadushchaya Rossiya* contain only ten chapters), is the mainstay of the journal. The novel is, of course, historical: it deals with ancient history, with Petersburg in 1914. But we who live in Petersburg, in the RSFSR, in 1921, we are Methuselahs, we are like the sleeper of H. G. Wells, awakening a hundred years later, and it is strange to us to read about our blind and charming youth—a hundred years ago, in 1914.

"An outside observer, coming to Petersburg from some lime-shaded Moscow lane . . ." These are the opening lines of the novel and, incidentally, an unwitting confession by the author himself. The outside observer from a Moscow lane is, of course, A. N. Tolstoy. He is a Muscovite, he belongs incurably to Samara and Nizhny-Novgorod. In his Petersburg you will not find the

This essay was also signed with the pseudonym Mikhail Platonov. *Gryadushchaya Rossiya* was a monthly which began publication in Paris in 1920. A. N. Tolstoy was one of its editors.

[1] Demyan Bedny (1883–1945), popular Communist poet who produced great quantities of propaganda verse.

eerie, spectral, transparent soul of the city that lives in the Peters-
burg of Blok, Bely, Dobuzhinsky. Alexey Tolstoy strolls through
Petersburg as an outside observer, though an acute and intelligent one. Chiefly, and most unexpectedly, intelligent. Until now,
Tolstoy knew how to conceal this with extraordinary skill—as,
I believe, Chukovsky pointed out in his article on A. N. Tolstoy.
And suddenly, in this new novel—intelligent conversations, intelligent people. Not many of them, and yet, and yet! In the past,
Tolstoy's whole charm was precisely in absurdity, in alogic. Now,
out of the pile of his former surprises and absurdities, you suddenly fish out a syllogism here and there. But Petersburg is all
straight lines, all geometry and logic. A man who comes here
from a crooked Moscow lane is therefore inevitably a mere
visitor. This is why *The Road to Calvary* is only an epic, without any of that lyricism which is inevitably present, as an implicit function, even in an epic by a Petersburg native writing
about Petersburg, about himself.

And one more thing: it is, of course, impossible to capture all
of Petersburg when the writer's palette consists solely of realistic
colors, without any admixture of Gogol and Hoffmann. There
must be sharpness, hyperbole, grotesquerie, there must be a new
kind of reality—the seemingly implausible reality which is revealed to the eye looking through a microscope. Alexey Tolstoy
is almost entirely devoid of this. Only in the beginning of the
novel does he rise for a moment over the heavy, three-dimensional Moscow world—in the passages where we get a glimpse
of the deacon who has seen an imp and spread the rumor that
"Petersburg will be an empty city," where the devil drives at
breakneck speed in a cab, and where a dead man looks through
the carriage window at a privy councilor. But this is only in the
first chapter, in which the author takes a highly concentrated,
skillful and clever (and this is especially notable—clever!) glance
at the history of Petersburg, down to our—no, not our days, days
that were a hundred years ago.

And here are these days, in the year 1914: "It was a time
when love, when kind and wholesome feelings were considered
outdated and cheap. Young women concealed their innocence,
husbands and wives, their fidelity. Destruction was considered in
good taste, and neurasthenia, a mark of refinement. . . . Worn
out by sleepless nights, drowning its anguish in wine, in mud,

in loveless love, in the sounds of the tango—the death hymn—
the city seemed to live in expectation of the dread and fateful day."

And this "dread and fateful day"—the day of war, followed
by revolution—wags a black finger menacingly in the novel here
and there. It is known that this day will come. It is even discussed
at the peaceful meeting of the "Philosophic Evenings" society
(so familiar!), where, sitting around the table, we see "the phi-
losopher Borsky, a former professor of theology, expelled from
the theological academy for his lapse into social democracy, the
writer Sakunin, author of cynical and remarkable books, devious
and cunning like an old serpent." The Social Democrat Akundin
speaks at the meeting, refuting the theory of the Messianic mission of the Russian peasant and calling for the "desperate experiment" of revolution.

And the historian replies:

> We foresee the triumph of your truth. You will be mas-
> ters of the elemental force, not we. . . . But when the ava-
> lanche rolls down to the very bottom, to the ground, you
> will discover that the higher justice, to the conquest of which
> you had called the people with factory whistles, . . . is noth-
> ing but chaos, where man wanders, stunned and lost. "I
> thirst," he will say, because there will not be a single drop
> of moisture within him. And you will not give him anything
> to drink. Beware: in the paradise you dream of you may
> find the most terrible of all revolutions—the revolution of
> the spirit.

How strange it is to read such articulate, astute words, so un-
like Nalymov's,[2] in a work by Alexey Tolstoy.

Tolstoy is unfaithful to Mishuka Nalymov only with the secondary characters of the novel, however: the principal characters
—the girl student Dasha, her sister Katya and Katya's husband,
a lawyer, the poet Bessonov, and the engineer Telegin—are at
all times enchantingly absurd and alogical, and if they are occasionally intelligent, it is the intelligence of the heart, never the

---

[2] The reference is to an early story by A. Tolstoy, "Mishuka Nalymov,"
in which he paints the life of the Russian provincial gentry. Mishuka Nalymov is the personification of the mindless, bearlike landowner who lives
only by impulse and brutish appetites.

mind. And you do not know why Katya suddenly goes with
Bessonov to a hotel, where he "takes her without loving her,
without feeling anything, as if she were a doll." And you do not
know why the preposterous Futuristic young lady, Yelizaveta
Kievna, goes with the same Bessonov, and perhaps to the same
hotel. Or why Dasha comes to him. You do not know, and—
most important of all—you have no desire to know. This is a
clear victory by the author: he succeeds in hypnotizing the reader
into mindlessness, into believing everything without question or
argument.

When Tolstoy speaks of the "magnificent absurdities" of the
Petersburg Futurist colony, he is altogether in his own, Nalymov
milieu (what a first-rate Futurist the world has lost in Tolstoy
himself!). "The Central Station for Fighting Banality" in the engineer Telegrin's apartment; the poems about "young jaws crack-
ing church cupolas like nuts"; the stroll along Nevsky Prospekt
on a spring day of young men in orange blouses and top hats,
with monocles on thick cords. These future "proletarians" and
erstwhile state poets are beautifully depicted.

The novel breaks off after the description of the strike of the
Obukhov workers—and the fateful day draws ever nearer. Its
scarlet light may redden the second half of the novel, published
by another Paris journal, *Sovremennye zapiski* [Contemporary
annals].

The parts published in *Gryadushchaya Rossiya* are sufficient
for critical conclusions. Alexey Tolstoy has finally come out of
his linden-shaded lane and taken up new themes. But though
the themes are new to him, his methods and technique remain
the same; to use the French proverb, he does not look for anything better than wheat bread.

Indeed, what can be better than wheat bread? What can be
better than Alexey Tolstoy of *The Lame Master?* And then, there
is always a risk of exchanging wheat bread for our present bread,
full of chaff. But the road of the truly great artists is always the
road of Ahasuerus; it is always the road to Calvary, always a
giving up of the bird in hand for the greater one in the sky.
Tolstoy clutches at his bird and fears the soaring one. For an
instant the huge wings rustle over his head: "Dasha looked at
her sister with stern, 'furry' eyes." And immediately Tolstoy is
frightened of these magnificent furry eyes, and shields himself

from the soaring bird with quotation marks. And diligently fences off every unusual image with quotation marks, or with "as if," "as though" and "it seemed." "It was as though the very air sang in the evening stillness"; "It seemed that the body had become light and pure, without a single spot"; "Dasha seemed to be purifying herself with solemn music."

But we, who live in the spectral city, we know that what seems already is. We know that the air really sings in the evening stillness, and that one really becomes spotless, and really purifies oneself with solemn music. Tolstoy himself can also transcend his Moscow body at moments and see this. "Katya had done something terrible and incomprehensible, something black. Last night her head had lain on a pillow, turned away from everything alive, loved, and warm, and her body had been crushed, shattered. This was how Katya experienced what Nikolay Nikolayevich called infidelity." Clearly, Alexey Tolstoy is capable of seeing; but why does he see so rarely, why is he afraid of vision?

Plotinus said, "He who sees becomes the thing he sees." Alexey Tolstoy has never seen Petersburg with the vision that Plotinus speaks about. He has merely written an excellent novel about Petersburg. He has told about Petersburg, he never showed it.

The rest of the material in the journal is chiefly the work of sinners hanging on for salvation to the only righteous man, Alexey Tolstoy. In the first issue there is a story by Dikhof-Derental, "Daddy," dealing with revolutionary life—one of those stories whose passport says: "Height, average. No distinguishing characteristics." There are also Boborykin's recollections, "Half a Century," about Hertzen, Lavrov, Mikhailov, Tkachev, M. Kovalevsky, Lev Tolstoy. The talented publicist and orator Alexinsky signs his name to a very feeble bit of fiction ("Tale about the Archangel Annail"). In the second issue we stumble unexpectedly upon another venerable debutant, G. E. Lvov, with a story, "The Peasants." The story is inept, clumsy, with occasional irritating lapses into the style of the folk epic, but there are also fresh peasant turns of phrase and expressions, from a genuinely peasant, not *paysan* vocabulary. The story is appended by a lengthy sermon on the topic "Animals decide their conflicts with their teeth, man is endowed with the capacity for deciding his conflicts with his heart." The sermon is both fine and timely, but even the most graceful church cupola won't do as a roof for a Russian peasant hut.

There are poems—by Ropshin, Minsky, Vladimir Nabokov (in the first issue), Amari, Wilkina, and Teffi (in the second issue). Reading these poems is like driving down a street in a provincial town in England: all the houses are clean and tidy, and one is like the other—not a stray curl or sagging window.

> I bless the cherished gift,
> The little fire, kindled by God,
> Fed by the warmth of the heart.
> But neither storms nor alarms
> Can fan it into a conflagration.

These lines are by Amari, but it seems to me that they apply not only to his verses, but also to those of his neighbors. The only one whose fire is not so "little" is Nabokov. His first two poems ("Requiem" and "Snowstorm") can be read with more than the eyes; the third ("After the Grave") was clearly extracted by the author from an old, carefully lined high school notebook.

To us, who have forgotten the sound of words that do not come from phonographs, there is a great deal of interest in the articles. G. E. Lvov contributes a fine programmatic article, "Our Tasks," to the first issue; it is sincere and without the slightest tinge of émigré ill will. The central idea of the articles is "Evil cannot destroy evil: only love has the power to do it. Love must conquer the world and purge it of the hate and malice which prevail today." Aldanov's article, "Fire and Smoke"— aphoristic, in the manner of Lev Shestov—discusses the bolshevism of Henri Barbusse, Romain Rolland and Anatole France, and draws a parallel between Konstantin Aksakov and Lenin. This parallel between the slavophile and Communist belief in Russia's messianic mission is most paradoxical and witty. The dry, uniformed lines by the prosecutors Mirolyubov and Iordansky, documenting the investigation of the execution of Nicholas II, are chilling; this chapter in the history of the former Autocrat of All the Russias has somehow remained behind a thick veil. And all political revolutions shrink to puny dimensions when you read Professor Anri's article, "The Modern Scientific Outlook," dealing with the revolution in science brought about by the law of relativity, discovered by Einstein. This is a new age in science. The first was before Aristotle; the second, from Aristotle to Galileo-Descartes-Newton; and the third, the new one, begins with Einstein. Yet we, stuffed to the ears with Demyan's fish soup of politics,[3] are first learning about it now, a year later, surreptitiously gathering a few crumbs here and there.

1921

[3] A pun referring both to Krylov's fable "Demyan's Fish Soup," in which a guest must finally run from an overhospitable host who feeds him plate after plate of fish soup, and to the prolific propagandist output of the Communist poet Demyan Bedny.

THE SERAPION
BRETHREN

A long room with columns in the House of the Arts—the studio. And here they are, around a green table: the quietest Zoshchenko; Lunts, who looks like my wonderful plush teddy bear; and somewhere, always behind a column, Slonimsky; and Nikitin —whenever you look at him, he seems to have an invisible brash cyclist's cap on his head. On winter evenings, during those days when no trolleys were running in the city, I used to come here from Karpovka to talk to them about language, plot, rhythm, instrumentation. On dark evenings they came here from the technological institute, from the abbey of Alexander Nevsky, from Vasilievsky Island. I watched them grow here—all except Vsevolod Ivanov and Konstantin Fedin: these came from outside; and Kaverin I remember seeing only rarely during the last days of the studio.

None of us older writers had gone through such a school. We are all self-taught. And, of course, there is always, in such a school, the danger of creating goose-stepping, uniformed ranks. But the Serapion Brethren have already, it seems to me, outgrown this danger. Each of them has his own individuality and his own handwriting. The common thing they have derived from the studio is the art of writing with ninety-proof ink, the art of eliminating everything that is superfluous, which is, perhaps, more difficult than writing.

Fedin is the steadiest of the lot; for the time being he still holds firmly in his hands the guidebook of old realism, with its exact schedule (without delays), and knows the name of the station to which he has taken his ticket.

The others have all been more or less derailed and are bumping along the crossties. It is not clear how they will end: some of them, perhaps, in catastrophe. This is a hazardous path, but true.

The most catastrophe-prone of the seven writers assembled in the first anthology of the Serapion Brethren are Lunts, Kaverin, and Nikitin.

Lunts is all shaken up; every particle within him is in a state of suspension, and there is no telling what color the solution will be when everything in it settles. From successful biblical stylization ("In the Desert") he skips to tragedy, from tragedy to a pamphlet, from pamphlet to a fantastic tale (I know these works). He is rougher and clumsier than the others, and he makes more mistakes. The others see and hear much better than he, but for the present he thinks better. He reaches out for broad syntheses, and the literature of the immediate future will inevitably turn away from painting, whether respectably realistic or modern, and from daily life, whether old or the very latest and revolutionary, and turn to artistically realized philosophy.

The same tendency can be sensed in Kaverin. This is not as noticeable in his *Chronicle of the City of Leipzig* as in his other, still unpublished works. Kaverin has taken a difficult course: he follows in the path of Theodor Hoffmann;[1] he has not yet climbed across this peak, but there is reason to hope that he will. While Zoshchenko, Ivanov, and Nikitin are working chiefly with language and ornamentation, Kaverin is obviously drawn to experiments with plot, to the problem of synthesis of fantasy and reality, the pungent game of destroying illusion and creating it anew. In this game he is skillful. But in the excitement of the game, he sometimes ceases to hear words, and his phrases turn out somewhat askew. But as Dr. Khorosheva said recently, in the presence of the Serapion Brethren, this is very easily cured. Kaverin has one weapon which, I think, no one else among the Serapions possesses—irony (the professor in the *Chronicle of the City of Leipzig,* the early parts of chapters 6 and 7). This sharp and bitter herb has until now grown very sparingly in our

---

[1] E. T. A. Hoffmann (1776–1822), German writer and composer, author of fantastic tales. The Serapion Brethren greatly admired his art and took their name from his story about the hermit Serapion.

ВЕЧЕР
—СЕГОДНЯ—
А. РЕМИЗОВ
Н. НИКИТИН
.ЗОЩЕНКО
.ЛУНЦ

Ю.А.
1921

Mikhail Zoshchenko

Russian fields; the more valuable the attempt to plant it, and the more uniqueness it lends the author.

Zoshchenko, Ivanov, and Nikitin are folklorists and painters, "icon painters." They do not look for new architectural or plot forms (although Nikitin has lately begun to do so), but take a ready form—the *skaz*.[2]

For the time being, Zoshchenko utilizes the simplest form of the *skaz*—that written in the first person. His entire cycle "The Stories of Sinebryukhov" is written in this form (the story in the anthology is taken from this cycle). Zoshchenko makes excellent use of the syntax of popular speech; there is not a single mistake in the order of the words, the verb forms, the choice of synonyms. He knows how to lend amusing novelty to the most worn, most hackneyed words by a (seemingly) wrong choice of synonyms, by intentional pleonasms ("to live a life of full family pleasure," "at one end, a hillock, at the other—vice versa—a hillock," "in his bottom underpants"). And yet Zoshchenko should not stop too long at this station. One must move forward, even if one has to bump over the crossties.

Nikitin is represented in the anthology by "Desi," a story altogether untypical of him. This is his first attempt to leave the rails of the *skaz* and create what I have on occasion called a *pokaz,* a "showing," in a concentrated, disjoined form. The story is made up of individual fragments, seemingly discrete, without cement, and only from a distance can it be seen that the rays extending from all the pieces meet in a single focus. A most interesting experiment in composition, but it overtaxed the author's resources; in the second part, "Epos" and "Sky," he lapsed back into an ordinary story. The result is a train consisting half of airplanes, half of cars. Naturally, the airplanes do not fly. But even if the experiment ends in a catastrophe, even if the author emerges from it black and blue, the attempt is still good; it shows that Nikitin does not seek to settle into a steady and untroubled existence, that he has no desire to become an efficient literary landowner. Indeed, he has already passed through the settled stage—with his excellent story "Stake," well-integrated and rich in fresh imagery. This story would have been the best in the

[2] A tale or story told by a fictional narrator rather than the author, in the language characteristic of the narrator and his milieu.

anthology, but was not included for reasons beyond the author's control.

Vsevolod Ivanov has strength enough for two, but his instruments are coarser than those of Zoshchenko and Nikitin. The *skaz* form he uses is not consistently maintained: every now and then he forgets that he must look at everything with Yerma's eyes ("The Blue Beastie") and think with Yerma's brain; every now and then "a leaf etched by the birch tree in the sky" will jump out at you. Altogether unnecessary and jarring is his attempt to convey folk speech with primitive naturalism, as though he were taking ethnographic notes. To convey a village morning symphonically, it is quite unnecessary to put a live rooster and a calf into the orchestra, next to the first violin. Ivanov can do very well without these ethnographic notes, especially since he is not even consistent in his usages, and his Yerma speaks the same words differently on the same page. This is simply careless work. It seems to me that Ivanov writes too hastily and too much; he does not search as intensely and restlessly as some of his neighbors in the anthology. And that's a pity, because he is not less talented than they are. What marvelous new images he can find when he wants to: "dark, airless huts—and the people in them like flies in bread, baked into it," or "water among the tussocks, heavy, sated." Strong, sturdy words, "like Irbit carts."

Slonimsky, like Lunts, is still searching for himself; he is still in the state of an Ahasuerus: plays, war stories, grotesques, contemporary life. With Kaverin and Lunts, he forms the "Western" group of the Serapion Brethren, tending to operate predominantly with architectural masses, with plot, but with relatively little ear or love for the Russian word itself, its music and its color. The latter is more within the ken of the "Eastern" group— Nikitin, Zoshchenko, Vsevolod Ivanov, and, partly, Fedin. Slonimsky's story, "The Wild One," is very dynamic and frequently verges on *pokaz*. Slonimsky has succeeded in shifting his rhythms with the appearance of various characters and with changes in the relative intensity of the action (chapter 1—Abraham—*lento;* 2—Ivan Gruda—*allegro;* 7—*presto*). Slonimsky does not have the rich imagery of Nikitin and Vsevolod Ivanov; some of his images are wrongly invested with the author's colors, not those of his characters ("Abraham . . . saw himself . . . wise as eternity." The tailor Abraham—and eternity. Doubtful.)

Fedin, I repeat, is somewhere off by himself in the entire group. Most of his comrades march under the flag of Neorealism, but he is still completely stuck in Gorky. I remember his excellent story "The Garden" (it was read at the competition at the House of Writers). Up to this time, he has not produced anything better than "The Garden." In his "Canine Souls," the dogs often think like Fedin, not like dogs. After "Kashtanka" and *The White Fang*,[3] writers, especially young writers, should beware of dogs.

The shadows of major literary figures still hang over most of the Serapion Brethren. But there is little point in searching for birth certificates. It has been written of Lenin that he is a descendant of Saratov gentry; does that change anything? It is sufficient to say that they are talented—each in his own way—young, and work hard. Some of them will probably make a contribution to the history of Russian literature; others, perhaps, only to the history of the Russian Revolution.

1922

[3] "Kashtanka," by Chekhov, and *The White Fang,* by Jack London.

ON SYNTHETISM

$$+, -, -\ -$$

These are the three schools in art, and there are no others. Affirmation, negation, and synthesis—the negation of negation. The syllogism is closed, the circle completed. Over it arises a new circle—new and yet the same. And out of these circles the spiral of art, holding up the sky.

A spiral; a winding staircase in the Tower of Babel; the path of an airplane rising aloft in circles—such is the way of art. The equation of the movement of art is the equation of a spiral. And every circle of this spiral, the face, the gesture, the voice of every school, bears one of these stamps:

$$+, -, -\ -$$

The plus: Adam—nothing but clay; the world—nothing but clay. The moist, emerald clay of grass; peach warm, the naked body of Eve against the emerald; cherry red, Eve's lips and breast tips, apples, wine. Vivid, simple, firm, coarse flesh: Moleschott, Büchner, Rubens, Repin, Zola, Tolstoy, Gorky, Realism, Naturalism.[1]

But now Adam is satiated with Eve. He is no longer drawn to the scarlet flowers of her body, he immerses himself for the first time in her eyes, and at the bottom of these eerie wells cut in the three-dimensional, clay world, he finds the misty glimmering of another world. And the emerald grass pales; the red,

---

[1] Jacob Moleschott (1822–93), Dutch-born physiologist and advocate of scientific materialism. Georg Büchner (1813–37) was a writer of the Naturalist school. Ilya Repin (1844–1930), eminent Russian realistic painter.

firm lips are forgotten; the embracing bodies untwine. This is minus—to the whole clay world; no—to all flesh. Because there, in the depths, in the fluid mirrors, is a new Eve, a thousand times more beautiful than this one, but she is tragically unattainable, she is—Death. And so—Schopenhauer, Botticelli, Rossetti, Vrubel, Verlaine, Blok, Idealism, Symbolism.

Years, minutes pass—and Adam quivers again. He has touched Eve's knees and lips. Again the blood rushes up to his cheeks; his nostrils quiver, drinking the green wine of the grass. Away with the minus! But today's artist and poet, today's Adam, is already poisoned by the knowledge of the other, once glimpsed Eve, and together with sweetness his kisses leave on the lips of this Eve a bitter touch of irony. Under the glowing flesh, Adam, who has gone through negation, who has grown wiser, knows the skeleton. But this makes his kisses still more ecstatic, his love still headier, the colors more vivid, the eye still keener, grasping the most fleeting essence of lines and forms. Thus synthesis: Nietzsche, Whitman, Gauguin, Seurat, Picasso—the new Picasso, still unknown to many—and all of us, great and small, who work in contemporary art, whatever it may be called— Neorealism, Synthetism, or something else.

Tomorrow we shall be gone. Tomorrow a new circle will begin, Adam will launch out on a new artistic experiment: this is the history of art.

The equation of art is the equation of an infinite spiral. What I want to do here is to find the coordinates of the present circle of this spiral; I need a mathematical point in the circle from which I can begin to study the equation. And I shall take Yury Annenkov as this point.[2]

There is a tactical axiom: every battle requires a group of self-sacrificing scouts doomed to cross a certain dread line, and to pave the earth beyond it with their bodies under the cruel laughter of machine guns.

In the battle between the antithesis and the synthesis—between Symbolism and Neorealism—the role of these self-sacrificing scouts was taken by the numerous clans of Futurists. The Hindenburg of art had given them a superhuman mission in which they had to perish, to the last man. This mission was the

---

[2] Yury P. Annenkov (b. 1889), a leading twentieth-century Russian painter, illustrator, scenic artist, and writer.

Ю.А.

Yury Annenkov

logical reduction of art to absurdity. They carried it out reck-lessly, heroically, honestly; their homeland will not forget them. They paved the earth under cruel laughter, but this sacrifice was not in vain. Cubism, Suprematism, nonobjective art were needed to show directions that should not be taken, to let us know what lies concealed beyond the line crossed by the heroes.

And this is precisely what they were—a scout detachment. And those among them whose life instinct proved stronger than reckless courage returned from reconnaissance to the unit that had sent them out, to rejoin the battle in closed ranks, under the banner of Synthetism, Neorealism.

This happened to Picasso. Such works as the portrait of Stra-vinsky, the sets for Diaghilev's ballet *Tricorne,* and others, are a turn toward Ingres. The same path might have been taken by Mayakovsky. And this is also how Annenkov has saved himself.

The lid of the scholastic cube seemed just about to slam shut over him, but his strong and vital artistic organism took the upper hand. Some invisible fire warped his straight lines. They bent and began to move: from the elementary formulas of the triangle, square, and circle, he fearlessly went on to complex in-tegral curves. But the lines were still broken; they tossed about like infusoria in a drop of water, like the needles forming in a saturated, crystalizing solution. Another moment—year—and the solution was strengthened by facets, living crystals, bodies: thus, Annenkov's *Yellow Mourning,* his vast canvas *Adam and Eve,* his portraits.

And today Annenkov is where all the more clear-eyed and life-loving have come, imperceptibly to themselves, from the dark Symbolist dugouts, from the trenches of *Mir iskusstva* [World of art]. It was here—to Synthetism and Neorealism—that Blok came before his death with his poem "The Twelve" (and it was not by chance that he chose Annenkov as his illustrator). It was here that Andrey Bely came, imperceptibly to himself, with *The Crime of Nikolay Letayev* and his last novel about Moscow. Sudeikin seems to be here, too, with his *Drinking Tea, Ride at Shrovetide,* and other recent paintings. And of course, Boris Grigoriev, with his graphics, his whole magnificent cycle *Russia* and his *Buyi-buyi* [Show booth]. And I am certain that many others—in Paris, in Berlin, in Chicago, and in London—of whom we know little, have come to Neorealism from various directions.

But Bely's Professor Letayev is at the same time a Scythian with a spear, flying on his horse across the steppe; and the drainpipe on the Kosyakov house is no longer a pipe, but time. And Annenkov's Adam walks toward Eve with a balalaika in his hands, and at his feet in paradise there is a little locomotive, a rooster, and a boot; and in his *Yellow Mourning* a jolly fellow with a harmonica sits astride the Great Dipper. Is it not absurd to speak of realism here, even if "neo"? After all, it is well known that a drainpipe is a drainpipe, and there are no roosters and no boots in heaven.

But this is known to Thomases. We know that, of the twelve apostles, only Thomas was not an artist. He alone could see nothing but what he could touch. And we who have been titrated through Schopenhauer, Kant, Einstein, and Symbolism, we know that the world, the thing in itself, reality are not what is visible to the Thomases.

Take something apparently very real and beyond question— your own hand. You see the smooth, pink skin, covered with delicate down. So simple, so unquestionable.

And here is a little piece of this skin under the cruel irony of the microscope: ditches, pits, furrows; thick stems of unknown plants—once hair; a huge lump of earth, or a meteorite which dropped down from the infinitely distant sky—the ceiling—just recently a mere speck of dust; a whole fantastic world—perhaps a plain somewhere on Mars.

Yet it is your hand. And who will say that the "real" one is this hand, familiar, smooth, visible to all the Thomases, and not the other—the fantastic plain on Mars?

Realism saw the world with the naked eye. Symbolism glimpsed the skeleton through the surface of the world—and Symbolism turned away from the world. These are the thesis and the antithesis. Synthesis approached the world with a complex assortment of lenses, and grotesque, strange multitudes of worlds are being revealed to it. It discovers that man is a universe where the sun is an atom, the planets are molecules, and the hand is, of course, the vast, shining constellation of the Hand. It discovers that the earth is a leucocyte, that Orion is but an ugly birthmark on a lip, and the flight of the solar system toward Hercules is but the cosmic peristalsis of the intestines. It discovers the beauty of a log of wood—and the corpselike hideousness of the moon. It discovers the most insignificant and most grandiose greatness of man. It discovers the relativity of everything. And is it not natural that the philosophy of Neorealism contains at the same time infatuation with life and the blowing up of life with that most terrible of explosives—the smile?

In our day, the only fantastic thing is yesterday's life resting on the immutable foundation of three whales. Today, the Apocalypse could be published as a daily newspaper; tomorrow we shall calmly buy a ticket for a journey by sleeper to Mars. Einstein broke space and time themselves from their anchors. And the art that grows out of this present-day reality—can it be anything but fantastic, dreamlike?

Nevertheless, there are still houses, boots, cigarettes. And next to the office which sells tickets to Mars is the store that sells sausages. Hence, the synthesis of the fantastic with the everyday in contemporary art. Every detail is palpable; everything has its measure, weight, and smell; everything is bursting with juice like a ripe cherry. And yet, out of rocks, boots, cigarettes, and sausages, we have the phantasm, the dream.

This is the very alloy whose secret was so well known to Hieronymus Bosch and the "hellish" Peter Breughel. This secret is known also to some of our young men, including Annenkov. His fantastic harmonica player riding stars, and his pig pulling a coffin, and his paradise with boots and a balalaika are, of course, reality, but a new reality, the reality of today. Not *realia*, true, but *realiora*. And it is not fortuitous but quite logical that in his work in the theater Annenkov is associated with the production of Gogol's *The Nose,* Dostoyevsky's *A Nasty Anecdote,* and Wedekind's *Lulu.*

After the geometrically philosophic earthquake produced by Einstein, the old space and time perished irrevocably. But even before Einstein, this earthquake was recorded by the seismograph of the new art; even before Einstein, the axonometry of perspective was shaken, the axes of the Xs, Ys, and Zs split into multiple rays. A single second holds not one, but hundreds of seconds. And next to the face in Annenkov's portrait of Gorky a street bristling with bayonets, a cupola, a dreaming Buddha hang suspended within the second. Adam, a boot, a train exist simultaneously in one painting. And in the plots of verbal paintings, we see side by side, on the same plane, mammoths and house committees of present-day Petersburg, Lot and Professor Letayev. There has been a displacement of planes in space and time. For the depiction of present, fantastic reality, the displacement of planes is a method as logically necessary as projection on the planes of Xs, Ys, and Zs is in classic descriptive geometry. The door to this method was rammed out by the Futurists, at the cost of their foreheads. But they employed it like a first-year student who has deified the differential but does not know that a differential without an integral is a boiler without a manometer. As a result their world—the boiler—exploded into a thousand disconnected pieces, words decomposed into meaningless sounds.

Synthetism employs integral displacement of planes. Here the pieces of the world set into one space-time frame are never accidental. They are welded by synthesis, and—whether nearer or farther—the rays issuing from these pieces invariably meet at one point; the pieces always form a single whole.

Take Annenkov's Petrukha and Katka, from Blok's "The Twelve." Katka: a bottle and an empty glass turned upside down; a cheap clock decorated with painted flowers; a black window with a bullet hole and cobwebs; forget-me-nots. And Petrukha: a bare autumn branch; croaking ravens; electric wires, a brigand's knife, and a church cupola. A seeming chaos of apparently contradictory objects, accidentally thrown onto the same plane. But take another look at "The Twelve," and you will see the focus where all these scattered rays are gathered, the strong links that bind the bottles and the sentimental forget-me-nots, the brigand's knife and the church cupola.

This is true of Annenkov's latest paintings. In his earlier works such integration of fragments is often impossible; there you have only independent, deified differentials, and the world is shattered into pieces only because of a mischievous infantile desire to kick up a row.

At times you also find there one of the Futurists' favorite errors: a hopeless attempt to fix upon the canvas the sequence of several seconds—to introduce into painting, a three-dimensional art, a fourth dimension: continuity, time (a dimension given only to words and to music). Hence, these "traces" of the supposedly moving hand in the portrait of Elena Annenkova (a drawing superb in its synthetic economy of line); the "traces" of the supposedly falling derby of the Bourgeois (illustration for "The Twelve"). But all this belongs to a stage that has clearly been outgrown by Annenkov. His latest works show beyond doubt that he has already understood that the strength of painting is not in crystalizing five seconds, but one; and that the strength of painting in our speeding-automobile era is in crystalizing not one, but one one-hundredth of a second.

All our clocks are, of course, mere toys; no one has a true clock. Today, an hour, a year are altogether different units of time from what they were yesterday, and we are unaware of this only because, floating in time, we do not see the banks. But art has keener eyes than we do, and the art of every epoch reflects the speed of the epoch, the speed of yesterday and today.

Yesterday and today are a stagecoach and an automobile.

Yesterday you traveled along the steppe road by unhurried stagecoach. A slow wanderer—a village church—is floating toward you. Unhurriedly, you open the window; you narrow your eyes against the steeple gleaming in the sun, the whiteness of the walls; you rest your eyes on the blue slits of sky; you will remember the green roof, the lacy sleeves of the weeping birch, like the sleeves of an oriental robe, the solitary woman leaning against the birch.

And today—by car—past the same church. A moment—it rises, flashes, disappears. And all that remains is a streak of lightning in the air, topped with a cross; beneath it, three sharp, black shapes cut in the sky, one over the other, and a woman-birch, a woman with weeping branches. Not a single secondary detail, not a single superfluous line, not a word that can be crossed out. Nothing but the essence, the extract, the synthesis, revealed to the eye within one one-hundredth of a second, when all sensations are gathered into focus, sharpened, condensed.

Annenkov did not paint this flashing church steeple. The picture is mine, verbal. But I know—had he painted it, this is precisely how he would have done it. Because he has a keen awareness of the extraordinary rush and dynamism of our epoch. His sense of time is developed to the hundredth of a second. He has the knack—characteristic of Synthetism—of giving only the synthetic essence of things.

The man of yesterday, the stagecoach man, may find this un-

Korney Chukovsky

satisfactory. But the man of today, the automobile man, will be led much further and deeper by the flash of lightning ending in a cross and the three silhouettes in the sky than by an excellent depiction of the church tower, drawn in detail in words or paint. Today's reader and viewer will know how to complete the picture, fill in the words—and what he fills in will be etched far more vividly within him, will much more firmly become an organic part of him. Thus, Synthetism opens a way to the common creative action by the artist and the reader or viewer. This is its strength. And it is precisely upon this principle that most of Annenkov's portraits are built, especially his line portraits and the rest of his recent work.

Gorky's portrait: a somber, crumpled face, silent. But the three wrinkles, which appeared just yesterday over his brows, speak; the red rhombus with the letters *R.S.F.S.R.* shouts. And in the background a strange combination: the steel network of a huge, fantastic city—and the seven-starred cupolas of old Russia, sinking into the earth, or, perhaps, rising from the earth. Two souls.

The portrait of Akhmatova—or, to be more exact, the portrait of Akhmatova's eyebrows. Like clouds, they throw light and heavy shadows on the face, and in them, so many losses. They are like a key to a piece of music; the key is set, and you hear the speech of the eyes, the mourning hair, the black rosary on the combs.

Remizov's portait: head rises from the shoulders, cautiously, as out of a burrow. All of him covered, wrapped up in Serafima Pavlovna's blouse, with a patch on the collar. The room is cold—or, perhaps, warm only near the stove. And a winter fly, revived by the stove, has just alighted on the forehead. But the man does not even have strength enough to raise his hand and brush away the fly.

Sologub—silvered, touched by frost, wintry. Pyast—face overgrown with stubble, rusty; lips and eyebrows tightly knit; cataleptic, motionless eye. Chukovsky—with a look of desperate fatigue, from lectures, meetings. Shchegolev—face grown loose, baggy, like a ready-made suit, but still smiling with one eye, and still elephant-footed, still absorbed in books. Laconic portrait of Annenkov: a cigarette rolled from the official *Izvestia,* and a single, intent look, intent precisely because the other eye was not drawn in. Some faces have been anatomized ironically by this close, intent look, but the irony is faintly discernible, and in order to find it, the sitter is tempted to take a look at the other side, the mirror side, where children and cats look for reality.

Some of these portraits, such as the portrait of Gorky, though conceived with synthetic sharpness, turned out unconcentrated, too wordy in execution. Others still bear the marks of Annenkov's Futurist infancy. But these are his early experiments in portraiture, and his recent works only gain by juxtaposition with them.

Portraits like those of Akhmatova and Altman are four-line Japanese haiku, models of skill in creating a synthetic image. They are done with a minimum of lines, no more than a few dozen—the lines can all be counted. But the dozens are invested with as much creative tension as yesterday's art invested in hundreds of lines. And therefore each of these lines carries a tenfold charge. These portraits are abstracts of faces, of people, and each of them is part of a biography of man in our time.

The last page of this biography—Blok in his coffin. And this merciless page could not but be the last, because it is not a portrait of the dead Blok, but a portrait of death itself—his, hers, yours. And after this face, already smelling of corruption, it is no longer possible to look at any living face.

1922

THE NEW RUSSIAN
PROSE

Russian literature in recent years is like Peter Schlemiel who has lost his shadow: there are writers, but there are no critics. The Formalists still don't venture to operate on living people but continue to dissect corpses. The living writers fall into the hands of amateur critics, and these judge literature with the same angelic simplicity as an engineer of my acquaintance judged music. To him, all of music was divided into two categories: on the one hand, "God Save the Tsar," on the other, everything else; if people got up, it meant that the music belonged to the first category; if they didn't, it belonged to the second—to the non–"God Save the Tsar" category. This is the only kind of response heard by the writer today. There is no literary, professional criticism. And so, willy-nilly, I, a writer of fiction, must step out of the circle and take a look from the side—who does what, and how?

Let us start from the left—the farthest left—the proletarian fiction writers. There are none.

They do exist, but thus far there are none who will survive tomorrow and enter the history of literature, if only through the back door. Despite the creation of special incubators, it proved impossible to hatch any kind of a proletarian literature, and it is not unusual today to hear an honest admission, such as: "It was a waste of time to try to create a proletarian literature by artificial means, by organizing Proletcults. The Proletcults have not produced anyone or anything."[1] And, indeed, they could not. Dogma, static positions, consonance—all these are obstacles to

[1] From a report to the Petersburg Soviet in 1922.

catching the disease of art, at least in its more complex forms. True, *Kuznitsa* [Smithy] and *Gorn* [Forge] have produced several genuine poets (Kazin, Obradovich, Alexandrovsky), but Andrey Bely is right when he says in one of his articles: "It is more difficult to write . . . in prose than in verse. And this is why, historically, prose appears much later than poetry." This "much later" is still very remote even for the most cultivated groups, such as *Kuznitsa* and *Gorn* in Moscow.

The extremely noisy company of Cosmists,[2] proliferating in the Petersburg newspapers like a host of parasites, threatens us in the weekly articles of its household critics with a downpour of new talents. But these obliging forecasts of their barometers are of small avail: the cosmos suffers from the same drought and the same crop failure in the field of prose. The largest number of promissory notes by friends seems to have been issued in the name of the author of a little book, *Hunger,* solemnly designated a novel. The heroine of *Hunger* (and, of course, she is not some common Marya or Darya, but—true to Verbitskaya's[3] brand of aesthetics—a "Fairy") says somewhere about her own face: "I can see no eyes, no nose. Something pallid glimmers, but the mind cannot grasp anything." This describes not only the Fairy's face, but the face of the whole book. Everything in it is a strict model of banality, down to "The petals have fallen, the fires burned down. Farewell, Sergey, farewell. I have buried him forever." This is the end not only of the story, but perhaps of the author as well.

Some of the Moscow Communist writers—Arosev, Neverov, Libedinsky—are stronger and more genuine. They till their pages with the good old wooden plow of realism. But Arosev occasionally digs up rather deep psychological roots (*Harvest Time* and *Recent Days*); Libedinsky (*A Week*) already tries to garnish his pictures of daily life with impressionism; and Neverov—well, Neverov seems to follow in the steps of Gleb Uspensky.[4] Nevertheless, it is quite clear that these writers are as certain as the Cosmists and the Smiths that revolutionary art is art depicting

[2] A group of proletarian poets in Saint Petersburg, analogous to the Moscow Kuznitsa group.

[3] A. A. Verbitskaya (1861–1928), author of numerous popular sentimental-erotic romances.

[4] Liberal realist writer (1843–1902).

the daily life of the revolution. They see nothing but the body—and not really the body, but hats, military style jackets, mittens, boots. As for the vast, fantastic sweep of the spirit of our epoch, which has demolished everyday life to pose the problems of being—it is not to be found in any of their works. They are the Peredvizhniki,[5] the Vereshchagins[6] of literature. And if there were a revolutionary tribunal in art, it would surely try these groups of prose writers for literary counterrevolution.

Next to them on the defendant's bench would be the Russian Futurists. The material evidence? *LEF* no. 1—"a journal of the left front in Art." Three most dynamic manifestos; an auto-salute: "We know that we are the best artists of the age"; truly masterful poems by Aseyev and Mayakovsky; and suddenly—right about turn!—from Aseyev to Avseyenko:[7] Brik's story "She Is Not a Fellow Traveler," a most successful parody on the drawing-room story in a contemporary setting. Even the "elegant" names of the heroes are obvious parodies: Strepetov! Velyarskaya! The author has played a clever practical joke at the expense of the editors of *LEF,* but, of course, this parody is not traveling with any kind of new art.

The Serapion Brethren, born of the Petersburg House of the Arts, were at first welcomed with great fanfare. But the articles bestowing laurel wreaths upon them have now given place to what are virtually articles of the criminal code. According to the newest data (provided by the Cosmists), it turns out that these writers "don't have a penny to their names," that they are "wolves in sheep's clothing" and "don't accept" the Revolution. The Serapion Brethren are not Mozarts, of course, but they also have their Salieris. And all this is unquestionably the purest Salierism: there are no writers hostile to the Revolution in Russia today—they've been invented to relieve boredom. And the pretext was that the Serapion Brethren do not regard the revolution as a consumptive young lady who must be protected from the slightest draft.

But then, the Serapion Brethren are generally a fiction, like

[5] Movement in nineteenth-century painting in Russia, deriving their name from the Society for Traveling Art Exhibitions.

[6] V. V. Vereshchagin (1842–1904), painter of realistic war scenes.

[7] V. G. Avseyenko (1842–1913), journalist and in his middle years author of novels exposing high society and the bureaucratic milieu.

the famous Putois of Anatole France. A variety of acts and even crimes were attributed to Putois, but Putois did not exist—he was invented by Madame Bergeret. In this case, I was partly this Madame Bergeret; however, today it is no longer possible to conceal that the Serapion Brethren are not brethren at all: they have different fathers. And they are not a school, not even a trend: what kind of trend can they be if some are heading east and others west? They are simply chance fellow travelers who met in a railway car and whose journey together away from literary traditions will last only to the first junction. Only a few of them will go on; the rest will stop at the station of impressionized realism embellished with folklore. Vsevolod Ivanov and Fedin will probably remain here, and possibly also N. Nikitin and Zoshchenko. Their rich load of words pulls the four of them down, toward the earth, to everyday life; with Hoffmann's Serapion Brethren these four have less than a nodding acquaintance.

Our artless critics, using the method of "God Save" and non– "God Save," have lavished particular praise on Vsevolod Ivanov. Someone has even called him "a new Gorky." This was evidently intended as praise, but to a writer such praise is a rather bitter pill. No one called Gorky in his day a new so-and-so, because he was Gorky, and no one else. And he became the Gorky of *Childhood* and "Yeralash" only after long work and thought.

Thus far, Ivanov gives no evidence of much thought; he does more sniffing than thinking. No other Russian writer has written so much with his nostrils as he does. Ivanov sniffs everything indiscriminately; his work abounds in the smells of "trousers wet with sweat," of dogs, rotting manure, mushrooms, ice, soap, ash, koumiss, tobacco, homebrew, "human paltriness," urine ("Dimitry's hands, reeking of urine"), and on and on—the catalogue can be continued endlessly. Ivanov's sense of smell is like an animal's—magnificent. But when he recalls that man, after all, is not a wood goblin, that he does not consist of nostrils alone, and attempts to philosophize, the results are often anecdotal, like the God-seeking conversations in *Colored Winds:* "Got any homebrew?" "Nope. And what d'you say about God?" Or the scene in the same book where the hero, mounting a peasant woman, suddenly remembers: "A man needs faith, but what kind of faith—who knows?"

Vsevolod Ivanov is beyond question a painter. But the art of the word is painting + architecture + music. He still hears too little of the music of the word, and architectural forms of plot construction are still outside his field of vision. This is why he failed to master the complex, polyphonic structure of the novel (*Blue Sands*). For the time being, he is totally immersed in daily life (the "daily life of the revolution"), and going deeper and deeper into it. Only the impressionism of his images gives him the right to a ticket in the same railway car with the Serapion Brethren.

"Everyone around me wonders why I am so neat and clean. They don't know I've been tumbling in the dust . . . that my only thought is how to make a better somersault. . . . I am heartsick. How get rid of it?" These lines are from the author's aside in a story by N. Nikitin. And this is what Nikitin could say about himself if some literary Vvedensky organized a "universal confession."

Nikitin's tumble sickness is especially noticeable in his latest works, and its origin is, of course, a healthy fear of banality. He is ready to say the strong, the apt word, and he can do it, but he is afraid. And the result is often something altogether nonsensical, such as "the seagull whooped its wing over the water," or "discerning the sky at his feet, right by the firmament," although he surely knows that "whooping" means shouting, and that the firmament cannot be at one's feet.

Tumbling is no cure for heartsickness. Heartsickness—pain— is the very crack in the soul through which genuine art (blood) seeps out. Fortunately and unfortunately for him, Nikitin has this crack. Hence such stories as "Pella," "Stones," and "Stake." Hence, too, he is far more restless than Vsevolod Ivanov, and there is less chance of his resting from his labors on "revolutionary life," folklore, and impressionist painting.

Zoshchenko sits at the same table with Nikitin and Ivanov: they gorge themselves on the same thing—the intricately patterned and decorated gingerbread of words. But Zoshchenko has none of Nikitin's tumbling or Ivanov's greedy indiscriminateness. Among the entire literary youth of Petersburg, Zoshchenko alone has an unerring command of popular dialogue and the *skaz* form (as does Leonov among the Muscovites. But more of him later.) Such instantly exact and finished mastery always gives rise to fear that the author has found for himself his *petit verre*. But Zoshchenko's excellent, still unpublished, literary parodies, and his short novella *Apollo and Tamara,* built on the very sharp borderline between sentimentality and parody on sentimentality, suggest that the author's range is perhaps broader than the *skaz* form.

Among Fedin's assets is the oddly mature story "The Garden," which even Bunin would sign his name to. In *Anna Timofeyevna* there is slight shift to the left. A further shift, I believe, is to be found in his still unfinished novel. For the time being, Fedin is more to the right and more canonical than the rest.

Three Serapion Brethren—Kaverin, Lunts, and Slonimsky—are traveling with long-distance tickets. They may, perhaps, get off somewhere halfway, without going to the very end. Slonimsky may run out of strength, and Lunts, of patience. But in the meantime, they have gone much further away from the traditions of Russian prose, bogged down in daily life, than their four comrades. The traditional disease developed by Russian fiction writers is a certain pedestrian quality of imagination, a plot anemia; everything is thrown into painting. But these three have architecture, plot structure, fantasy—though at the cost of painting. Nevertheless, their kinship with Hoffmann goes beyond their passports.

This is especially true of Kaverin. His geography consists of Heidelbergs and Württembergs, inhabited by magisters, burgomasters, and fraus. Words to him are *a, b, c, x, y*—mere designations, the same in any language. He does not know of any concrete number words, and he knows nothing of painting, because he has plunged himself entirely into architecture. And here his experiments are very interesting: he obtains strong alloys of fantasy and reality; he skillfully sharpens his composition by playing at exposing his own game; he knows how to deepen his perspective philosophically, as though by parallel mirrors ("The Fifth Wanderer"). To become a highly original writer, Kaverin ought to transfer his Nuremberg at least to Petersburg, to color his words a little, and to recall that these words are Russian.

Lunts, like Kaverin, is all in algebra, in blueprints, not in painting. His stories have not yet emerged from the exercise stage, and may not emerge from it: his plot tension is usually so great that the thin shell of a story cannot contain it, and the author chooses the form of a movie scenario or play instead. His play *Outside the Law,* constructed in some algebraic Spain, bears far more deeply on the Revolution and contemporaneity than any story or play on revolutionary daily life.

M. Slonimsky is still a hybrid; at least, this is what he is in his only book of stories *The Sixth Rifle Unit*. These are stories of daily life (the war, the front, 1917), but the screen on which the incidents flicker is not solid, it frequently stirs and sways, and there is a feeling that fantasy may momentarily break through it.

As passengers of individual railway cars often do, the Serapion Brethren keep the door of their car locked. But, in fact, there is still room in it for many others. For Olga Forsh, of course, among Petersburg writers—not so much because of her stories, as because of her plays. In her stories, the age is shown primitively, arithmetically; in her plays, it is expressed in implicit functions, in a very profound, stirring form (*The Rabbi, Copernicus*). Of Moscow writers, there is, of course, room for Pilnyak, Pasternak, Leonov, Budantsev, Ognev, Malyshkin.

Among the literary youth of Moscow, Pilnyak is the senior member (he began publishing before the February Revolution) and, for the time being, the most outstanding. He clearly springs from Bely, but, like every sufficiently strong creative individual, he is anxious to cut the umbilical cord as quickly as possible, which is why he dedicates his latest work to "Remizov—the master whose apprentice I was." This is merely instinctive self-defense against Bely.

What is valuable in Pilnyak is, of course, not that he takes his clay only from the pits dug by the Revolution, and not his two-color journalism, but that he seeks new forms for his material and works simultaneously both on the painting and the architecture of prose. Very few writers do this today.

In Pilnyak's compositional technique there is an element that is new and very much his own: this is the constant use of the technique of "shifting planes." One thematic plane suddenly, abruptly succeeds another, sometimes several times on the same page. This method, as such, was used in the past as well—in the form of a constant alternation of two or several plot threads (Anna plus Vronsky; Kitty plus Levin; and so on). But no one has done it with such a frequency of fluctuation: Pilnyak has shifted from direct to alternating current, from two- or three-phase to multiphase current. This was used most successfully in one of his first stories, "Ivan and Marya."

In Pilnyak's latest works we see an interesting attempt to create
a composition without heroes—a task parallel to Toller's *"Massenmensch."* Focusing on the crowd, the mass, is just as possible
as pouring walls of concrete instead of building them of individual
bricks. But the pouring of concrete walls requires a steel frame.
And Pilnyak never has such a frame; his plots are, thus far, of
the simplest type, without a backbone; his novels or stories, like
angleworms, can always be cut into pieces—and every piece will
crawl off painlessly in its own direction. This is why he has not
yet succeeded in his attempt to construct a plotless and heroless
story ("The Third Capital"). No matter how insistently the
author stresses that "there are no heroes," the story turns out to
be, not of concrete but of brick, not of the *Massenmensch* but of
Menschen.

It seems to me that Pilnyak has not yet heard the language of
our epoch—rapid and sharp as code. In his works, especially the
latest, the syntax is Karamzin's,[8] lost in the shifting sands of his
periods. Only an air pump could read them aloud: no human
breath can suffice. Perhaps to reinforce these periodical quick-
sands, the author resorts to a variety of "shocking" typographical
tricks—which, after Bely, can scarcely shock anyone. I remember a certain "modern" conductor in Penza arranging his orchestra in a series of diamonds, angles and semicircles—in order to
play a medley from *The Demon.* But Pilnyak does not offer the
reader a medley. He has words, he has an original compositional
method, and Penza tricks only spoil his works.

Moscow has always been closer to Penza than Petersburg—
and always will be. And this geographic destiny makes itself felt.
There is still the hand of the Penza conductor in the motley pages
of Budantsev, with their varied type (in the novel *Rebellion*):
long primer, italics, brevier, corvinus, capitals, bold, demi-bold.
But under all this chaff, under the still-breaking line of rhythm
and the style weighed down by participles, you feel the pliant body
of urban, present-day language, the strong skeleton of plot, a
fresh and keen eye. His symbols are ruled by rampant impressionism. This fully protects the author from banality, but sometimes leads him to images obviously nourished in a laboratory
jar. In places, Budantsev successfully employs verbal instru-

[8] N. M. Karamzin (1766–1826), eminent writer and historian.

mentation—an art with which no one else among the writers of the younger generation seems to be acquainted.

And again, Penza: "abyss," "bottomless," "infinite," "faceless," "mad." This is Malyshkin, suffering for Leonid Andreyev's sins. Thus far, he has produced only two stories, but he has great sweep, and all he needs is to leap across the Penza abyss. In his story "The Fall of Dair," Malyshkin succeeded in creating what Pilnyak has not yet achieved: a thousand-headed, nameless hero.

Ognev may find himself in Pilnyak's wake. In his story "Eurasia" we find the same multiphase plot development. Later, however, he reveals his own elements—a synthesis of fantasy and daily reality (in the story "Cabbage Soup of the Republic"), perhaps the only correct coordinates for the synthetic presentation of our time. The same coordinates are chosen from the very beginning by Leonov in his stories—with a still greater tendency toward the fantastic, and even toward myth. This is a guarantee of wide range, a guarantee that the author will not solidify and settle into daily life. Leonov is of good stock, unquestionably descended from Remizov; hence his language, ruddy and firm, very Russian, but without any slang.

Pasternak has chosen the most difficult, but also the most promising path. He is a writer without kith or kin. He is not a new so-and-so, but immediately Pasternak, although he has published, I believe, only one story and one novella (*The Childhood of Luvers*). His own, new contribution is not in the area of plot (his work is plotless) or vocabulary, but in an area where almost no one else is working—in syntax. His symbolism, however, is also very sharp and very much his own. He seeks no external modernity, with flags and shots, and yet he belongs entirely to contemporary art.

Such is the young generation of prose writers. Those who consider themselves politically at the extreme left occupy the extreme right benches of old-time Realism. At the center is impressionized daily life and folklore. At the left, builders of plot, the purely fantastic, or the fantastic growing out of daily life. And the left is precisely here, because here we find the greatest swing away from the erstwhile traditions of Russian prose.

These traditions—fine easel painting, genre, psychologism—are still strong in the older writers. The earthquakes of recent years have not changed their technique; the epoch has expressed itself only in the monumental character of their edifices, their novels, and in their use of material from contemporary life.

However, these edifices are only beginning to be opened for inspection. Because of their specific gravity, the older writers came within the cone of explosion, and the blast of 1917 scattered them in every direction. Only now do they begin to emerge from printless deserts, and we learn of works mostly by rumor. In some Crimean wilderness Sergeyev-Tsensky silently finished the huge building he had begun during the war, his novel *The Transformation* (as yet unpublished). Prishvin has written a novella *Ape Slave,* which contains so much of today we shall read it only in some remote tomorrow. Ivan Novikov, B. Zaitsev, and Shmelyov are also working on novels seeded by the epoch. Shmelyov's superb story, "It Was" (in the *Nedra* [The depths] anthology), in which daily life is ready every moment to swirl into delirium, may be taken as a promise that Shmelyov will have sufficient strength to encompass the age in his novel as well.

In *Nedra* and *Novaya Moskva* [New Moscow] a large group of prose writers (Trenyov, Nikandrov, Shishkov, A. Yakovlev, and others) is still clinging to the good old realistic slice-of-life manner. These writers may be stronger, more stable, and more talented than some of the younger ones, but they represent the old Moscow, not the new.

Among the writers scattered abroad, thrown into the bits of Russia in Berlin, Paris, and Prague, there are few pussy willows (a pussy willow blooms anywhere, even in a bottle of water). Kuprin, Merezhkovsky, Gippius, and Bunin have stopped blooming (although only recently we have been told of new Bunin stories). Of Bely's two branches, only one—the poetic branch—has sent forth new shoots. Remizov still draws his nourishment from the little box of Russian soil he brought with him to Berlin; the expected results of Steinach's operation are still to be seen in his case. But there are also two productive names: A. N. Tolstoy and Ehrenburg—and their work can vie with that which has been turned out in Petersburg-Moscow Russia.

Tolstoy's *Road to Calvary* cannot properly be called a new novel. It is the last old Russian novel, the last fruit of Realism, of the real Tolstoy—Lev. Nevertheless, for A. N. Tolstoy this novel is new: until now his heroes thought with anything but their heads; here they have suddenly begun to think with their heads. From lack of practice, this does not always turn out successfully. When he makes Burov, in the *Road to Calvary,* discourse on love and say that love is a lie, he discovers gunpowder for the one-thousand-and-first time; the last Schwarzes before him were Artsybashev and Vinnichenko. But Gvozdev on the "herd" and the "inch," Zhdanov on "the law of man and the law of humanity," on the antinomy of freedom and equality—these are something else again, these are the real thing, Faustian. True, the novel moves along the rails of plot according to a mail-train schedule; true, the author encloses every daring epithet that slips through in quotation marks; true, the wineskin is old, but it is filled with good wine. Gulping down some of the pages, the reader becomes intoxicated. Because it is given to A. N. Tolstoy to know what love is (many of our young writers know it only from anatomy textbooks).

In his latest novel, *Aelita,* Tolstoy attempted to transfer from the mail train to the airplane of the fantastic, but all he managed was to jump up and plop back on the ground with awkwardly spread wings, like a fledgling jackdaw that has fallen out of its nest (daily life). Tolstoy's Mars is no further than some forty versts from Ryazan; there is even a shepherd there, in the standard red shirt; there is "gold in the mouth" (fillings?); there is even a house manager who "secretly held out two fingers like horns to ward off the earthmen"—he had evidently paid an earlier visit to Italy with his *barin.* The only figure in the novel that is alive, in the usual Tolstoyan fashion, is the Red Army soldier Gusev. He alone speaks, all the others recite.

The language of the novel: next to vivid, original expressions, you suddenly read something totally bald, such as "memory awakened the recent past." And the "recent past" predominates. Language and symbols have suffered the same fate here that women sometimes do after a bout of typhus: the hair is clipped—and there is no longer any woman, she turns into a boy. Tolstoy was compelled to clip the customary symbols and the details of everyday life, but he did not succeed in inventing new ones.

And, finally: *Aelita* has many rich relatives, beginning with Wells and Zulawski. In the pages of *Krasnaya nov* [Red virgin soil], *Aelita* undoubtedly blushes over her acquaintance with such a patented "mystic" as Rudolph Steiner: *Aelita* read about the seven races, Atlantis, and vegetable energy in Steiner's *Chronicle of Akasha.*

Ehrenburg is perhaps the most contemporary of all Russian writers, in and out of Russia. He has such a lively sense of the coming international that he has become in advance a non-Russian writer. We might call him a general European, even a kind of Esperanto writer. And this is true of his novel *Julio Jurenito* as well.

There is a story about a young mother who was so full of love for her coming child, so anxious to see it, that she did not wait nine months, but gave birth after six. The same thing happened with Ehrenburg. However, this may be due simply to an instinct for self-preservation: if *Jurenito* had been carried to full term, until ready to be born, the author might not have had sufficient strength to give birth. But even as it is—with a soft spot on the crown where the skull has not yet knitted, with bits of skin here and there still missing—the novel is significant and, in Russian literature, original.

Perhaps most original of all is that the novel is intelligent, and Jurenito is intelligent. With small exceptions, Russian literature of the last decades has specialized in fools, idiots, dullards, and sainted halfwits, and if anyone tried to show intelligent men, they did not turn out intelligent. In Ehrenburg's case, they did. Also his irony. This is the weapon of a European; among us, there are few who know it. Irony is a rapier; we have the cudgel and the whip. Ehrenburg impales on his rapier, successively, imperialist war, morality, religion, socialism, the state—any state. But it is here that he reveals the pieces which have not yet been overgrown with skin. Next to superb chapters, reminiscent of Anatole France, we find abortive newspaper feuilletons (such as chapters 6 and 15).

But the abortiveness is revealed most of all in the language. At times, the novel reads like a translation from another language into one that is not very Russian. Faulty syntax, poor choice of words. And this is all the more regrettable because, next to dreadful, rusty expressions, we find grains of gold (the intellectual has a "thin, straggly beard, as though it had come up in a year of drought"; women in a cafe have "thickly painted targets for kisses").

Three small books of Ehrenburg's short stories (*Improbable*

Stories, Thirteen Pipes, and *Six Tales about Easy Ends*) are three points through which we can trace the trajectory of Ehrenburg's formal shifts. In the first book, daily life is intertwined with the fantastic, and the language is still Russian. The second is a shoot from *Jurenito.* In the third, the language is compact, sharp, quick, telegraphic, international; there is an unquestionable kinship with the newest French prose (the Dadaists, Cendrars, Jules Romain's *Donogoo-Tonka*). Perhaps this is why even the peasants in this book speak like *paysans* (Yegorych in "Mercure de Russie," Silin in "Colony No. 62").

All the numerous blemishes in Ehrenburg's language can be explained (though, of course, not excused) by the fact that he is a convinced constructivist; hence, both in his novel and in his stories, his first concern is not ornamentation, not color, but composition. And it must be said that his compositional inventiveness is frequently more ingenious than that of his colleagues working in the same area on this side of the border. (In *Jurenito,* the device of introducing the author as one of the characters is highly successful; the construction of the story in the form of a scenario for a film is new to Russian prose, although it is borrowed from Jules Romains.) Ehrenburg closes the left wing of contemporary Russian prose.

And so the circle is complete. Dozens of names, titles, sleepless nights, achievements, mistakes, falsehoods, and truths. But this is life. Only lifeless mechanisms move along faultlessly straight lines and compass circles. In art the surest way to destroy is to canonize one given form and one philosophy: that which is canonized quickly dies of obesity, of entropy.

Such entropy has threatened Russian literature in recent years, but its viability proved stronger. Our literature still has life and fighting spirit, reduced, for the time being, to a struggle of formal trends. Of these, Symbolism is no longer in the field: it exists only on the bookshelf, firmly bound. On the other hand, primitive Realism, its cheeks reddened with left-wing political views, is crawling out into the open, shaking off the dust of forty years. But today, when exact science has exploded the very reality of matter, Realism has no roots; it is the refuge of old men and of old young men. In exact science, analysis is increasingly being replaced by synthesis, microscopic problems—by the problems of

Democritus and Kant, the problems of space, time, the universe. And these new beacons clearly stand before the new literature: from "real life" to the realities of being, from physics to philosophy, from analysis to synthesis.

Bare depiction of daily life, even if it be archcontemporary, no longer fits the concept of contemporary art. The recording of daily life is arithmetic: single units or millions—the difference is merely quantitative. In our age of great syntheses, arithmetic is powerless; we need integrals from 0 to ∞, we need relativism, we need daring dialectics, we must "contemplate every accomplished form in its movement, that is, as something transient" (Marx). Daily life can enter the new prose only in synthetic images, or only in the form of a screen for some philosophic synthesis. And, of course, the situation is not affected by the attempts—even if they are very talented attempts—of the prose writers of the center to rejuvenate genre painting and impressionism with folklore. The analytic work of word-searching is coming to its completion; the argonauts who have sailed off for the golden fleece of the word are already approaching argot, *langue verte*. The pendulum is clearly swinging in the opposite direction: toward broader formal problems, problems of plot and composition.

Life itself today has lost its plane reality: it is projected, not along the old fixed points, but also the dynamic coordinates of Einstein, of revolution. In this new projection, the best-known formulas and objects become displaced, fantastic, familiar-unfamiliar. This is why it is so logical for literature today to be drawn to the fantastic plot, or to an amalgam of reality and fantasy. In the West today dozens of writers are working with the fantastic—philosophical, social, or mystical: Harald Bergstedt, Aage Madelung, Colerus, Brehmer, Meyrink, Farrere, MacOrlan, Benoît, Randolph, Bernard Shaw, and even Upton Sinclair (his novel, *They Call Me Carpenter*). Russian literature, too, is gradually beginning to flow into this channel: A. N. Tolstoy's *Aelita*, Ehrenburg's *Julio Jurenito*, the present author's *We*, and works by younger writers—Kaverin, Lunts, Leonov. Coming into closer contact with the West also holds out the hope of curing the old sickness of Russian prose writers, which has already been discussed—plot anemia.

Another extreme may develop: some writers may simply be diverted into thoughtless games, into adventure novels; this has happened in the cases of Pierre Benoît and MacOrlan in France. But such novels reflect only one color in the contemporary spectrum. To reflect the entire spectrum the dynamics of the adventure novel must be invested with a philosophic synthesis of one kind or another. Despite their fine technical equipment, many of the young writers named earlier still lack such synthesis. Yet this is what is so sharply needed today. Everything that should have been and could have been destroyed has been destroyed. Now we have desert, and salt-laden, bitter wind. How populate this desert, how build it up? *Horror vacui* exists not only in nature but also in man.

If it were necessary to find a single word to define the point toward which literature is moving today, I would choose the word *Synthetism:* synthetic formal experiments, the synthetic image in the system of symbols, synthesized life, synthesis of the fantastic and of daily reality, experiment in artistic-philosophic synthesis. And dialectically: the thesis, Realism: the antithesis, Symbolism; and now the new, third stage, synthesis, which will include simultaneously the microscope of Realism, and the telescopic lenses of Symbolism, leading off into infinities.

1923

ON LITERATURE,
REVOLUTION, ENTROPY,
AND OTHER MATTERS

Name me the final number, the highest, the greatest.
But that's absurd! If the number of numbers is infinite,
how can there be a final number?
Then how can you speak of a final revolution? There is
no final one. Revolutions are infinite.

Yevgeny Zamyatin, *We*

Ask point blank: What is revolution?

Some people will answer, paraphrasing Louis XIV: We are the revolution. Others will answer by the calendar, naming the month and the day. Still others will give you an ABC answer. But if we are to go on from the ABC to syllables, the answer will be this:

Two dead, dark stars collide with an inaudible, deafening crash and light a new star: this is revolution. A molecule breaks away from its orbit and, bursting into a neighboring atomic universe, gives birth to a new chemical element: this is revolution. Lobachevsky[1] cracks the walls of the millenia-old Euclidean world with a single book, opening a path to innumerable non-Euclidean spaces: this is revolution.

Revolution is everywhere, in everything. It is infinite. There is no final revolution, no final number. The social revolution is only one of an infinite number of numbers: the law of revolution is not a social law, but an immeasurably greater one. It is a cosmic, universal law—like the laws of the conservation of energy and

[1] N. I. Lobachevsky (1793–1856), Russian mathematician who pioneered in non-Euclidean geometry.

107

of the dissipation of energy (entropy). Some day, an exact formula for the law of revolution will be established. And in this formula, nations, classes, stars—and books—will be expressed as numerical quantities.

The law of revolution is red, fiery, deadly; but this death means the birth of new life, a new star. And the law of entropy is cold, ice blue, like the icy interplanetary infinities. The flame turns from red to an even, warm pink, no longer deadly, but comfortable. The sun ages into a planet, convenient for highways, stores, beds, prostitutes, prisons: this is the law. And if the planet is to be kindled into youth again, it must be set on fire, it must be thrown off the smooth highway of evolution: this is the law.

The flame will cool tomorrow, or the day after tomorrow (in the Book of Genesis days are equal to years, ages). But someone must see this already today, and speak heretically today about tomorrow. Heretics are the only (bitter) remedy against the entropy of human thought.

When the flaming, seething sphere (in science, religion, social life, art) cools, the fiery magma becomes coated with dogma—a rigid, ossified, motionless crust. Dogmatization in science, religion, social life, or art is the entropy of thought. What has become dogma no longer burns; it only gives off warmth—it is tepid, it is cool. Instead of the Sermon on the Mount, under the scorching sun, to up-raised arms and sobbing people, there is drowsy prayer in a magnificent abbey. Instead of Galileo's "But still, it turns!" there are dispassionate computations in a well-heated room in an observatory. On the Galileos, the epigones build their own structures, slowly, bit by bit, like corals. This is the path of evolution—until a new heresy explodes the crush of dogma and all the edifices of the most enduring stone which have been raised upon it.

Explosions are not very comfortable. And therefore the exploders, the heretics, are justly exterminated by fire, by axes, by words. To every today, to every evolution, to the laborious, slow, useful, most useful, creative, coral-building work, heretics are a threat. Stupidly, recklessly, they burst into today from tomorrow;

they are romantics. Babeuf[2] was justly beheaded in 1797; he leaped into 1797 across 150 years. It is just to chop off the head of a heretical literature which challenges dogma; this literature is harmful.

But harmful literature is more useful than useful literature, for it is antientropic, it is a means of combating calcification, sclerosis, crust, moss, quiescence. It is utopian, absurd—like Babeuf in 1797. It is right 150 years later.

We know Darwin. We know what followed Darwin—mutations, Weismannism, neo-Lamarckism. But all of these are attics, balconies; the building itself is Darwin. And in this building there are not only tadpoles and fungi, but also man. Fangs are sharpened only when there is someone to gnaw on. Domestic hens have wings only for flapping. The same law is true for hens and for ideas: ideas nourished on chopped meat cutlets lose their teeth, like civilized, cutlet-eating man. Heretics are necessary to health; if there are no heretics, they should be invented.

A literature that is alive does not live by yesterday's clock, nor by today's but by tomorrow's. It is a sailor sent aloft: from the masthead he can see foundering ships, icebergs, and maelstroms still invisible from the deck. He can be dragged down from the mast and put to tending the boilers or working the capstan, but that will not change anything: the mast will remain, and the next man on the masthead will see what the first has seen.

In a storm, you must have a man aloft. We are in the midst of storm today, and SOS signals come from every side. Only yesterday a writer could calmly stroll along the deck, clicking his Kodak (genre); but who will want to look at landscapes and genre scenes when the world is listing at a forty-five-degree angle, the green maws are gaping, the hull is creaking? Today we can look and think only as men do in the face of death: we are about to die—and what did it all mean? How have we lived? If we could start all over, from the beginning, what would we live by? And for what? What we need in literature today are vast philosophic

[2] François Babeuf (1760–97), French revolutionary who demanded economic, social and political equality; executed under the Directory for plotting to overthrow the government.

horizons—horizons seen from mastheads, from airplanes; we need the most ultimate, the most fearsome, the most fearless "Why?" and "What next?"

This is what children ask. But then children are the boldest philosophers. They enter life naked, not covered by the smallest fig leaf of dogma, absolutes, creeds. This is why every question they ask is so absurdly naïve and so frighteningly complex. The new men entering life today are as naked and fearless as children; and they, too, like children, like Schopenhauer, Dostoyevsky, Nietzsche, ask "Why?" and "What next?" Philosophers of genius, children, and the people are equally wise—because they ask equally foolish questions. Foolish to a civilized man who has a well-furnished European apartment, with an excellent toilet, and a well-furnished dogma.

Organic chemistry has already obliterated the line between living and dead matter. It is an error to divide people into the living and the dead: there are people who are dead-alive, and people who are alive-alive. The dead-alive also write, walk, speak, act. But they make no mistakes; only machines make no mistakes, and they produce only dead things. The alive-alive are constantly in error, in search, in questions, in torment.

The same is true of what we write: it walks and it talks, but it can be dead-alive or alive-alive. What is truly alive stops before nothing and ceaselessly seeks answers to absurd, "childish" questions. Let the answers be wrong, let the philosophy be mistaken —errors are more valuable than truths: truth is of the machine, error is alive; truth reassures, error disturbs. And if answers be impossible of attainment, all the better! Dealing with answered questions is the privilege of brains constructed like a cow's stomach, which, as we know, is built to digest cud.

If there were anything fixed in nature, if there were truths, all of this would, of course, be wrong. But fortunately, all truths are erroneous. This is the very essence of the dialectical process: today's truths become errors tomorrow; there is no final number.

This truth (the only one) is for the strong alone. Weak-nerved minds insist on a finite universe, a last number; they need, in Nietzsche's words, "the crutches of certainty." The weak-nerved lack the strength to include themselves in the dialectic syllogism. True, this is difficult. But it is the very thing that Einsten succeeded in doing: he managed to remember that he, Einstein, observing motion with a watch in hand, was also moving; he succeeded in looking at the movement of the earth from *outside*. This is precisely how a great literature, which knows no final numbers, looks at the movements of the earth.

The formal character of a living literature is the same as its inner character: it denies verities, it denies what everyone knows and what I have known until this moment. It departs from the canonical tracks, from the broad highway.

The broad highway of Russian literature, worn to a high gloss by the giant wheels of Tolstoy, Gorky, and Chekhov, is Realism, daily life; hence, we must turn away from daily life. The tracks canonized and sanctified by Blok, Sologub, and Bely are the tracks of Symbolism, which renounced daily life; hence, we must turn toward daily life.

Absurd? Yes. The intersection of parallel lines is also absurd. But it is absurd only in the canonic, plane geometry of Euclid. In non-Euclidean geometry it is an axiom. All you need is to cease to be plane, to rise above the plane. To literature today the plane surface of daily life is what the earth is to an airplane— a mere runway from which to take off, in order to rise aloft, from daily life to the realities of being, to philosophy, to the fantastic. Let yesterday's cart creak along the well-paved highways. The living have strength enough to cut away their yesterday.

Whether you put a police inspector or a commissar into the cart, it still remains a cart. And literature will remain the literature of yesterday even if you drive "revolutionary life" along the well-traveled highway—and even if you drive it in a dashing troika with bells. What we need today are automobiles, airplanes, flickering, flight, dots, dashes, seconds.

The old, slow, creaking descriptions are a thing of the past; today the rule is brevity—but every word must be supercharged, high-voltage. We must compress into a single second what was held before in a sixty-second minute. And hence, syntax becomes elliptic, volatile; the complex pyramids of periods are dismantled stone by stone into independent sentences. When you are moving fast, the canonized, the customary eludes the eye: hence, the unusual, often startling, symbolism and vocabulary. The image is sharp, synthetic, with a single salient feature—the one feature you will glimpse from a speeding car. The custom-hallowed lexicon has been invaded by provincialisms, neologisms, science, mathematics, technology.

If this becomes the rule, the writer's talent consists in making the rule the exception. There are far more writers who turn the exception into the rule.

Science and art both project the world along certain coordinates. Differences in form are due only to differences in the coordinates. All realistic forms are projections along the fixed, plane coordinates of Euclid's world. These coordinates do not exist in nature. Nor does the finite, fixed world; this world is a convention, an abstraction, an unreality. And therefore Realism —be it "socialist" or "bourgeois"—is unreal. Far closer to reality is projection along speeding, curved surfaces—as in the new mathematics and the new art. Realism that is not primitive, not *realia* but *realiora,* consists in displacement, distortion, curvature, nonobjectivity. Only the camera lens is objective.

A new form is not intelligible to everyone; many find it difficult. Perhaps. The ordinary, the banal is, of course, simpler, more pleasant, more comfortable. Euclid's world is very simple, and Einstein's world is very difficult—but it is no longer possible to return to Euclid. No revolution, no heresy is comfortable or easy. For it is a leap, it is a break in the smooth evolutionary curve, and a break is a wound, a pain. But the wound is necessary: most of mankind suffers from hereditary sleeping sickness, and victims of this sickness (entropy) must not be allowed to sleep, or it will be their final sleep, death.

The same disease often afflicts artists and writers: they sink into satiated slumber in forms once invented and twice perfected. And they lack the strength to wound themselves, to cease loving what they once loved, to leave their old, familiar apartments filled with the scent of laurel leaves and walk away into the open field, to start anew.

Of course, to wound oneself is difficult, even dangerous. But for those who are alive, living today as yesterday and yesterday as today is still more difficult.

1923

THE DAY AND
THE AGE

1

To the female sparrow it undoubtedly seems that her gray little
mate does not twitter, but sings—and sings not a bit worse than
the nightingale: that, in fact, he can put the best of nightingales
to shame. Such a sparrow world has prevailed in our literary
criticism in recent years. The she sparrows have listened to their
mates with melting hearts, adoring them in all sincerity. And the
sparrow flocks are teeming all around us to this day—just as they
do during the Lenten season in March, pecking out treasures in
the yellowed ruts with deafening chatter. But now we are beginning to hear nonsparrow voices as well, with sufficient courage
to tell themselves and others that the chirping, enchanting as it is
(to the mate), and highly useful (for breeding purposes), is,
nevertheless, nothing more than chirping.

Fortunately, songs that give pleasure not only to she sparrows
but to birds of any breed, and to man as well, are still heard, and,
like all songs, they are, above all, *truthful*. And they can be distinguished at once.

Truth is the first thing that present-day literature lacks. The
writer has drowned himself in lies, he is too accustomed to speak
prudently, with a careful look over the shoulder. This is why our
literature fulfills so poorly even the most elementary task assigned
to it by history—the task of seeing our astonishing, unique epoch,
with all that it contains of the revolting and the beautiful, and
recording it as it is. The interminable, century-long decade of
1913–23 might well have been a dream; one day man will
awaken, rub his eyes—and the dream will be gone, because it has

113

not been told. What remains in our literature of the war? For the purpose of hatching patriotic eggs, it was considered useful to wrap them in a thick layer of tinsel. And almost nothing remains today except the tinsel.

The tinseling turns out to be a hereditary disease: it was inherited by our present-day, postrevolutionary literature, and three-quarters of this literature in solidly tinseled. Our virtuous modesty is so great, that the moment naked truth flashes its bare knee or belly before the footlights, we hastily throw an operatic toga over it.

In America there is a society for the suppression of vice which once decided, in order to prevent temptation, that all the naked statues in a New York museum must be dressed in little skirts, like those of ballet dancers. These puritan skirts are merely ridiculous, and do little damage: if they have not yet been removed, a new generation will remove them and see the statues as they are. But when a writer dresses his novel in such a skirt, it is no longer laughable. And when this is done not by one, but by dozens of writers, it becomes a menace. These skirts cannot be removed, and future generations will have to learn about our epoch from tinseled, straw-filled dummies. They will receive far fewer literary documents than they might have. And it is therefore all the more important to point out such documents where they exist.

2

In all our "literary and social" journals, the department of belles lettres plays only a subsidiary role; it is merely a vestibule for the uninitiated, meant to lead them into the sanctuary of the other department. Literary documents are, perhaps, more likely to be found in anthologies, where literature is offered not only to entice the public to a "concert meeting" (at one time such meetings were in fashion everywhere, but today they survive only in the literary field), but to draw the public to a concert proper.

And so, here are four of the latest anthologies: *Nedra,* no. 1; *Nashi dni,* no. 2; *Krug,* no. 3; and *Rol,* no. 3.

Nedra [The depths] is clear kin to the former *Zemlya* [Land]. Its name seems to suggest that the layer of black earth has been dug to great depths, and that treasures which have lain buried for many years have at last been brought into the light.

In one sense, at least, this is true. The staleness of many years can indeed be felt in most of the treasures extracted from "The depths." This fully applies to Veresayev's *Dead End,* and to Serafimovich's *The Iron Stream*—a battle painting after Vere-shchagin, occupying 164 pages and laid in the year 1918.

The Iron Stream—iron wrested from underground. What, one might ask, could be better? But send a sample of this iron to any factory laboratory, and you will discover that it has long been rusting in the cellars of *Znaniye* [Knowledge]. In accordance with the good old *Znaniye* traditions, two pages are devoted to singing "You Have Fallen in the Fatal Struggle."[1] This is followed by a series of Ukrainian nationalist songs, ending with "What Does the Muscovite Want?" In the *Znaniye* tradition, too, and harking back to Andreyev's "Red Laugh," are such gems as "mad sun," "The mother laughs with an unutterably joyous, ringing laugh," "kisses her child madly," "down with war—that's wildly understandable," "the light quivers madly," "over the blue abyss," "bottomless deeps," "the mirage vibrates with fiery vibrations."

But there is something else here too, something that was not to be found in the Serafimovich of *Znaniye.* When we read, "Picking his way out of the crowd toward the windmills with an inexplic-ably red face, with the first faint growth of a little black mustache, in a sailor hat"—a sentence without a subject—we are clearly in the presence of "modern style," verging on Przybyszewski.[2] And coming upon such phrases as "Again irrepressible astonish-ment rose in the minds of those who were running amid tension toward salvation," we suspect the beginnings of instrumentation —almost in the manner of Bely.

And also, in *Znaniye* there was never any of that tinsel which abounds today in Serafimovich's iron, mined from "the depths." The figure of the "contemptible compromiser" Mikeladze is built according to every tinsely code. But the thickest overlay of tinsel is reserved for the ending—the apotheosis of the hero, whose figure is assembled in strict conformity to all the known operatic rules, which, as everyone knows, demand that "the heart be stamped with a fiery brand" and that tears "roll down the wind-

---

[1] Opening words of a revolutionary funeral march.

[2] S. Przybyszewski (1868–1927), Polish Neoromantic writer, exalted feeling at the expense of reason, wrote in a highly charged emotional style.

beaten faces of all the passersby, and down the faces of the old men," and "tremble brightly in the eyes of the young girls."

Yet the ore mined by Serafimovich for his *Iron Stream* is so rich that even its operatic processing could not entirely devalue it. Some of the scenes are memorable. There are occasional apt images (Horpyna's husband has "hands like hooves"; the cossacks have "frenzied, beefy eyes"); one flashing second in the mountains is done well (p. 111). But these are as scarce as the righteous in Gomorrah.

Sergeyev-Tsensky chose one of the simplest forms of the *skaz* for "The Professor's Story": the Red Army commander Rybochkin tells the author the story of his life. There is no trace here of that tense, agitated language, the last ripples of which were still present in "Movements." The neoclassicism of this story is entirely justified by the form chosen and is, of course, vastly superior to operatic peudoclassicism. The web of the story is strong and honest from beginning to end. Only one page (p. 194)—a philosophic excursion by the author—lapses from literary to journalistic prose. And yet, perhaps it is precisely this page that lifts the story above the level of a mere "picture of contemporary life."

The only modern piece in *Nedra* is Bulgakov's "Diaboliad." The author unquestionably possesses the right instinct in the choice of his compositional base—fantasy rooted in actual life, rapid, cinematic succession of scenes—one of the few formal frameworks which can encompass our yesterday—1919, 1920. The term "cinematic" is all the more applicable to this work since the entire novella is two-dimensional, done on a single plane; everything is on the surface, and there is no depth of scene whatever. With Bulgakov, *Nedra* loses its classical (and pseudoclassical) innocence for what I believe is the first time, and as happens so frequently, the provincial old maid is seduced by the very first brash young man from the capital. The absolute value of this piece, somehow too thoughtless, is not so great, but good works can apparently be expected from its author.

In its choice of poems, *Nedra* still clings to its Realistic virginity—and clings to it so rigidly that the verses of Kirillov, Polonskaya, and Oreshin have the sameness of ten-kopek coins: of the six poems published, four even have the same meter—iambic tetrameter.

3

The earth, as we know, rests on three whales. An anthology, as
we know, must rest on one. In *Nedra* (no. 3) the deputy whale
is Serafimovich; in *Nashi dni* [Our days] the temporary acting
whale is Shishkov. In *Nedra* we have Ukrainian opera; in *Nashi
dni,* the melodrama *The Gang.*

It seems to be an epidemic disease today: the writers of fiction
have forgotten how to finish their works. The endings are always
worse than the beginnings. The roots of this may lie in our epoch
itself, so like a novel the end of which even Shklovsky[3] cannot
compute with his arithmetic. This ending sickness afflicts Serafimovich. Shishkov suffers from the same disease: at the finish
of *The Gang* he limps into melodrama.

The subject matter of *The Gang* is well chosen. It is not spur-
ious, Meyerholdian, but genuinely of the "rearing earth." It deals
with an elemental uprising of Siberian peasants against Kolchak[4]
—with that "Bolshevism of the soil" which Blok considered to
be the whole essence of the history of our recent years. This
theme is curiously intertwined with another, at first glance quite
unexpected: Lenin and the schismatic's leather rosary; Bolsheviks from among the Old Believers. The author contrives to pass
unscathed through this psychological paradox: the Old Believer
partisans demolish churches and chop off the heads of priests
with a clear conscience—because those churches and those
priests are Nikonian, of the antichrist. Very forthrightly, with
brutal, Gorky-like directness, without covering the truth in any
Quaker skirts, Shishkov shows us a paralyzed old woman thrown
out of a window, a priest sawed in two, a public execution.
Shishkov has coped successfully with the staging of these most
difficult scenes, but beginning with act 3—with chapter 10
of his novel—his actors launch into melodrama: they gurgle,
wheeze, growl, howl, moan.

" 'The scum, why didn't they wait!' Naperstok wheezed
hoarsely."

"Growling and squealing, he gnawed his own hands, tore his
clothes, howled and rolled on the ground."

---

[3] Victor Shklovsky (b. 1893), writer and critic, one of the founders of
the Formalist school which stressed literary technique and devices.

[4] A. V. Kolchak (1870–1920), one of the leaders of the White forces in
the civil war following the revolution.

" 'Blood! Blood!' he howled."

" 'Father, father,' Zykov wheezed, shaking."

" 'Ah, you! Ah—' Zykov cried out wildly, terrifyingly. He clutched his hair and moaned."

And so on.

And here are a few additional comments by the author on his characters:

"Zykov, in a short black coat with a red sash, a black-bearded giant." "Zykov—on his horse; the horse gallops, his nostrils blowing smoke, his hooves striking fire." Zykov's fighting unit is "like rock, like flame, like an avalanche from the mountains." He himself is "out of a fairytale, all of him made of cast iron and will." The heroine Tanya "leaned against him, her face sad and lovely like a fairy tale." "The sad, lovely girl from a sad Russian fairy tale broke out of the fairy tale."

It is obvious that Shishkov, together with Zykov, is in love with this "fairy-tale Tanya" to the point of tears. And, together with Tanya, he is in love with Zykov. And, together with someone else, he hates the executioner Naperstok. All this is fine. But steam will work obediently only when it is compressed in a steel cylinder. There is lots of steam in the bathhouse, but no work can be gotten from it.

All the mistakes of *The Gang* are mistakes in ornamentation, in color. Compositionally, the novel is successful. The reader gradually becomes accustomed to the growling of the actors; after a while (the instinct of self-preservation), he stops noticing it and is carried along by the plot.

In composition, the obstinate Old Believer Shishkov seems to be abandoning the canon: the novel is constructed of pieces, with rapidly changing stage sets—several changes in every chapter.

Around the whale of *Nashi dni*—*The Gang*—there is a gamboling shoal of lesser stories. Most of them leave no trace. Yesterday I was served a cutlet at dinner—I think it was a cutlet, I don't remember. I don't remember its taste; all I know is that I ate it and had no heartburn.

Lyashko's "Stirrups" leave you with heartburn.

"The old man's words are imbued with vanity and ignorance," "Veniamin felt that they were blind and sticky." Such writing was done in the age of the "decadents" of blessed memory. At that time writers did not know the art of *showing* emotion; they

described it. And "Stirrups" is full of description of emotions:
"anger boiled in his blood," "muffled the ripples of anxiety,"
"angrily transferred the things that agitated him from his breast
to the canvas," "shame bared his skull," "excitement ebbed," "his
heart ached with smoldering bitterness." All of these were found
in the space of two or three pages.

Like *The Gang*, "Stirrups" is melodrama—but a tinselly melodrama. The reader who accepts Shishkov's melodrama will never
believe in a melodrama which grows out of an artist's sale of his
"ideological" painting to the "well fed." This artist is obviously
straight out of the Association of Artists of Revolutionary Russia
(AKhRR).

K. Fedin's "About 1919" is a fragment from his still unfinished novel.

In 1919 people carefully collected every scrap of fabric, even
the tiniest; there was a textile famine. Today anthologies and
journals carefully collect in their pages fragments of novels—a
symptom of literary famine. And perhaps, of the nonmetaphori-
cal hunger of the writer, who must try to get two skins off every
novel. We can sympathize with the author. But there is not much
point in being a literary Cuvier and attempting to guess at the
skeleton on the basis of a single tooth. Fedin's novel is not a fossil.

Ognev's "The End of the Antenna" is unquestionably the best
of Pilnyak's stories. Pilnyak's entire laboratory is in evidence:
the same constant shifting of planes, the same "multiphase current," the insertion of documents, typographical tricks. But the
old Pilnyak strung all of this on cotton thread, which kept breaking all the time; the Pilnyak perfected by Ognev has strung his
pieces on a firm rod of plot. In the perfected Pilnyak's story,
compositional work proceeds side by side with ornamental work;
there are quick and sharp syntactic moves. The vocabulary is
varied—from radio terms to folk expressions; the symbols are
simple and bold ("a *wide, spacious* smell," *"trifling* globe"—
trifling to the radio waves that circle it).

Minor errors don't count (there are no "benzine diesels" anywhere in the world; and no one in the world puts diesels in airplanes; and no one in the world should use anapests in prose,
in the manner of Bely, as Ognev does on pages 301 and 307).
"The End of the Antenna" is an excellent story; it belongs to
"our days" both in theme and in technique. But still, Ognev's

excellent story is the best of Pilnyak's stories. And since Pilnyak patented his form first, Ognev must—alas!—look for another way. He will undoubtedly have strength enough to do this.

4

The third anthology is *Krug* [Circle]. The first two issues were breaths of fresh air. The third suddenly has a dense smell of naphthalene from way back in the 1860s. Just recently Luna-charsky[5] repented his former patronage of Futurism and took under his wing a certain Ostrovsky. Could this most recent slogan—"Back to Ostrovsky!"—have affected *Krug* as well?

But if only it were "back to Ostrovsky"! It is back to Uspensky, and not Gleb, not Nikolay,[6] but A. Uspensky. What this Uspensky, the author of "Retraining," needs is simply training of the most elementary kind; he needs to learn at least the rudiments of the technique of the short story, he needs to learn how to sew on his moral with a needle at least a little smaller than the huge burlap needle he uses today.

The only modern element in the story is its theme, the post-revolutionary province. The author's purpose is not art, but a sermon; he wants to "expose" this province—and not rudely but as patriotically as possible. Even such a curtsying satire, however, was deemed too dangerous by the editors, and the story was published with a fig-leaf "preface" glued on in the appropriate place.

Inspired by the very latest of the Russian writers he has read —Denis Fonvizin[7]—A. Uspensky begins by labeling his heroes: Abcin (a teacher, of course!), Taxov (of the Finance Department—obviously!), Sedulov, Silensky. After that, these allegorical figures stride across the pages, while the author, his hand inside the lapel of his frock coat (a long one—surely below the knees) moralizes to them:

"Ah, Duncetown, Duncetown! How good it would be to dry out the mud you're wallowing in; to clean you up, to tidy you

---

[5] A. V. Lunacharsky (1883–1950), critic, People's Commissar of Education from 1917 to 1929.

[6] Gleb and Nikolay Uspensky were radical writers of the latter half of the nineteenth century.

[7] D. I. Fonvizin (1745–92), leading playwright, famous for his satirical comedies, particularly *The Minor*.

and dress you up; to teach you to partake of the new happiness
—rational and splendid!"

The exhortation to "plant the seeds of the reasonable, the
good, the eternal"[8] does not appear anywhere in the story. But
the author clearly winds up every oration about his native Duncetown with precisely this homily—and old ladies, male and female, wipe away their tears.

It would, however, be libelous to say that A. Uspensky rests
blissfully on Fonvizin; he reads current newspapers, and in doing
this, he is himself Sedulov, and he culls from them the most tinselly clichés. One feels sorry for the sedulous author, and even
sorrier for the rich anecdotal material he ruins in working it over.

The innocence of the Naturalism of the 1860s, unclouded by
any compositional or stylistic heresies, prevails in Aizman's
novel, *Their Life, Their Death,* and in the stories by Shishkov
("The Black Hour") and Fedorovich ("A Tale about the God
Kichag and Fyodor Kuzmich").

Aizman's novel is from the French, a là Zola. Shishkov's story
belongs to his very old (and, generally, old) ethnographic series
—the form he began with. The present day may be found only
in the topic of Fedorovich's story.

Fedorovich's signboard calling his story a *skaz* should receive
no more credence than the signboard over a store—"Vasily
Fyodorov from Paris." This is not a *skaz,* it is simply a story,
occasionally freshened by folk expressions in the author's asides.
One day perhaps he will succeed in producing a *skaz:* he has a
good sense of dialogue and of the humor inherent in folk speech.
The author (or the editor?) with quite a serious mien provides
notes explaining the Ukrainian words used by his characters. The
plot is as instructive as the notes; it concerns the overthrow by
a Communist cell of the statue of Alexander I ("Fyodor Koz-
mich"), around which a folk legend has been created. The author
has succeeded, however, in avoiding tinsel, although the subject
offers ample opportunity for its use.

The four other authors represented in *Krug* have also been
caught in the charmed circle of the *skaz* form: Babel ("The
Sin of Jesus"), Leonov ("Yegorushka's Death"), Forsh ("Two
Bases"), and Rukavishnikov ("The Buffoon's Tale").

[8] A quotation from "To the Sowers," a poem by N. A. Nekrasov,
radical nineteenth-century poet.

ю. А
1925

Isaac Babel

Of the four, Babel is the most successful with the form. The entire little story, including the author's comments, is composed of elements of folk dialogue; the needed synonyms are chosen with great skill, and clever use is made of the syntactic deformations typical of folk speech. Work over the ornament did not, as so often happens, make the author forget his compositional problem. And one more thing: Babel remembers that, in addition to eyes, tongue, and the rest, he also has a brain, which many writers today treat as a rudimentary organ—something like an appendix. The little story is raised above the material of daily life and illuminated by serious thought.

In Leonov's *skaz,* the three-dimensional screen of daily life also expands occasionally into the fantastic (the appearance of the little monk Agapy). But at the end it is as though the author suddenly looked down upon the earth, felt dizzy, and made a hurried dive back into the plane of reality. The flight of Yegorushka and Agapy on "human birds," which promised to develop into something important, is revealed by the author to have been nothing more than a dream; a lame ending is attached to the story (again the "end sickness").

The entire story is built in a kind of churchly manner, and becomes cloying in spots. This is the result of an overabundance of affectionate diminutives and occasional transpositions of word order ("of northern lights the flames," "soft and damp, the earth," and so on). Leonov's vocabulary is rich and bold, as it always is, with many very organic neologisms. The mistakes in the story are good mistakes: they result from the difficulty of the tasks the author sets himself, and a fondness for difficult tasks is a good sign.

The task which Olga Forsh set herself was much easier: she sought to capture in a lively *skaz* form a piece of "revolutionary life"—the religious revolution taking place today. The form is followed consistently and skillfully; yet this is only the plane surface of daily life, and only the already canonized *skaz* form. One prefers to see a writer make good mistakes in a difficult undertaking—they are more valuable than easy achievements.

Rukavishnikov's experiment in versified *skaz* is most interesting. The rhythmic structure of the folk epic (Rukavishnikov attempts to revive this form) and the rhythmic structure of literary prose, essentially analogous, have not yet been adequately analyzed. Bely's attempt to approach the problem with a metric standard was a failure; the same standard is applied by Malishevsky in his confused and flabby preface.

The rest of the poems in *Krug* are comfortably old-fashioned, all the way down to Nasedkin's line about someone "joyous, faceless, laughing quietly by the water." Yesenin is the only one to try something new: I believe this is the first time he has attempted the ode form. But alas, how close he comes to the tinsel of the numberless odes produced today! This may be partly the fault of the editors, who embellish Yesenin's poem with a long string of ellipses.

5

Next to the solid *Nashi dni,* the well-fed *Nedra,* the rotund *Krug,* a lean little stranger with an odd name, *Rol,* timidly sits down on the edge of a chair. The men in frock coats and riding breeches don't notice him, and yet the stranger is worth talking to—and talking about.

Not its verse; here we find the same golden mean of different degrees of purity. But of its four prose writers, two—Lidin and Ivan Novikov—are superior to a good many in its solid neighbors.

In the paintings of the French Impressionists one often sees color reflections on faces—green from leaves, orange from oranges, raspberry red from an umbrella. Similar extraneous reflections have colored Lidin's face from his very first stories, colored by Bunin. Today he is in the shadow of Tolstoy, and Lidin's face shows Tolstoyan hues. But this is as natural as the fact that there is a sky over us. And under this sky, Lidin's "One Night" turned out to be dense and full-bodied. Its topic, close to our time, is the recent war. The plot, skillfully developed, with effective pauses, is combined with a language made fresh by seemingly simple shifts in its symbolism ("the sun fleck of a shy smile," "the stars poured out strongly"). And behind this external fabric, one senses a certain synthesis which lends the story perspective and depth.

There is even greater synthesis and deeper perspective in Ivan Novikov's story, "Angel on Earth."

The myth about the angel who rebelled against his Lord is the most beautiful of all myths, the proudest, the most revolutionary, the most immortal of them all. Novikov's story is a variation on this myth, woven into our earthly (and our Russian) life: Novikov's rebellious angel goes to work as a laborer for a village priest, then he leaves the priest to call the village poor to revolt. In the end he leaves men because he is unable to shed blood.

The story is steeped in summer heat, the heat when everything blooms and runs with sap, when people bloom with love. It is also the heat when eerie, copper clouds gather at sunset, when the sky bursts into flames and collapses. The sense of the impending resolution of both the love situation and the rebellion in the coming storm keeps the reader tense to the very last. But on the last page we see that Novikov has not escaped the general epidemic of poor endings (luckily, those who survive this sickness develop immunity!). The rose bush that springs up at the end by the author's will must be chopped down—to avoid a rosy ending.

The language of the story, solemn and measured, is good if only because it violates the present-day canons, which demand a jumping, telegraph-code prose.

6

This word, "present-day," which slipped in inadvertently, is nowadays the most widely used yardstick in measuring art. What is of today is good, what is not of today is bad. Or, the contemporary is good; the uncontemporary is bad.

But that is just the point: there can be no such "or." The "present-day" and the "contemporary" do not exist within the same dimensions. In practice, the "present-day" has no dimension in time—it dies tomorrow. But the "contemporary" exists in the temporal dimension of the epoch. That which is of the day greedily clutches at life, indiscriminate in its choice of means: it must hurry, it has only until tomorrow. And hence, that which is of the day is invariably shifty, nimble, servile, lightweight, afraid to dig an inch deeper, afraid to see the naked truth. The contemporary, that which is of the age, is *above* the day, it may be out of tune with it, it may be (or may seem to be) nearsighted— because it is farsighted, because it looks ahead. The present-day takes from the epoch only its coloration, its skin; it lives by the law of mimicry. But the contemporary takes its heart and its mind from the epoch—it lives by the law of inheritance.

And so, the formula we cited earlier may be revised in favor of another, shorter one: the contemporary in art is good, the present-day, bad. If we apply this to the new literature, to all that parades today with the passport of belles lettres, we shall, unfortunately, find that there is much more in it of the day than of the age. And it would be well if this proportion, this ratio of the day to the age, did not grow—as do the philistines we see sprouting like weeds from every crack, choking out man.

1924

THE GOAL

All of our literature is still permeated by the poisons of war. It is built on hatred—on class hatred, its components, its surrogates. It is not possible to build on negative emotions. Genuine literature will come only when we replace hatred for man with love for man. True, our age is a cruel, iron age; true, it is an age of wars and rebellions. But this is why a respite from hatred is all the more necessary—for hatred has a destructive effect upon the human psyche. What comes after the abolition of classes is not a time of automatic equality, of sheer animal well being, but a time of enormous upsurge of the highest human emotions, a time of love.

Yet, what our future will be depends on us. For the moment, we give no thought to fostering the high emotions which belong to an era when collectivism is being realized. Edicts, resolutions, paragraphs: trees—and no wood behind the trees. What can excite the imagination in "The ABC of Politics"? Nothing.

"Art has always served the ruling classes." This dictum might waken the enthusiasm of a fascist, an imperialist, but not a revolutionary, not a *dialectician.* The entire difference in the nature of the present ruling class is that it rules *temporarily,* that it rules in order to cease ruling as soon as possible—in order to free mankind of the yoke of any state and any rule. The difference is that the present ruling class knows (should know, I feel) all this. Yet this is precisely what is being lost sight of.

The germ of the future is always in the present.

It is true that artists of every kind—the majority of artists—have always been unprincipled and corrupted by skepticism. The

127

majority of them have always been lance-knights, mercenaries who sold themselves to the highest bidder. But this law of buying and selling talent is a law of capitalist society. A society planning to rebuild life on different, new, nobler foundations can no more accept this shameful law than it can accept without objection the sale of their bodies by women. From my (heretical) point of view, a stubborn, unyielding enemy is far more deserving of respect than a sudden convert to communism—such as Sergey Gorodetsky, to take one example. The spectacle of service to the ruling class based on the advantages accruing from such service should certainly provoke no jubilation in a revolutionary. A revolutionary should be nauseated by such "service," which quite naturally degenerates into a lackey's servility. This can please only such typical products of the transitional period, entirely devoid of a sense of smell, as Gorbachev or Lelevich; and, perhaps, men like Averbakh, who are not very far removed from them.[1]

What these young men have in their hands is not pen and ink, but a whip and a piece of roast beef. Basically, their criticism reduces itself to the command: "Sit up and beg!" To them, a writer is merely a mutt who must be taught to stand on his hind legs—then he is given a morsel of meat, and everything is just fine.

No, my dearest comrades, it is not *just fine*. The Revolution does not need dogs who "sit up" in expectation of a handout or because they fear the whip. Nor does it need trainers of such dogs. It needs writers who fear nothing—just as the Revolution fears nothing. It needs writers who do not seek immediate benefits— just as the Revolution does not seek immediate benefits (it is not by chance that it teaches us to sacrifice everything, even life, for the sake of the happiness of future generations: this is its ethic). It needs writers in whom the Revolution awakens a true, organic echo. And it does not matter if this echo is individual in every writer. It does not matter if a writer ignores such-and-such a paragraph adopted at such-and-such a conference. What matters

---

[1] G. E. Gorbachev (1897–1942), G. Lelevich (1901–45) and L. L. Averbakh (1903–?) were Communist critics who demanded strict control of literature and total subservience of art to the aims of the party. As head of the RAPP, Averbakh was virtual dictator of Soviet literature from 1929 to 1932, subjecting nonconformist writers to vicious persecution. He disappeared during the Great Purge in the 1930s.

is that his work be sincere, that it lead the reader forward instead of back, that it disturb the reader rather than reassure and lull his mind.

But where forward? And how far forward? In the answer to these questions we find the basic error of the majority of today's critics and the majority of writers who are obediently following critics incapable of thinking dialectically.

We feel that the correct answer to these questions should be: the farther the better, the more valuable. Reduction of prices, better sanitation in the cities, tractorization of the village—all this is very good; it is, naturally, a movement forward. I can imagine an excellent newspaper article on these topics (an article that will be forgotten the next day). But I find it difficult to imagine a work by Lev Tolstoy or Romain Rolland based on improvement of sanitation. I find it difficult to imagine readers truly, deeply moved by such a sanitary Tolstoy.

It is time, at last, to understand that the stubborn limitation of writers to the area of "minor affairs" creates only a philistine, subservient literature, and nothing more. It is time to understand that literature, like science, is divided into major and minor branches, each with its own tasks. There is a firm division of surgery into "major" and "minor." "Major surgery" carries science forward; "minor surgery" fulfills daily, current needs. "Major surgery" conducts the experiments of Carrel and Voronoff; "minor surgery" bandages a sprained arm. Astronomy is divided into major and minor: the former seeks to determine the course of the solar system; the latter recommends methods of determining a ship's position at sea. If we compel Carrel to bandage sprains, we shall obtain one more male nurse; of course, this would be useful, but stupid, for in gaining a male nurse, humanity would lose a scientific genius.

Our criticism is pushing Russian literature today into the role of male nurse; the name of the sickness that afflicts Russian literature is malenursism. No wonder Marietta Shaginyan (whom all the Gorbachevs have recently invested with the formal title of "Left Fellow Traveler") lost patience and cried out in her book, *Daily Life and Art,* that one of the reasons why "the writer is sick" is lack of "projections of the future." She made a single mistake: this is not one of the reasons, but the only reason, to which, broadly speaking, all the others reduce themselves.

The purpose of art, including literature, is not to reflect life but to organize it, to build it. (For the task of reflecting life there is a minor art—photography.) What does it mean for literature to "organize life"? Averbakh understands it thus: "Dairy cooperation in a peasant country is a matter of enormous importance. Dairy cooperation will be the topic of the works of new writers, because it is a matter of the social experience of the new epoch." This sounds like a malicious anecdote, but this malicious anecdote, mocking Averbakh, was invented—for the edification of posterity—by Averbakh himself.

Dairy cooperation—when it is the concern of a specialist, not Averbakh—is a most estimable matter. It may be a tiny step, to be measured perhaps in centimeters, but a step, nevertheless, to a given future—one of a million means toward the attainment of our goal. It is the specialist's task to talk about means, about centimeters. An artist's task is to talk about the goal, about kilometers, thousands of kilometers. The organizing role of art consists of infecting the reader, of arousing him with pathos or irony—the cathode and anode in literature. But irony that is measured in centimeters is pathetic, and centimeter-sized, dairy-cooperative pathos is ridiculous. No one can be carried away by it. To stir the reader, the artist must speak not of means but of ends, of the great goal toward which mankind is moving.

1926(?)

A PIECE FOR AN ANTHOLOGY ON BOOKS

When my children come out into the street badly dressed, it hurts me. When street urchins throw stones at them from behind a corner, I suffer. When a surgeon approaches them with forceps or a knife, I think I would prefer that he cut my own body.

My children are my books: I have no others.

There are books of the same chemical composition as dynamite. The only difference is that a piece of dynamite explodes once, while a book explodes a thousand times.

Man ceased to be an ape, vanquished the ape, on the day when the first book was written. The ape has not forgotten it to this day: try and give it a book—it will immediately spoil it, tear it up, befoul it.

23 December 1928

MOSCOW—PETERSBURG

"Moscow is feminine, Petersburg masculine," wrote Gogol exactly one hundred years ago. This may seem to be a chance quip, a grammatical pun,[1] but it contains so acute an insight into something basic in the character of each of these two Russian capitals that we recall it even today, after a hundred years.

Petersburg has since become Leningrad, but it has remained Petersburg far more than Moscow has remained Moscow. Moscow has surrendered herself to the Revolution more impetuously, recklessly, and submissively than Petersburg. And indeed, the victorious Revolution has become the fashion, and what true woman will not hasten to dress according to fashion? Petersburg accepted the new without such haste, with masculine composure, with greater circumspection. It went forward more slowly, and understandably so: it had to carry a great load of cultural traditions, especially perceptible in the realm of art. Without such cumbersome baggage, traveling light, the Moscow muses rushed headlong, overtaking not only Petersburg, but also Europe, and at times good sense as well. "If it be fashion, then Moscow must have fashion all the way!" Gogol twitted Moscow; he knew this feminine weakness of hers.

But this headlong chase after novelty is not only a feminine trait; it also comes of youth. The new Moscow, which exists alongside, above, and through the ancient, the six-hundred-year-old one, is only sixteen! The unexpected, motley combinations of the old and the new in Moscow make the head spin. Petersburg

[1] In Russian Moscow and Petersburg (*Moskva, Peterburg*) are, respectively, feminine and masculine nouns.

is more severe: today, as in Gogol's day, it "dislikes gaudy colors." Petersburg will remain a window on Europe, on the West. Moscow has become a door through which America has flooded in—by way of Asia, from the East.

Of course, this is merely a schematic sketch. In life, especially in mirror life—in art—there is no such geographic precision: Here you can see an unruly Moscow forelock dashing along Nevsky Prospekt, or a noisy Moscow square hushed under the austere shadow of the Petersburg Bronze Horseman. Yet despite these admixtures and through all the changes, the individual face of each of these two capitals remains discernible in every mirror. And this may be seen most distinctly, perhaps, in the stone mirror of architecture, in the marks left by the Revolution in Petersburg and Moscow.

Petersburg grew up as an imperial city, a city of the government; it was built by the treasury, the state, the system. A large proportion of the buildings which give it its character—the magnificent works of Rastrelli, Guarengi, Thomon and Voronikhin—were produced by the era of Catherine the Great, Alexander I, and Nicholas I. Fortunately, the tastelessness of the last emperors did not succeed in leaving its imprint on the northern capital; by this time, the basic architectural composition of Petersburg had been completed. It was in this shape that it met the Revolution as well, and its completeness, it architectural finality account for the preservation of its former character after the Revolution. There was almost no room for the new anywhere, except on the city's outskirts. And it is only there that the Revolution has left its imprint; it is there that Leningrad is slowly growing up around Petersburg, with such elements as the well-designed block of new buildings for workers near the Narva Gate, with its huge and excellently equipped theater and House of Culture, and similar Houses of Culture in other workers' districts.

Tsarist Moscow came into being quite differently, in an oriental manner—capriciously, vividly, scattered without plan or system over a large area. No one's single will directed its growth. In contrast to imperial Petersburg, it was the capital of landowning and merchant—chiefly merchant—Russia. Men who had made their fortunes somewhere in the backwoods of the Urals or in Old Believers' monastery villages along the Volga would settle in

Moscow and build their homes in accordance with the notions of style brought from their native regions. These one-family homes, unceremoniously standing next to modern multistory giants, are as typical of Moscow as palaces are of Petersburg. And in addition to the one-family homes, there are the churches —the multitude of churches which strike the eye, most of them ancient, dating back to the fourteenth and fifteenth centuries, a heritage of the days when Moscow was the capital of pious tsars.

After the Revolution, when Moscow became once more the capital city, it was flooded with vast numbers of institutions and officials, produced by the new socialist economy. An extremely acute housing crisis, such as has never been experienced by any European capital, necessitated the hasty building of new houses. Yielding to these, the old small houses and the churches began to disappear from the central streets of Moscow (the disappearance of the churches was also connected with the antireligious policies of the government).

The face of a city and of its individual districts is especially altered by the demolition of such distinct buildings as churches. People who saw the old square on the banks of the Moskva River with the Church of the Savior will not recognize it today: the golden cupola which had been visible from a distance, and the huge yellowish white body of the church are no longer there. This enormous building did not possess great architectural value, but one cannot help regretting the loss of such ancient buildings as the Simonov Monastery, the Chudov Monastery in the Kremlin, and the old Sukharev Tower which lent so much beauty to the square at the end of Myasnitskaya Street. In other instances, the demolition of such old buildings proved justified from the point of view of architectural composition. Thus, the view of the Kremlin's Red Square gained substantially from the removal of the Iversk Kremlin Gate and the Iversk Chapel. Now the magnificent Cathedral of Vasily Blazhenny, formerly shut out by the gate of the chapel, can be seen against the blue sky from Okhotny Ryad.

What strikes the eye in old Moscow is the intrusion of America, or, rather, the popular Berlin version of America—Constructivist combinations of stone cubes in the manner of Corbusier. But Moscow taste demands "all-out fashion," and Moscow has tried to out-Corbusier Corbusier himself; some of its new buildings are still drier, more abstract and bare than the model they are patterned on. A typical example of this style is the dark, grim cube of the Lenin Institute on Tverskaya Street, in the very center of Moscow. Some of the left-wing Moscow architects have proclaimed this American-Berlin style proletarian (and hence, the most fashionable). However—the proletariat refused to believe them and protested vigorously when these dreary cubes began to rise in workers' districts. As one of the most prominent Moscow architects, Shchusev, admitted, "We have found that the simplified Constructivist type of architecture is not always acceptable or understandable to the masses. . . . The boxlike, poorly designed exterior of the buildings quickly wearied the eye. . . . It became necessary to study the works of the great masters of earlier epochs. . . . Architecture cannot solve its tasks without mastery of the two related arts—painting and sculpture."

Of the two related arts, sculpture might have been expected to come to a new flowering in revolutionary Russia. The victorious revolution manifested a clear desire to immortalize itself by setting up appropriate monuments in the streets and squares of both capitals. These monuments multiplied prodigiously during the early postrevolutionary years, but disappeared just as rapidly, since they were usually made of the most perishable materials, including plaster. This lack of foresight was highly fortunate: hastily made, clashing with their architectural surroundings, these figures, busts, and heads contributed little to the adornment of the revolutionary capitals. Indeed, today some of them might, in the new Soviet terminology, be attributed to intentional sabotage. How else, for example, is one to characterize such early monuments as the bust of Marx in Petersburg (by Matveyev), which depicted the founder of Communism with—a *monocle* in his eye? As we know, Marx did, in fact, wear a monocle, but this bourgeois accessory hardly fitted the canonized image.

The imperial period, of which there are few visible marks in Moscow, left an entire chronicle of bronze and stone in the streets and squares, embankments and parks of Petersburg, beginning with the magnificent Bronze Horseman created by Falconetti and sung by Pushkin. Revolutionary Petersburg had enough taste and restraint to preserve all these monuments, with but a few exceptions. And Petersburg had enough sense of style to place one of its few permanent (not temporary) revolutionary monuments, the figure of Lenin, not in the center of the city, among Empire buildings and monuments of emperors, but nearer the workers' suburbs, nearer to Leningrad—in the square near the Finland Station. Moscow treats the old monuments with less ceremony; thus, two years ago, old Muscovites found with astonishment that the monument to Minin and Pozharsky had moved from its old place to one nearer the Cathedral of Vasily Blazhenny. In its new permanent monuments, as in its new buildings, Moscow prefers the geometric style (the white obelisk in the Alexandrovsky Garden, the gray one in the former Skobelev Square). Unfortunately, for the time being there is not a single new monument either in Moscow, or in Petersburg, that can be said to rise above mediocrity, to possess a bronze voice even remotely approaching in power that of the Petersburg Bronze Horseman.

A typical Petersburg building with columns, on the Neva embankment, is the Academy of the Arts, the home of another neighbor of architecture—painting. In the eighteenth century, when the academy was founded, Petersburg was already the capital of Russian painting. Shortly before the war and the Revolution, seeds of the new French art were brought into Russia through the Petersburg "window on Europe," and their crossbreeding with the old Russian painting produced the richest sprouts in the group of artists who had united under the name of the World of Art. These artists felt confined in Petersburg, now transformed into Leningrad, and most of them have since become residents of Paris or New York. But the traditions created by them and the works of the masters who remained true to Petersburg proved sufficient to preserve the city's primacy in this field even today, when Moscow has become the official capital. It is, of course, impossible to speak of the Petersburg and Moscow schools of painting. Diffusion is even more natural in this area than it is in others. Yet Moscow can be recognized even here.

In the history of Moscow during the "troubled times" the names of pretenders are recorded side by side with those of tsars. Nor has the city escaped its share of pretenders today. Before the

Revolution, they masked themselves behind such names as Streetcar B and Jack of Diamonds. These groups belonged to one family—the Futurists. After the Revolution, the Futurists exchanged their old slogans for those of October: they proclaimed themselves the plenipotentiary representatives of the revolution in painting and declared their art proletarian. For several years raspberry-colored and blue Cubist workers graced revolutionary banners and placards, but then the story of the proletarian style in architecture repeated itself: the models of proletarian art adopted by snobs were not accepted by the proletariat. The reaction here was even sharper and expressed itself (formally) in a swing of the pendulum from the extreme left to the extreme right. The vacant residence of proletarian artists was usurped by new pretenders—the Akhrovtsy (AKhRR—derived from the Association of Artists of Revolutionary Russia). This group attempted to revive a primitively naturalist, highly tendentious genre. The artistic results of their activities proved so feeble that they lost their position even more speedily than the Futurists, who had at least entertained a sincere desire for a renewal of form in painting, although they had carried it far "to the left of good sense." Petersburg waited with great restraint for the end of the era of pretenders, and it seems that the crisis has resolved itself during the past year: all Soviet artists have joined a single association, which bases its principles not only on fashionable political slogans, but also on the demand for genuine mastery. The artistic leadership in this association seems likely to remain in the hands of painters close to the World of Art.

A crisis of another, specifically Soviet type, though parallel to that observed in European art as well, is the crisis in the area of easel painting. The Stankovists [Society of Easel Painters] are still working both in Moscow and in Petersburg, but chiefly for themselves—or, at best, to show their paintings at an exhibition and then hang them on the walls of their studios. With the end of the era of New Economic Policy, all the nouveaux riches who hastened to demonstrate their advanced culture by the purchase of paintings, have disappeared without a trace. The budget of the present Soviet citizen precludes all luxuries, including paintings. Neither is the state, which has thrown all available funds into the development of industry, capable of spending much to support artists. Economics have brought painters face to face with the need to seek a way out in works accessible to the mass consumer—in colonizing the realm of applied art.

The beginning of this colonization had been made by Petersburg back in the years of war communism: it launched a great exodus of artists into the book field—to work in book illustration. A number of publishers sprang up in Petersburg, gathering around them first-rate artists and leaving a legacy of small museums of art on the shelves of booklovers (these include the excellent publications of such houses as Akvilon, Petropolis, and Academia). With the demise of the NEP, these private publishing houses were liquidated as capitalist enterprises, but their cultural traditions and their technical forces remained and have concentrated during the past two years chiefly around two publishing houses—the cooperative Izdatelstvo Pisatelei [Writers' Publishing House] and the Academia, which was taken over by the government. Petersburg was followed, somewhat later, by Moscow, and fine literary publishing houses appeared there as well. In the meantime, however, the best examples of fine book publishing are still produced in Petersburg. At any rate, both Moscow and Petersburg are witnessing the characteristic phenomenon of the mass migration of artists from the easel to the book.

A relatively small number of painters found the door open to another area, measured not by the centimeters of the book page, but by the dozens of meters of stage sets. In this field, Moscow has taken the unquestioned lead, and for a long time "all-out fashion" was dictated both to Petersburg and to the rest of Russia by Meyerhold. This new fashion of "Constructivist sets, which expelled all traces of painting from the theater and abolished theatrical costumes (replacing them by the same "industrial clothing" for all characters), was parallel in its schematic character and bareness to what was taking place in other fields as well. Fortunately, Meyerhold is the product of long Petersburg schooling, and, most important of all, he is far more talented than his left-wing neighbors in the other arts. Therefore, the scenic artists who worked in accordance with his principles produced a number of extremely interesting works (such as those of the Moscow artists Nivinsky, Rabinovich, and Shlepyanov, and the Petersburg artists Dmitriev and Akimov). But this skeletal, geometric fashion has already been abandoned even by its orginator. Side by side with a return to colorful sets and rich costumes (especially in opera and the ballet), the last word today is the method of "concentrated realism," which demands the construction on the stage of "three-dimensional sets" and the furnishing of the play with a minimum of "real things."

Of the seven sisters, the feminine element is, of course, most pronounced in Thalia and Terpsichore. The theater comes to life only when it is fructified by the male principle—the playwright. The actor becomes a true artist only when he gives himself up completely to the chosen role. The director is only an experienced educator who follows his own way of molding the child to the hereditary pattern invested in it by the author. And if "Moscow is feminine, and Petersburg masculine," where, then, but in Moscow could the theater find its most fertile soil? And could one have expected anything but the total victory of the Moscow theaters? In this field Petersburg yielded itself to the mercy of the victor and acknowledged her supremacy all the way. True theater lovers in Petersburg no longer attend their own dramatic theaters; they wait for visits from Moscow.

This does not mean that all is serene in the victorious camp. It is still far from the weary equilibrium of age; the struggle still goes on between Russian theatrical Moscow and the latest, "American" Moscow. America, the drive toward the unusual, toward sensation, toward the dazzling trick, the purely American unceremoniousness in remaking the play to one's own taste, effective, restless, always in "the latest" fashion—this, of course, is pure Meyerhold. His impetuous American thrust pushed Stanislavsky's Art Theater to the background during the first postrevolutionary years. Meyerhold was proclaimed the leader of the revolutionary theater. He is a member of the party, an honorary Red Army soldier, the dictator of the Meyerhold Theater. The Theater of the Revolution, the Studio of the Maly Theater, Tram (the Theater of Working Class Youth) are his vassals. His scouts penetrate even into the former "imperial" Maly Theater and into the Vakhtangov Theater created by Stanislavsky's pupils, where productions in the Meyerhold style can often be seen.

But the too rapid American "prosperity" led to a crisis. Along with the retreat from the extreme left positions in all areas of art, the tastes of the theatergoer and (which was even more important in terms of practical consequences) the tastes of the Moscow authorities clearly shifted toward Stanislavsky about two years ago. Even before that, Meyerhold entered a period of failures with the production of Mayakovsky's *The Bathhouse.* He recouped his position to some extent, though far from fully, by his productions of *The Inspector General* and *Woe from Wit.*[2] But even his brilliant directorial imagination could not save the poor play *Introduction,* produced last season. Just recently, Meyerhold's Petersburg vassal, the Alexandrinsky Theater, turned from him: direction of this theater came into the hands of an old pupil of Stanislavsky.

This theatrical shift from the extreme left to the center is also reflected in the repertoire, in which we see the reappearance of the classics, pushing the often second-rate Soviet plays into the background. From the period of risky experiments, the Moscow theater is moving over to a calmer and more organized activity, to a consolidation of its victories. The defeated Petersburg theaters glow only with the reflected light of Moscow. The only fort which has not yet hoisted a white flag is the Petersburg Theater of Opera and Ballet, the former Mariinsky Theater, which still competes for first place with the Moscow Bolshoi.

The first postrevolutionary decade was a difficult period for opera and ballet, both in Petersburg and in Moscow. The companies of those two theaters were bled more severely than dramatic companies by the loss of first-rate artists abroad. These losses were recouped more rapidly by the Petersburg Mariinsky Theater, which had inherited from the imperial era both a wealth of tradition and a better school, especially in ballet. Another troubled area was in the repertoire: attempts were made to sovietize it at forced speed. But the light skiff of opera and ballet turned out to be ill adapted to the transportation of the heavy load of utilitarianism. Most of the "industrial" propaganda ballets and operas were fiascoes (the ballet *Bolt* in Petersburg, the opera *Breakthrough* in Moscow, and so on). This caused a turn to the classic repertoire, expressed even more sharply in opera and ballet than in drama. In addition, Petersburg also found another solution: it opened its window on Europe and produced a series

---

[2] By Gogol and Griboyedov, respectively.

of skillfully and sharply interpreted new European operas (Krenek's *Leap Over the Shadow,* Berg's *Wozzek,* Schreker's *Distant Tone,* and others). "Opera and ballet are the king and queen of the Petersburg theater," said Gogol a hundred years ago, and so they remain today. And the decisive role in this was played, perhaps, by the "individuality," the character, of the northern capital. Opera and ballet live only halfway in the feminine element of the theater; the other half lives in the realm of music, and the roots of Russian music have long been in Petersburg.

If we should draw a map of the musical resources of Russian song, the richest veins will be found in the north. Here, in the Novgorod, Olonetsk, Archangel, and Mezen villages, the old ceremonial, group dances, and lyrical Russian songs survive to this day; in the Moscow environs they have long been replaced by factory songs and musically impoverished *chastushka*s.[3] The famous Petersburg Mighty Five (which included Rimsky-Korsakov, Moussorgsky, Borodin) were nurtured on the wealth of folk music. The first Russian conservatory was also founded in Petersburg. It was from Petersburg that Stravinsky, Prokofiev, Glazounov, Rachmaninoff, and the conductor Koussevitzky went forth to conquer the world with Russian music. Who among those who had been in Petersburg before and during the war can forget its brilliant musical evenings? The magnificent columned hall of the Gentry's Assembly, filled by the Petersburg intelligentsia. The gallery above, packed with students looking down over the railing. On the stage, Koussevitzky with his magical baton. At the piano, Scriabin.

Much has changed since. The Gentry's Assembly hall has become the home of the Leningrad Philharmonic Orchestra. Scriabin is dead, and not only physically: his attenuatedly sensuous mysticism is no longer audible today; this recent idol is quite forgotten. Koussevitzky is no longer in Petersburg, and, we must admit, there are no new great Russian conductors (the best concerts are given under the batons of foreign visitors). But the Philharmonic Hall still draws the flower of the intelligentsia, both that which has survived from old Petersburg, and that which has

[3] Comic four-line ditties.

grown up in Leningrad. In Moscow the situation is quite different: there, such brilliant assemblies can be seen chiefly in the theaters; but the Petersburg audiences have remained, above all, music lovers.

The highly complex, almost mathematical, nature of music creates for it an ironclad protection against the microbes of dilletantism, which penetrate much more easily into the fields of painting, literature, and the theater. Therefore, the processes observed in other realms of art were not so painful in music. The musical organization which tried to exploit political slogans (the RAMP[4]) died in infancy. There have been almost no attempts to replace the organic development of new content in music by the fabrication of hastily made musical homunculi. The various stages of the struggle between formal movements are developing far more slowly. The "left wing" in music, related to the new French composers, as well as to Schoenberg, Hindemith, and Stravinsky, is still dominant (and the most vivid and talented representative of this wing is the young Petersburg composer Shostakovich, author of the opera *The Nose,* based on Gogol's story, and a number of ballet, orchestral, and piano works). But recently a new group has arisen in Petersburg (clustered around the composer Shcherbachev), which seeks to restore melody, lost in the drive for sharpness and originality of harmonization typical of the extreme left. This phenomenon is parallel to the retreat of "Meyerholdism" before "emotional" theater. And, in complete analogy with the theater there has been a stress in recent years on the classic repertoire, especially Beethoven, whose music, it is claimed, is "optimistic" and puts the listener into a "healthy, cheerful mood." Among the Russian composers abroad, Stravinsky has the greatest appeal for the public. The first performance of Stravinsky's *Oedipus* and *Les noces*—by the excellent Petersburg chorus under Klimov's direction—was one of the most important events in Soviet musical life.

But if one thinks of outlandish, "American" notions in music, the first place in devising these belongs, of course, to Moscow. It was Moscow, for instance, that invented "Persimfans"—the first symphony orchestra to repudiate the authority of the conductor and to conduct itself collectively. The Moscow Edisons are build-

---

[4] Russian Association for Proletarian Music.

ing instruments for the production of "electromusic," the "music of the future." It was only in Moscow that an attempt could have been made to leap across time into a still more distant and utopian future. Several years ago, during a revolutionary holiday, the new capital heard a symphony by a young Moscow composer, performed on factory whistles. It proved impossible, however, to conduct these "voices of the city," and the result was chaotic cacophony. Incidentally, even the timbre of Moscow's voice has changed radically, has become Americanized, since the removal some five years ago of all its church bells. Petersburg—and even more so, Leningrad—has preserved the music of the bells to this day.

The greatest amount of material for assessment, for a summing up, is, of course, provided by literature. And naturally so, for here are gathered the elements of all the arts: in composition —architecture; in characterization—the chisel; in landscape— paint; in verse—music; in dialogue—the theater. The characteristic Moscow and Petersburg overtones heard in the voices of the other arts sound with particular clarity and fullness in Soviet literature. It is here, perhaps, that we can see most distinctly that "Moscow is feminine, Petersburg masculine," and that the winds of Europe blow over Petersburg and the winds of America, over Moscow.

Before the Revolution, the highroad of Russian literature ran through Petersburg. This was Russia's literary capital. For many decades, Moscow remained merely the Russian province, and was regarded as such by the residents of Petersburg. "Petersburg is fond of poking fun at Moscow, at her awkwardness and lack of taste," noted Gogol, adding that Moscow, in turn, "accuses Petersburg of not knowing how to speak Russian." Even Pushkin had counseled learning true Russian from "the old women of Moscow—her bakers of communion bread." And he learned from them himself. Nevertheless, like Gogol, he remained a son of Petersburg, the poet of the "northern Palmyra." The beautiful Neva and the bronze Peter rearing his horse on its banks, the Petersburg canals, the palaces mirrored in their glass, the ghostly fogs and delirious white nights, and the people bearing within themselves something of the madness of those nights, of the destructive rages of the Neva, suddenly overflowing its granite banks and sweeping everything in its path—all this is forever imprinted in Russian literature, from its golden age—from Pushkin, Gogol, Dostoyevsky, and Lev Tolstoy—through the last spokesmen of the silver age—Blok, Sologub, Bely, Remizov. The lens of major literature was rarely, and even then somehow accidentally, turned on Moscow. Tolstoy alone divided himself almost equally between Moscow and Petersburg. The others, whenever they abandoned Petersburg in their pages, seldom halted midway in Moscow, preferring to this provincial capital the Gogolian exoticism of the true Russian province.

Thus it was that throughout the nineteenth century the Petersburg tradition was built and developed in literature—and Russian literature was built in Petersburg. It was here that almost all the influential Russian journals were published; it was here that all the large publishing houses were concentrated; and it was here that literary movements were born and grew. It was here, too—within our memory, on the eve of the war—that the long reign of the Realist dynasty, concluded with Bunin and Gorky, was succeeded by the age of the Symbolists, who had sent their vice-regents to Moscow as well. Moscow recognized them and obediently paid them tribute until its sudden rebellion on the eve of the catastrophe, on the eve of the war. It was not, however, a serious rebellion, but rather an extravagant, hysterical outburst ("Moscow is feminine," quipped Gogol): under the title "A Slap in the Face of Public Taste," the Russian Futurists published their first manifesto in Moscow (in 1912), proposing that "Pushkin, Dostoyevsky, and Tolstoy be thrown overboard from the ship of today," not to mention "all those Gorkys, Bloks, Sologubs, Bunins and the rest." The young men who raised these modest demands were laughed at in Petersburg and soon forgotten. It never occurred to anyone that these young men would soon occupy the captain's bridge on the ship of literature. No one (with the exception of the visionary poet Alexander Blok) sensed that the guns of social revolution were already loaded and were just about to fire.

In Lev Tolstoy's novels a fallen bomb always spins on the spot for a long time before exploding, and the hero experiences, as in a dream, not seconds, but months, years, a lifetime. The bomb of revolution fell in February 1917, but it spun for a long time; for many months after that everyone lived as in a dream, awaiting the explosion itself. When the smoke of this tremendous explosion had cleared at last, everything turned out to be upside down—history, literature, men, reputations.

Unexpectedly for Petersburg—and even more unexpectedly for herself—Moscow became the capital, the seat of the new government. Unexpectedly for many people, the new government turned out to be extremely interested in the destinies of art generally and literature particularly. Literary policy at that time was formulated hastily, on the run, and the run was toward the left, as far left as possible, in typical Moscow fashion.

And here a clear dividing line immediately appeared between Moscow and Petersburg: without a second thought, Moscow obediently rolled left; Petersburg resisted, refusing to throw its accumulated riches "overboard from the ship of today." Needless to say, the Symbolists, who had grown up in the hothouse atmosphere of the ivory tower, found it impossible to breathe in the cyclone, in which ozone was mixed with clouds of dusty rubble. But even Gorky at that time was in some measure a member of the Petersburg camp, of the literary opposition. The new government found only two groups which enthusiastically accepted everything, without the Petersburg objections. These were the Futurists, already prepared by Moscow in advance of the Revolution, and the new Proletcult, consisting chiefly of poets with genuine proletarian passports. Naturally, both these groups were supported by the government. But the Proletcult was only a nursery, an incubator, an attempt to create new proletarian talents by laboratory methods and in the shortest possible time. To the astonishment of the directors of this laboratory, it soon became apparent that even proletarian talents were born in the natural manner and subject to the natural laws of slow and difficult growth, as evidenced by the earlier example of such a writer as Gorky. The feeble Proletcult voices, breaking like those of fledgling roosters, were easily drowned out by the powerful basso of the leader of the Futurists—Mayakovsky.

A poet of vast temperament and extraordinary mastery of versification, he succeeded for several years in hypnotizing the audience, and even the working-class audience. He succeeded even in winning over to Futurism some of the Communists assigned to watch over literature. The blood kinship between Russian Futurism and bourgeois Italian Futurism was forgotten,

ю.А.
1923

Sergey Yesenin

as were the snobbish prerevolutionary lorgnettes and yellow blouses of Mayakovsky and his friends. The inventors of the yellow blouse were the first to win the red mandate—the right to represent the revolution in literature.

To put it more precisely: not in literature generally, but only in poetry. In the Futurist journal *LEF* prose, poverty-stricken and amateurish, appeared very rarely, somewhere on the out-skirts. Throughout its existence, Futurism did not create a single prose writer. Even Mayakovsky, who on several occasions had secretly confessed to the author of the present essay that he had "finally got down to writing a novel," had evidently also failed to master the task he had set himself. And this is highly character-istic of Futurism, a movement which was above all emotional, "feminine." Out of these emotions, the Futurists may have com-posed occasional odes glorifying the logical element of reason, but Futurism, by its very nature, proved ill suited for the logical work of plotting a novel, or even a story.

It was quite natural, then, that the new literary group which soon came into competition with the Futurists was also a group of poets, and also born in Moscow. These were the Imaginists, who disputed the right of the Futurists to call themselves the extreme left—and hence, the most fashionable. Where the Futurists brandished the proletarian emblem of the new Russian coat of arms, the hammer, the Imaginists had every reason to adopt as their symbol the still unclaimed peasant sickle, for by this time, by the beginning of the NEP, the peasantry had already come forward as a new social force. Thus, the greatest peasant lyric poet, Yesenin, who had begun to write before the Revolution, had as much right to say "Imaginism—is I!" as Mayakovsky had the right to say "Futurism—is I!" The building of a poetic work on the image—even if it was a new image—was essentially nothing new. It needed the enchantment of Yesenin's melodic gift, the romantic aura of the biography of this Moscow François Villon, to compel attention after the cast-iron thundering of Mayakovsky and to win a place next to Mayakovsky on the Mos-cow Parnassus of those years.

It is both curious and characteristic that Futurism and Imaginism proved incapable, as poetic schools, of striking root among the literary youth of Petersburg. Quite another spirit reigned here, more "masculine," more skeptical, more inclined to build the new not on totally denuded ground, but on the foundation of the earlier, Western culture, even if it was branded by the odious designation of "bourgeois." Both Yesenin and Mayakovsky were hostile to the West: the former, in the name of a unique brand of Slavophilism, in the name of faith in a Bolshevik-peasant Russia; the latter, in the name of a new, Moscow-American, supermechanized, Communist Russia. Of all the Petersburg poets of those years, Blok was the only anti-Westerner (witness his magnificent poems, "The Scythians" and "The Twelve"). However, his revulsion against the West reached such extremes that it grew into a certain revulsion against the revolution itself when the dry Marxist skeleton began to protrude more and more insistently from under its original elemental forms.

But Blok spoke only for himself; he walked alone, followed by no one. This became especially obvious when Blok failed to win reelection as chairman of the Petersburg Poets' Union and was replaced by Gumilyov. Gumilyov is known abroad chiefly because he was shot by the Cheka, and yet he must take his place in the history of the new Russian literature as an important poet and leader of the typically Petersburg poetic school—the Acmeists. The compass of Acmeism clearly pointed west. The helmsman of the Acmeist ship sought to rationalize the poetic element and gave major stress to work on poetic technology. It was not accidental that, in the field of art, Blok and Gumilyov were enemies. And it is not accidental that a seemingly paradoxical phenomenon has been observed in Soviet poetry in recent years: in order to learn how to write, the younger generation of proletarian poets studies the poems of the rationalist romantic Gumilyov, rather than those of Yesenin or the author of the revolutionary poem "The Twelve," Blok.

The poetic school of the Acmeists existed at that time in Petersburg not only figuratively, but literally, in the shape of the Literary Studio (attached to the Petersburg House of the Arts), which played a major role in the development of Soviet literature. At this studio, Gumilyov gave a course in poetics and conducted a poetry seminar. Similar work in the department of criticism was performed by the young critic V. Shklovsky, and in the department of prose, by the author of the present essay.

It would, perhaps, not be an exaggeration to say that the cold, unheated lecture rooms of the Studio, where both the lecturers and the audience often sat wrapped in overcoats, produced what in a formal respect was the most interesting group of Soviet prose writers (Zoshchenko, Vsevolod Ivanov, Kaverin, Slonimsky, and Lunts). The name of the Serapion Brethren, adopted by this group, is known to anyone who has followed the evolution of postrevolutionary Soviet literature, and in itself indicates the definitely Western literary orientation of the group. Certain Marxist literary circles had in those years already exhibited a tendency to return to the naturalist Russian prose of the 1860s, which had set itself propagandist rather that artistic goals. As a counterbalance to this artistically reactionary trend, the Serapion Brethren, in their manifesto of 1922, gave first place to questions of the writer's craft and protested against the demand that writers turn out works solely on topical subjects. This position, as well as certain elements of romanticism (built, however, not on abstractions, as was the case with the Symbolists, but as extrapolations of reality), brought the Serapion Brethren close to the Petersburg Acmeist trend.

Thus, the city of Gogol, Pushkin, and Dostoyevsky saw the emergence of fresh, firm shoots of a new Russian prose. On the other hand, Moscow, the home of Yesenin's ringing songs and the magnificent growling of Mayakovsky, brought forth a single new and original prose writer—Pilnyak. And it must be said that he was a typical product of the Moscow soil. While in the works of the majority of the young Petersburg prose writers we find a masculinely strong plot, constructed with engineering precision, Pilnyak's plots are always as unclear and tangled as the ground plan of Moscow itself. Where the Serapion Brethren are akin to the Acmeists, the vivid embroideries of Pilnyak's prose bear a recognizable likeness to the motifs of Imaginism, down to its unique kind of a new Slavophilism and faith in the messianic mission of the new Russia.

The birth of a new prose in Petersburg and the new poetry of Imaginism and Futurism in Moscow—this whole revival in literature began long before the NEP, during the years of Russia's total economic collapse. Literature emerged from lethargy much earlier than economics. In literature, therefore, the sharp turn from war communism to the NEP, which opened a new chapter in the history of the Russian revolution, meant little more at first than a continuation of the previous chapter. The relaxation of the political regime, the appearance of a number of cooperative and private publishing houses, merely created more favorable conditions for the development of literary trends which had begun before the NEP. And these trends of the first years of the NEP are stamped even more distinctly with the individual characteristics of Petersburg and Moscow.

It was not by chance that Petersburg became the home of Vsemirnaya Literatura [World Literature], a publishing house founded by Gorky. As though recalling once again its role as a window on Europe, Petersburg flung this window wide open, and European works, in the excellent translations provided by Vsemirnaya Literatura, poured out in editions of many thousands to all ends of Russia. Neither was it by chance that with the reemergence of "thick" monthlies Petersburg produced the two nonpartisan journals. *Sovremenny zapad* [Contemporary West], and *Russky sovremennik* [The Russian contemporary], edited by Gorky, A. Tikhonov, and Zamyatin, while Moscow produced the two semiofficial literary journals *Krasnaya nov* [Red virgin soil] and *Novy mir* [New world], edited, respectively, by the Communist critics A. Voronsky and V. Polonsky.

Sovremenny zapad continued the cultural policies of Vsemirnaya Literatura. *Russky sovremennik,* which gathered in its pages all the best representatives of the old literature and the most talented young writers, was the only journal which had the courage in those years to engage in polemics with the biased, sectarian criticism of some of the Communist literary groups. This journal had a brief existence, not more than about two years, but it will remain one of the most characteristic monuments of the Petersburg literary line of the NEP period.

Under the stimulus of the NEP, both capitals, Moscow and Petersburg, changed even externally with astonishing speed. The recently boarded-up shop windows once again glittered with lights. Still embarrassed by their bourgeois appearance and taking cover behind semiofficial signboards, cafes and restaurants dotted the streets. Instead of machine-gun fire, the streets resounded with the hammering of boilermakers, bracklayers and carpenters, especially in Moscow, where the very acute housing shortage made it necessary to build with American speed. Words like *building* and *plans* peppered the pages of the press—still, for the time being, as exotic novelties. To people who had witnessed only various forms of destruction for several years, there was, indeed, something magically new, almost miraculous, in construction. And it did not take long before this newest, constructivist motif reflected itself in literature.

And, of course like all the other "newest," "latest" developments, this occurred in Moscow. Futurism and Imaginism acquired a new rival—Constructivism, a new poetic school whose loudest spokesman was the poet Selvinsky. This superfashion was the very embodiment of Moscow's Americanism, and indeed, a more complete and logically consistent embodiment than Futurism. "Constructivism rejects art as the product of bourgeois culture. . . . Constructivism seeks to create a new, constructive man. Invention and technology are the two means toward the attainment of this goal." Such were the theses of Constructivism. We must say "were," because this curious literary school, like many others, ceased to exist in the very next chapter as a result of the critical carnage instituted by a new privileged literary group, the RAPP (of which more will be said later).

The carnage, however, was still in the future; the fields of Soviet literature still flowered peacefully and produced rich harvests. By this time, two first-rate new poets came to maturity— Pasternak in Moscow and N. Tikhonov in Petersburg. Having passed through the stage of the short story, prose soon came to the monumental form with the appearance of the first examples of the new Russian novel, where the same material—the Russian revolution—was refracted through the most diverse prisms of the individual authors. Like first love, these first novels proved far fresher, more sincere and full-throated than the subsequent works of the same writers (Pilnyak, Leonov, Fedin, Forsh, and others).

The renewed orchestra of literature still lacked one instrument —criticism. It is highly characteristic that the beginning in this area, particularly responsible and demanding a wide cultural background, was, again, made by Petersburg, where the Formalist school was organized during the early years of the NEP. This was the first serious attempt to create a scientific, objective method of criticism, as opposed to the usual subjective critical methods, based solely upon the esthetic or political tastes of the given critic. Proceeding from a definition of the essence of art as a sum of the methods employed, the Formalists held that the task of the literary critic was objective analysis of the methods employed by the writer. True, this conception of the critic's role limited itself to abstract anatomy; it did not yet contain the principle of living medicine (which alone justifies the existence of criticism). Nevertheless, side by side with Formalism, all the other critical methods, which offered literature the most diverse prescriptions, were little more than primitive quackery. Formalism, which united under its banner a group of extremely talented young scholars (Eichenbaum, Tomashevsky, Zhirmunsky, Shklovsky, and Tynyanov), had only had time to take its first steps. Sooner or later, anatomy would have been followed by scientifically based therapy, very close in spirit to the positive trends in Soviet literature. However, Formalism did not live to enter this stage. Like many other literary groups, it did not survive the onslaught of the RAPP and went out of existence.

It is time to disclose the meaning of this mysterious designation, RAPP—the Russian Association of Proletarian Writers. Organized during the early years of the NEP, it began at that time to snipe at the rest of literature in its journal *Na postu* [At the post]. This sniping gradually intensified to a steady barrage toward the end of the NEP and became an all-out assault in 1927–30, when the Communist party's general policy took a sharp new turn—from the NEP to the Five-Year Plan and the collectivization of agriculture.

Seeking to take control not only of material production, but also of the "intellectual output"—art and literature—the victorious class raised a number of slogans which the RAPP adopted as its battle cry. It demanded a "Five-Year Plan in literature" and "the hegemony of proletarian literature." The group of young Communist writers in Moscow who headed the RAPP decided without false modesty that they could take upon themselves the role of masters of Russian literature. They would rebuild the psychology of the Fellow Travelers at the same crash tempo that was applied to the economic Five-Year Plan and transform them, if not into Communists, then at least into sufficiently orthodox "allies." Unfortunately, these candidates for supremacy did not possess the high artistic authority commensurate with their ambition. In formal skill, in the diversity of ideas, and in the number of talented writers, the advantage was unquestionably on the side of the Fellow Travelers. The flock turned out to be superior to the shepherds. The RAPP could not possibly win literary hegemony in free artistic competition, at least in the foreseeable future. Only one alternative remained to the impatient conquistadores—to establish their authority by artillery methods.

Their party positions proved most favorable for artillery action. For a certain time, literary criticism was a virtual monopoly in the hands of the RAPP. A carefully planned barrage was opened at individual prominent Fellow Travelers and entire literary groups. The critical shells were invariably filled with the same standard gas: the charge of political unreliability. This concept now included "formalist deviations," "biological deviations," "humanism," "apolitical approach," and so on. Sincerity, talent, and the writer's artistic resources usually remained outside the field of vision of the critics. But although this critical method was not burdened with excessive erudition, it nevertheless unerringly achieved its end. The targets were left no choice but to withdraw into the dugouts of their desks and disappear from the field of print.

Moscow, Petersburg, individuality, literary schools—everything was leveled, equalized; everything vanished in the smoke of the literary carnage. The shock produced by incessant critical bombardment was so great that an unheard-of psychic epidemic flared up among the writers—an epidemic of penitence. Entire processions of literary flagellants passed through the pages of newspapers: Pilnyak flogged himself for his novella *Mahogany,* which had been declared criminal by the masters; the founder and theoretician of Formalism, Shklovsky, repudiated the Formalist heresy forever; Constructivists repented their lapse into Constructivism and disbanded their organization; the old anthroposophist Andrey Bely swore in print that he was really an anthroposophic Marxist. This epidemic found its most favorable soil in Moscow, which lent itself more easily to emotions. Among the Petersburg writers, flagellants were the exception. Both Moscow and Petersburg, however, submitted to the RAPP dictatorship.

This chapter in the history of Soviet literature was marked by an obvious decline. "To be in literature is to serve, not to be in service" wrote a Petersburg writer later (in the Leningrad journal *Zvezda,* no. 4 [1933]). "Art is not the soulless artisan hackwork which was demanded of us by certain RAPP comrades of unhappy memory, who turned their group into a kind of assay office for the new Soviet literature." In the life of the country this was a period of momentous events. The radical agrarian revolution, the feverish industrialization—these should have given artists a wealth of material, but not, of course, as a matter of "doing a job," of working under command, of hurried production, which contradict the very essence of the creative process—a process far more complex than the commanders of the RAPP imagined. Some of the most important writers, who understood (or, rather, felt) the danger of such "service," almost ceased to appear in print (Babel, Seifulina, Sergeyev-Tsensky, and others). Others chose to withdraw from this danger into past centuries. Thus, the sudden revival of the Russian historical novel (A. N. Tolstoy, Olga Forsh, Yury Tynyanov). And characteristically, this, again, took place in Petersburg.

At the same time, however, both Petersburg and Moscow writers produced a number of works on the most topical subjects: industrialization, "wrecking activities," defense, and so on. Successful works in these areas were but rare exceptions, and those were produced solely by Communist writers (Sholokhov, Afinogenov), for entirely understandable reasons. These writers were not compelled to give constant proof of their reliability at the expense of artistic truth. Most of the novels and plays written by Fellow Travelers as a matter of obligatory service, without genuine creative enthusiasm, turned out to be considerably inferior to their authors' general level (Pilnyak's *The Volga Falls into the Caspian Sea,* Katayev's *Vanguard,* Leonov's *Sot,* N. Tikhonov's *War,* N. Nikitin's *In the Line of Fire, The Busy Workshop* by Forsh, and others).

It became increasingly obvious that all was not well in literature. The symptoms of literary anemia developed with alarming speed where only recently there had been flourishing health. Clearly, some energetic treatment was needed to put the patient back on his feet.

The surgical operation was performed unexpectedly, without any preparation, in April of 1932. By resolution of the Central Committee of the Communist party, the RAPP was dissolved, and its activity was officially declared to be a hindrance to the further development of literature. Similar measures were taken in connection with kindred organizations active among painters and musicians.

This was an unquestionable victory for the civilized, "Petersburg" policy in art—a victory particularly perceptible in literature. Abolishing the hegemony of the RAPP, a hegemony entirely disproportionate to the true correlation of artistic forces, proved to be as easy as turning a page. The next page opened a new and far more promising chapter in Soviet literature. There was a redistribution of literary forces in accordance with their relative artistic merit—and, naturally, the influence of the fellow travelers immediately rose. Again the voice of Petersburg was heard more clearly and confidently in literature. Throughout the preceding years political weather in literature had been set by the Moscow *Literary Gazette*. Now the Petersburg writers acquired their own newspaper, *Literary Leningrad*. In setting forth its program, this newspaper resolutely gave first place to the traditional goals of the "Petersburg line": "The newspaper must become a laboratory of literary craft, a laboratory of the word, of language, of plot."

The fruitless occupation of "weighing ideology on an apothecary's scale" (a definition coined by *Literary Leningrad*) has given way to genuine literary debate. The scholastic prescription of the "dialectic method," which had but yesterday been regarded as obligatory in creative art, has been retired to the archives. The latest literary discussions reflect a struggle between two artistic methods—romanticism and realism, with the latter clearly ascendant for the time being. The latest slogan is return to classic, monumental simplicity (paralleling the European tendencies of "clarisme"). It is highly characteristic that, among contemporary "bourgeois" writers, Moscow has shown particular interest in the American left-wing urbanist, John Dos Passos.

The surgical operation of 1932 has produced its results. Soviet literature has experiencd that upsurge of vital energies that is familiar to anyone convalescing from a serious illness. But was the operation radical? Will there be no relapse?

Paris, December 1933

Евгений Замятин

THE PSYCHOLOGY
OF CREATIVE WORK

In surgery there are two subdivisions: major surgery and minor. Major surgery is the art of operating, and only a man with a special talent for it can be a good surgeon. Minor surgery is a craft, and anyone can learn to apply bandages or lance abscesses. Astronomy is also divided into major and minor; the latter is that part of applied astronomy required for such things as determining a ship's position at sea, verifying a chronometer by the sun, and so on.

The same subdivisions, it seems to me, exist in art. There is major art and minor art. There is creative work, and there is craft. Only Byron could have written *Childe Harold;* but anyone who has had adequate training can translate it. Only Beethoven could have written the *Moonlight Sonata;* many can play it— and quite well. Writing *Childe Harold* and the *Moonlight Sonata* is creation—it belongs to the realm of major art. Translating *Childe Harold* or playing the *Moonlight Sonata* belongs to the realm of craft, of minor art. And obviously, while minor art, craft, can be taught, creation, major art, cannot: it is impossible to teach anyone to write *Childe Harold*s or *Moonlight Sonata*s.

This is why I repudiate from the very start the announced title of my course. It is not possible to teach anyone how to write novels or stories. In that case, you may ask, what are we doing here? Wouldn't it be best to say good night and go home? To this I will answer: No, there is still enough for us to do, after all.

This essay, as well as "Theme and Plot" and "On Language," was part of Zamyatin's series of lectures on the technique of fiction, given in 1920–21 at the House of the Arts in Petrograd.

Craft—minor art—is inevitably a component of major art. In order to compose his *Moonlight Sonata,* Beethoven first had to learn the laws of melody, harmony, counterpoint. He had to learn musical technique and the technique of composition, which belong to the realm of craft. In order to write *Childe Harold,* Byron had to learn the technique of versification. Similarly, those who wish to devote themselves to creative work in the field of prose must first learn the techniques of literary prose.

The development of art is subject to the dialectic method. Art functions pyramidally: all new achievements are based on the utilization of everything that has been accumulated below, at the foundations of the pyramid. Revolutions do not occur here; this field, more than any other, is governed by evolution. And we must know what has been done before us in the field of verbal art. This does not mean that you must follow in trodden paths: you must contribute something of your own. A work of art is of value only when it is original, both in content and in form. But in order to leap upward, it is necessary to take off from the ground. It is essential that there be a ground.

There are no laws, and there can be no laws, on how to write: everyone must write in his own way. I can only tell you how I write, how writing is done generally. I can tell you not how to write, but how not to write.

And so, our main topic will be the technique of the art of prose writing. Those with creative capacity may be helped to break out of their shells with greater ease and speed; to those without such capacity, our work can only be a matter of curiosity; it can provide them with some information concerning the anatomy of literarure. This may be useful for critical work. Those who have a voice must learn to "place it" properly, as singers say. This is the second task. But those who have no voice naturally cannot be taught to sing.

If I were to promise you in all seriousness to teach you to write novels and stories, it would be as absurd as promising to teach you the art of loving, or falling in love, for that is also an art, and also requires talent.

I did not use this analogy fortuitously. To an artist, creating an image means being in love with it. Gogol was unquestionably in love—and not only with the heroic Taras Bulba, but also with Chichikov, and Khlestakov, and the lackey Petrushka. Dostoyevsky was in love with the Karamazovs—with all of them, the father and the brothers. In *Foma Gordeyev,* Gorky created the figure of old Mayakin. This was to be a negative character: he is a merchant. Yet Gorky is clearly in love with him. When I was writing *A Provincial Tale,* I was in love with Baryba, with Chebotarikha, however grotesque, however repulsive they were. But there is, perhaps, beauty in ugliness, in hideousness. Scriabin's harmony is essentially ugly: it consists throughout of dissonances. Nevertheless, it is magnificently beautiful.

I speak about this not to prove the axiom that creative art cannot be taught, but to describe the process of creation, insofar as this is possible, and insofar as I am familiar with it from my own experience.

Like being in love, writing is at the same time a joyful and a tormenting process. Another analogy may be even closer—motherhood. No wonder Heine wrote in his *Gedanken:* "Every book must go through its natural process of growth, like a child. No honest woman gives birth to her child before nine months."

This is a most natural analogy because a writer, like a woman, like a mother, creates living people who suffer and rejoice, mock and are laughed at. And like the mother, who creates her child out of herself, the writer also creates his people out of himself, nourishes them with his own self—with a certain nonmaterial substance which is part of his being.

There is a dearth of material that could give us an insight into the creative process itself. Writers rarely speak about it. And understandably so: the creative process takes place chiefly in the mysterious realm of the subconscious. The conscious, *ratio,* logical thought, plays a secondary, subordinate role.

At the moment of creative activity the writer is in a state similar to hypnosis: the mind of a hypnotized man receives and elaborates only the impressions created by the material given to him by the hypnotist. You can pinch or prick the skin of a hypnotized man, let him smell spirits of ammonia, he will not feel anything. But let the hypnotist give him a drink of water and say that it is champagne, and the subject will immediately experience all the associations, the taste, and the emotions connected with champagne: he will say that he is happy, describe the taste of the champagne, and so on. In short, he will become involved in a creative process. But as soon as the subject is released from the will of the hypnotist, the creative process is ended: he will no longer be able to create wine out of water, he will no longer be able to perform the miracle of Cana in Galilee.

It has often occurred to me that under hypnosis a writer might, perhaps, be able to write ten times faster and more easily. Unfortunately, no experiments have been made in this direction. The difficulty of creative work is that the writer must combine within himself both the hypnotist and the subject. He must hypnotize himself, put his own consciousness to sleep; and this, of course, requires very strong will power and a very lively imagination. No wonder many writers use narcotics when working in order to put the conscious mind to sleep and stimulate the subconscious, the imagination. Przybyszewski could not write without a bottle of cognac; Huysmans—and he was not alone in this —used morphine. Andreyev drank the strongest tea while at work. Remizov drinks coffee and smokes. I cannot write a single page without a cigarette.

All this, I repeat, is done to lull the conscious mind and subject it to the subconscious. Any effort to analyze the creative process inevitably results in bringing the conscious mind to the fore; the hypnotized man awakens, creative work is halted, and with it, of course, the attempt at analysis. I have tested this many times myself. This is the reason why writers provide so little information on the creative process. We find only vague statements that writing is difficult, or that it is a joyful experience, or a painful one.

Chekhov wrote to L. Gurevich:[1] "I write slowly, with long intermissions. I write and rewrite, and often throw away what I have written without finishing it." In another letter, he wrote: "I am writing and crossing out, writing and crossing out." In his last period, he no longer wrote, but, as he jestingly described it, "drew" (with colored ink).

We know what Tolstoy's and Pushkin's manuscripts look like —how many corrections and variations there are in them, and consequently, how much creative torment.

In the second part of Maupassant's *Strong as Death* almost every sentence was changed and restructured. There are five versions of the closing sentence alone! Maupassant wrote those pages at a period when his illness was becoming more and more

---

[1] L. Ya. Gurevich (1866–1940), editor and critic.

pronounced. You clearly feel that you are in the presence of the phenomenon I spoke about earlier: the author was no longer able to hypnotize himself, his conscious awareness; the conscious mind analyzes every word, revises it, reorders it.

Flaubert wrote about his work on *Salammbo:* "If your book is to sweat truth, you must be filled with your subject to your ears. After that begins the torment of the phrase, the anguish of the assonance, the rack of the period." "I have just completed the first chapter—and I don't find anything good in it; I am tormented by despair day and night. The more experience I acquire in my art, the more agonizing this art becomes to me. Imagination does not grow, but the demands of taste are constantly increasing. I think that few have suffered for literature as much as I." And, "What an accursed plot! The main difficulty is in finding the true note. This is achieved by extreme condensation of thought, attained naturally or by an effort of will, but certainly not by simply visualizing the immutable truth in a whole series of real and convincing details."

It is this "extreme condensation of thought" that I have called self-hypnosis, and it is the most essential condition for creative work and the most difficult to achieve.

Sometimes this state of self-hypnosis, the "condensation of thought," comes of its own, without an effort of the will—and this, in effect, is what we call inspiration. But this happens seldom. To write a long work, one must by an effort of will bring about the state of condensation of thought, and this cannot be taught. It stems from a certain organic capacity, which can only be developed further if it is present in the first place.

The moment of creative work is also similar to the dreaming state, when the conscious mind is half asleep, while the subconscious and the imagination work with utmost vividness.

That this comparison is true is attested by many writers, who often say that the solution of a given creative problem has come to them while asleep. It was in his sleep that some of the lines of his *Gypsies* came to Pushkin. Hamsun always has paper and a pencil on his night table, to jot down what comes to his mind suddenly when he awakes in the middle of the night. I have also found this to be true in my own experience.

In man's ordinary state, thought works logically, in syllogisms. In creative work, thought moves—as in a dream—by association. A word, an object, a color, an abstract concept bearing on the novel or story awaken a host of associations in the writer's mind. It is then the task of the conscious mind to select the most suitable of them. The stronger the writer's powers of association, the richer, the more original and striking his imagery. Hoffmann's extraordinary wealth of associations lends his stories the quality of fantastic dreams. Gorky recently read us his recollections of Andreyev. These recollections contain the following quote from Andreyev, who also possessed a great capacity for association: "I write the word 'spider web,' and my thought begins to unwind, and I recall a high school teacher who spoke in a slow drawl and had a mistress who worked in a pastry shop; he called this young woman 'Milly,' and her friends on the boulevard called her 'Sonka the Bubble.' " What extensive and fantastic associations suggested by a single word, "spider web." The writer's creative mind works as the minds of others do during sleep. We may accidentally touch in our sleep the mother-of-pearl button on our sleeve. In the ordinary state, when the mind works soberly and controls our sensations, this may arouse no associations and no feelings. But during sleep, when the conscious mind is subordinate to the subconscious, the sensation of the button is immediately associated with the touch of a cold steel knife. And in a fraction of a second, we see an entire picture: the knife of the guillotine—we are condemned to death—prison—a ray of sunlight on the door from the narrow window—the glitter of the lock—the click—in a moment the executioner will enter and lead us to the block.

This capacity for association—if it exists—can and should be developed by exercises. And we shall try to do so. Later on, we shall see that one of the subtlest and most potent artistic methods is the suggestion to the reader of specific associations, essential for the effect the writer intends to produce.

1919–20

THEME AND PLOT

How does a plot come into being? Where does the writer get it from? From life? But did Tolstoy know all the characters who people his *War and Peace*—Bolkonsky, Pierre, Natasha, the Rostovs? Had he ever seen Napoleon, who died decades before the writing of *War and Peace?* Had Hoffmann ever seen the archivist Lindhorst and the student Anselmus, whom he had put into a glass bottle? Had Dostoyevsky ever seen the Karamazovs? Had Andrey Bely known his geometric Senator Apollon Apollonovich, and Lipanchenko, and Alexander Ivanovich, and all the other characters in his *Petersburg?* Of course not. All these people, all these living people—Bolkonsky, Pierre, Natasha, the Rostovs, the Karamazovs, Senator Apollon Apollonovich—all of them had been given birth by the writer, who created them out of himself.

True enough, Tolstoy's *Childhood* tells about people who had really lived. The same is true of Gorky's *My Childhood;* in Gorky's other works we also frequently encounter people drawn from life. We find this seemingly direct transposition of living people to the pages of a book in the works of Realist writers, especially in works of an autobiographical character. But even here, we can be sure, events and persons are shown differently from what they had been in reality: the actual people and events merely served the writer as material. And this applies even

Like the preceding essay, originally given as a lecture (see note p. 159).

165

more to Symbolists and Neorealists, whose works abound in the fantastic and grotesque—in things which do not happen in reality.

To the writer, life serves only as material. The form of the entire edifice, its architecture, its beauty, its spirit are all created by the author himself. The architect Bramante built Saint Peter's in Rome of stone. But stone is merely dead material; it was Bramante who breathed life into it. In his painting *Ivan the Terrible,* Repin painted Ivan from a model; but he transformed the living model into Ivan. The writer does the same. The events observed, the people encountered are to the writer little more than the stone was to Bramante or the model to Repin. A writer who can only describe actual life, who can only photograph the people and events he had actually seen, is creatively impotent and will not go far.

Out of the stones which the writer takes from life the plot may be developed by one of two methods—inductive or deductive. In the former, the process of building the plot occurs as follows: some trivial and often unremarkable occurrence or person strikes the writer's imagination and gives him the initial impulse. The writer's creative imagination at such a time is evidently in a state that may be compared to that of a solution in the process of crystallization. It is enough to throw the last pinch of salt into the saturated solution, and the entire solution begins to solidify, crystal growing on crystal until there is a whole fantastic structure. The same thing happens here: the impulse provided by the person or incident seen plays the role of the last pinch of salt; association, the role of the cement which binds the individual crystals of thought. The idea, the generalization, the symbol which gives depth to the plot, comes later, after a large portion of the story has crystallized itself.

The other method is deduction: the writer first concerns himself with an abstract idea and then embodies it in images, events, characters. Either method is equally legitimate. But the latter, deduction, is the more dangerous, for the writer who uses it risks slipping into scholasticism.

As an example of the inductive method of plot construction, I should like to cite an incident related by Korney Chukovsky in his recollections about Leonid Andreyev. Andreyev once read the diary of Utochkin, who wrote: "In the evening light our prison is extraordinarily beautiful." This led to the story "My Diary," which ended with these words. Another example is Chekhov's *The Seagull*. One day Chekhov was strolling with the painter Levitan along a beach in the Crimea. Seagulls were flying over the beach and the water. Levitan shot one of them and threw it on the sand. This death of a beautiful bird, so wantonly and casually killed, struck Chekhov with its needlessness. This incident remained in Chekhov's memory and led to the creation of his play *The Seagull*.

Sometimes the fact that provided the original impulse for the plot drops out of the work altogether. This happened in the case of my novella *The Islanders*.

Examples of the deductive method of plot construction may be found in many Symbolist works, such as Minsky's play *Alma,* or Sologub's *Deathly Charms,* obviously written *à thèse*—to prove Dulcinea's superiority over Aldonsa. The plots of Artsybashev's *Sanin* and *The Breaking Point* and of Gorky's *The Mother* were also clearly created by the deductive method. This method is used in works of a didactic nature and, as I have said before, it is dangerous, for the resulting plots seldom achieve faultless literary form.

And so, we now have some idea of how plot originates. Now, suppose we have the plot—in embryonic form. What is the next step? Do we need a plan, a scheme of the novel or story in order to go on?

It is difficult to give a general answer to this question. On the basis of my own experience, however, I would say that it is best not to hurry with the plan. A plan drawn up at the very outset restrains the work of the imagination, of the subconscious, and limits the associative capacity. The creative process becomes too rational, even contrived. I would recommend beginning with something else: with bringing the principal characters to life. Secondary characters may, of course, appear and come to life later, as the work proceeds. But the principal figures always exist from the very beginning. And you must seek—by that very method of condensation of thought which Flaubert spoke about —to animate these figures, to bring them to life before you. You must get to see them—see them before all else, with all their peculiarities, all their salient traits. You must know how each of them walks, smiles, greets people, eats. Then you must note each one's manner of speech. In other words, you must judge your characters as you would judge any stranger you meet: first you observe them from without, and then, proceeding from the specific qualities, you form a general opinion by the method of induction. By the time you come to know your dramatis personae externally, you will also know them in great detail internally. You will know each one's character; you will know precisely and unerringly what each of them can and must do. And it is then that the plot will crystallize—in its true and final shape. And it is only then that you can safely map out the plan of the work.

This, then, is what should be done in practice: first you sketch the portraits of the principal figures, you carefully think through —or, rather, "feel through"—all their individual characteristics. Then, if you intend to write a long work, it is a good practice to sketch some of the scenes—and it does not matter whether these scenes will occur at the beginning or at the end of the work. After that, you can develop the plan further, and, making use of the sketches, start writing the work from the beginning.

When you are doing the first draft, it is best to write rapidly, preferably without stopping to polish details. Recalcitrant passages are best skipped, to be finished later. The important thing is to give form to the plot, the story. It does not matter if the first draft suffers from overlong passages, redundancies, superfluous details: all of this can be removed in your subsequent work. And there is a great deal of work still to be done. You must remember: every story, novel, or novella must be rewritten at least twice, not counting the preliminary sketches. And you must read it aloud to yourself. This is essential for several reasons: (1) to utilize, wherever necessary, the device of verbal music; (2) to correct all disagreeable sound combinations; (3) to make sure there are no rhythmic mistakes. But reading aloud is not enough to achieve correct phrase structure, correct word sequence, precision of epithets; it is too rapid a process. It is essential to rewrite the work once, twice, three times—as many times as necessary.

During this rewriting you begin to condense and delete. Crossing out is an art that is, perhaps, even more difficult than writing. It requires the sharpest eye to decide what is superfluous and must be removed. And it requires ruthlessness toward yourself—the greatest ruthlessness and self-sacrifice. You must know how to sacrifice parts in the name of the whole. Sometimes a detail, an episode, seems enormously valuable and interesting, and it is such a pity to eliminate it. But in the end, after you have done so, you will always find that it was for the best. And the deleted part can be used later, in another work.

It is always best to understate, rather than overstate. Unless he is a dunce, the reader has teeth sharp enough to chew what you give him; he should not be presented with masticated material. You must not write for cretins. A story, a novel may be considered completely ready and finished when you can no longer cut out of it a single chapter, a single sentence, a single word. Everything that can be eliminated must be ruthlessly eliminated, leaving only the vivid, the essential. Nothing superfluous. Only then can you say that your work is created and alive.

If it seems to you that an incident, an anecdote, a character is too interesting and valuable to eliminate, you must tie this incident or character to the plot with indissoluble, living threads; you must change the plot in such a way as to make the incident or the incidental character essential to it.

Plot development in the modern novel or story follows the same psychological law as it does in drama: introduction of the conflict, action, denouement. This is normal for a novel or novella. In contemporary novels, however, the last part of the formula, denouement, is often omitted. The curtain drops before the last act; it is up to the reader to guess the denouement himself. This method is acceptable only in cases where all the psychological data for the denouement have already been presented, and the reader can easily draw his conclusions from the first two parts of the formula.

A long story also frequently contains all the three elements of drama. But in short stories, the author often takes only one of the parts of this formula: either the conflict alone or the action alone or, directly, nothing but the denouement. Good examples of stories containing all three elements are Chekhov's "The Misfortune" and "The Siren." A story presenting only the initial conflict is his "Hunter." A story with nothing but the denouement is "The Malefactor." A story with nothing but action is his "Easter Night." In most cases, however, even short stories contain all three elements.

We know that classical drama was based on the law of unity: unity of time, place, and action. With the development of theatrical technique, these strict demands were relaxed, and modern dramaturgy no longer insists that the action occur in the same place and within a time span of twenty-four hours. The law of unity of action and unity of dramatis personae remains in force, however, because it derives from psychological, rather than technical, considerations.

The law of the unity of dramatis personae remains in force for the novel, the novella, and the story as well. The technical problems of the theater do not exist here: you are not constrained by the demand for unity of time or place; but unity of the dramatis personae in the modern novel or story is a must. The same group of people—or, perhaps, the same principal character—must be present throughout the work. The principal character may be surrounded by any number of secondary ones. These may disappear as the need for them passes, they may be episodic, but the hero, or heroes, remain throughout. It must be noted here that accidental, episodic characters are a shortcoming in a literary work; they break up its architectural harmony. And a skillful writer will always succeed in making these chance characters essential to the plot, to the development of the story line. I have deliberately emphasized that the demand for unity of the dramatis personae is normal for the new, modern novel or story.

In the early stages of the history of literary prose, this demand, as a rule, was not fulfilled. The prose works of the Middle Ages, or even of the eighteenth century, were built on the episodic principle. Good examples of this are *Scheherazade* and the *Decameron*. Lesage's *Gil Blas* appears to be bound by a single hero, but in essence—almost as in *Scheherazade*—it is only a matter of one person telling a series of tales.

The drama is also subject to another law, which I would call the law of emotional economy. The same thing is true of fiction. This law is based on the fact that strong emotions are followed by a reaction, fatigue, and a lowered emotional receptivity. Therefore, the strongest psychological effects must be reserved for the end of the novella, novel, or story. If they are brought in earlier, the reader will not be able to respond to the subsequent situations which have a lesser emotional charge.

This law of emotional economy has its corollary—the need for interludes. Emotional intensification in a literary work should be followed by a breathing spell, by a lessening of tension. The reader cannot be subjected to *forte* all the time, or he will turn deaf. The tempo and the volume of the sound must vary. This rule applies equally to the novel, the novella, and the long story. Very short stories of two or three pages can reach the reader even if they are written throughout in a high key; the reader's attention will have no time to slacken. He can read and respond to the story in a single breath. In a longer work, the breathing spell, the interlude, can be achieved by one of several methods.

The simplest, but also the crudest and most primitive method is to insert episodes. In other words, the narrative is interrupted by additional, inserted stories, essentially unconnected or connected very tenuously with the basic plot. There are many examples of this: Dostoyevsky's story about the merchant Voskoboynikov, the stories of Akhilla and of the dwarf in Leskov's *Cathedral Folk*. All of this achieves its purpose, but, as I have said, it spoils the architecture and disrupts the harmony of the work.

Other methods are the author's lyrical disgressions and comments. These were often employed by Gogol, as in his "Troyka." Among the new writers, we find such digressions in Remizov and Bely, both of whom derive from Gogol. This device, however, although it achieves its end, giving the reader a rest and diverting him from the flow of the plot, has a serious drawback: it permits the reader to awaken for a time, it cools him and weakens the spell of the work. It is as though an actor were to remove his makeup in the middle of the play, say a few words in his own voice, and then go on. Especially bad is the device of comments by the author, telling the reader about the feelings of his heroes which had already been shown in action. This is always superfluous; this is chewing the cud. An example of this is Chekhov's "The Husband."

Another means of achieving an interlude is description of the landscape or the situation in which the action is taking place.

This method is far more appropriate and acceptable than the others. It also achieves its purpose without introducing any alien element into the work. The landscape and the surroundings can become vital and essential elements. But this demands that the author tie them in organically with the plot.

Chekhov understood this very well. In one of his letters he says: "Description of nature is appropriate and does not interfere with the story only when it is relevant, when it helps to evoke in the reader the desired mood." The landscape, the surroundings, must not be neutral: they must be related to the plot and the emotions of the characters—either by paralleling them or by contrasting with them. Then, in addition to the direct purpose of creating an interlude, you also achieve an auxiliary gain: the reader is prepared for the events to follow. Another result is artistic economy. Examples of this may be found in Chekhov's "Dying to Sleep" and "Agafya," Zamyatin's *The Islanders,* Bunin's "An Evening in Spring."

In any event, both the landscape and the surroundings should be described briefly, in a few lines, as in Chekhov's "The Sea Was Vast." You must learn to see in the landscape and the surroundings either something very simple and therefore not likely to strike the eye, or some original image.

The most difficult and complex, but at the same time the most artful and effective method of creating interludes is that of the intertwined plot. In the story, novella, or novel written by this method several principal characters, connected with one another, move in their various relationships throughout the work, creating more than one story line. When the reader is tired of following the experiences of one pair of characters, his attention is diverted to another or a third. Examples of this are *The Islanders* (Mrs. Dewly and Campbell, Campbell and Didi, Didi and O'Kelly—all of them indissolubly linked with one another), and Chekhov's "In the Barn."

Before concluding my remarks about plot, I want to mention still another failing of the majority of Russian writers, including many of the greatest: I am referring to the poverty of plot, of intrigue in Russian novels, novellas, and stories. This is especially true of the newest writers. A wealth of inventiveness in plot construction may be found in the works of Tolstoy, Dos-

toyevsky, Leskov, and, among secondary writers, Boleslav Mark-
evich. After that, Russian literature devoted itself to perfecting
form and language, to deepening psychological analysis and elab-
orating on social problems. Plot itself was forgotten. Form and
psychology have been developed in our fiction to the point where
they probably outstrip even the western European models, but
this has been done at the expense of plot. Russian literature today
has no equals of such masters of plot and intrigue as Dumas and,
later, Maupassant, Flaubert, Bourget, Conan Doyle, Wells, and
Heinrich Mann. In recent years, only third-rate writers, or, to be
more precise, hacks like Verbitskaya and Nagrodskaya, have
been interested in plot, in cultivating the story line. But true
masters of literary prose have treated the problem of plot with
disdain and even seem to have regarded concern with plot beneath their dignity. And that is too bad. As a result, according
to library statistics, third-rate hacks like Verbitskaya win the
largest number of readers. And such artists, such masters of the
word as Bunin remain on the shelves. Bunin's plots are often dull.
And we must not forget the incontrovertible aphorism which
states that "every kind of literature is good except dull literature." The present-day writer will have to give special attention
to plot. We must keep in mind, first of all, that the reading
public is changing. Formerly, it consisted chiefly of intellectuals,
many of them capable of enjoying the esthetic forms of a work,
even if these were achieved at the expense of plot. The new
reader, more primitive, will unquestionably have a far greater
need for interesting plots. There is also another factor, a psychological one, which compels the writer to pay more attention to
plot: life has become so rich in events, so unexpected and fantastic, that the reader has inevitably developed a different scale
of emotions and different demands on literature. Literary works
must not be inferior to life; they must not be poorer than life
itself.

Among artificial devices for heightening the reader's interest
in the plot of a work, I want to mention three. The first is what
I would call the pause. This is employed in the intertwined plot.
The story is interrupted at a moment of heightened dramatic
tension, and the author turns to a second, parallel plot, thus filling in the deliberate pause. Such a pause naturally whets the

reader's impatience to learn the end of the dramatic event so unexpectedly interrupted. An example of this is found in Leskov's "The Sealed Angel."

The second device is to delay the appearance or postpone the action of the characters.

The third device consists of deliberately tangling the plot. By artfully placed hints, the author prompts the reader to form false conclusions about the outcome of a given conflict and then confronts him suddenly with the actual resolution. An example of this is found in "The North" (Zamyatin).

1919–20

ON LANGUAGE

What is the difference between poetry and prose? And is there such a difference? Poets still claim the privilege of constituting a separate church in art. But to me it is clear: there is no difference between poetry and literary prose. They are one and the same thing.

The division exists only in the old theories of literature, but today it has lost its meaning. Today we cannot distinguish where poetry ends and prose begins.

The internal devices of poetry and prose are the same: metaphor, metonymy, and so on. The external devices of poetry and prose differed in the past. Today we have verse without rhyme. We have verse without definite rhythm—free verse. In the newest prose, on the other hand, we often find the use of definite rhythm; we also find in it frequent use of verbal music—the whole arsenal of the newest poetry: alliteration, assonance, instrumentation. Hence, it is only poems with a definite meter, representing only one specific form of poetry, which differ sharply from prose—in their externals. In their other aspects, there is no qualitative difference between them and literary prose.

In the newest literary theory I see a division of all literary works into two categories: lyrical and epic. In other words, the revelation, the verbal portrayal, of the author's personality—and the portrayal of others, external to the author. A lyrical work is a journey on our own planet, the planet where we live; an

Like the two preceding essays, originally delivered as a lecture (see note p. 159).

175

epical work is a journey through interplanetary space, through vacuum, for people are surely different planets, divided from one another by frozen space, with a temperature of −273°C.

And so, if we were to speak of any qualitative difference between poetry and prose, we might define it as follows: poetry occupies itself chiefly with the lyric; prose, with the epic. And achieving true mastery in literary prose (as compared to poetry) is as difficult as making an interplanetary journey (as compared with a journey on our own planet).

Strictly speaking, only the lyricist is a narrator, a true narrator about himself. The epic writer, the genuine master of literary prose, is always an actor, and every epic work is acting, theater. The lyricist experiences only himself. The epic writer must experience the emotions of tens, often thousands, of other, alien personalities; he must incarnate himself in hundreds and thousands of images. "While the writer is creating his work," wrote Heine, "he experiences something akin to what Pythagoras describes in his theory of the transmigration of souls; it is as though he were living in different forms; his inspiration has all the qualities of recollection." Obviously, the writer must be a great and talented actor, a dramatic genius. As with actors, his range is often limited. Gogol was a comic actor, and he failed whenever he attempted tragic or noble roles. Turgenev, on the other hand, was a born lover, a romantic lead, and he could never have succeeded in a comic role. On the whole, however, the writer's range is immeasurably wider than that of an actor in the theater; the writer's capacity for reincarnation is far richer. In some writers, it reaches astonishing, incredible proportions: Dickens was such a writer.

Let us dwell for a moment on this thesis: an epic work—that is, the usual example of literary prose—is *theater, acting*. The writer is an actor. What, then, is the practical conclusion to be drawn from this with regard to language and style? The conclusion will depend on the theory of acting we adopt as most suitable for us.

The classic Greek theater, as you know, followed the theory of conventional acting. The actors did not trouble about compelling the audience to forget that it was watching actors on a stage. They played in crude, conventional masks; the sets were conventional. The modern style of acting without a mask, in makeup, would have been regarded as a crime against art, as bad taste. The classic manner of acting survives to this day in Japan and China. Conventional acting is addressed to a primitive viewer, with a fresh and keen imagination, a viewer who has no need of illusion. But such a viewer has long disappeared in Europe, and with him this type of theater. The only area where it survives is in the field of grotesque comedy.

A new theater has come into existence which seeks to create an *illusion* of actual life, to compel the viewer to forget that he is watching acting on a stage. It is the theater of realistic acting. And within it there are two schools: I would call them the school of external acting and the school of internal acting. The former is represented in our country by actors like Yuriev and theaters like the Alexandrinsky and the Moscow Maly. The latter is represented by Stanislavsky and such theaters as the Moscow Art and its Studios. And it is the latter school, the school of internal acting, which demands that the actor reincarnate himself, feel his way into the personage portrayed—an approach which, to my mind, is an essential psychological condition for the writer.

I would describe this theory of acting—the theory of the Art Theater—as Neorealist. If we adopt it, the conclusion will be clear: the writer must reincarnate himself wholly into the characters, the milieu he is portraying.

If you are writing about provincial life, you must yourself at that moment live the life of the province, among provincials; you must think like a provincial; you must forget there are such places as Petersburg, Moscow, Europe, and that you are writing, perhaps, mostly for Moscow and Petersburg, rather than Chukhloma or Alatyr. If you are writing about Carthage, Hamilcar, Salammbo, you must forget that you live in the nineteenth century A.D., you must feel and speak like Hamilcar. If you are writing about a modern Englishman, you must think in English and write in such a way that what you have written in Russian will read like a good translation from English.

Let us recall what Korney Chukovsky told us about Andreyev: in "Black Masks" he was the duke Lorenzo; in "The Seven Who Were Hanged" he was the terrorist. He was always an actor; he was always acting in life as well. We know of Flaubert that, when he was writing *The Temptation of Saint Anthony,* he was constantly haunted and tormented by all the devilish temptations and torment experienced by Saint Anthony. When he was writing about the suicide of Madame Bovary, he felt it all himself. Maupassant, having created his Horla, suffered from this Horla. In short, true writers reincarnate themselves into their heroes.

I apologize for turning from Maupassant to myself. But I shall have to speak about myself, my work, and my experiences quite often—precisely because they are most familiar to me and the material is near at hand. I remember someone asking me whether *The Islanders* was not a translation from the English.

Consequently, the conclusion from what I have said above, the demand that must be made on language in literary prose is that it must be the language of the milieu and period portrayed. The author must be entirely invisible. The principle that the language of dialogue must be that of the milieu portrayed has long become the unchallenged rule. But I extend this thesis to the entire work: all of the author's comments, all the descriptions of the surroundings, the characters, the landscapes must be couched in the language of the milieu portrayed.

Let us take, for example, a story about fishermen. It would be a mistake, in describing the head of one of the fishermen, to compare it, let us say, with a globe or the head of a hippopotamus. The image may be fine in itself, but it would never have occurred to a fisherman. This image will take the reader outside the atmosphere of the milieu you are portraying, whereas the sense of that milieu must be consistently present throughout the story or the novel.

When I speak of the "language of the milieu portrayed," I do not mean to say that you must write about Englishmen only in English, about Ethiopians only in Ethiopian, or about peasants only in peasant dialect. Naturally, we shall write about them all in Russian. If we take the statement literally, we shall end up in absurdity. What language do you use in writing about a she-wolf—as Chekhov did in "White Forehead"? Or about a horse, as Kuprin did in "Emerald"? Or about fools, or mutes? At this rate we should end up with a "Poem of Silence," as Kruchenykh did.[1]

To make myself understood correctly, I must qualify my state-

---

[1] A. Y. Kruchenykh (b. 1886), Cubo-Futurist poet, later member of LEF. Since 1930 he has published only occasional articles and bibliographies.

ment. When I spoke about "the language of the milieu," I did not mean the literal language of the milieu, but an artistic *synthesis of the language of the milieu,* a stylization of it. In writing about peasants, it is by no means necessary to use the crudest forms of peasant speech. This would be in bad taste and would attest to the writer's ineptness. An experienced writer always knows how to create an artistically synthesized impression of the actual language of the milieu without crude extremes or distortion—be it the language of the peasant, the intellectual, the Ethiopian, or the horse. One must select and introduce into the text only such typical, colorful, rare, and original words as will create the impression of the language of the given milieu, rather than banal and hackneyed words which have been used a thousand times.

Every milieu, era, nation has its own language structure, its own syntax, its own way of thinking. And this is what we must absorb and utilize. The characteristic deviations in language are not grammatical, but syntactic. The most characteristic elements, and at the same time the elements which least distort literary language, are the word order and the choice of synonyms. It is these—the syntax, the word order, the synonyms—that we must study, learn to feel, and endeavor to reproduce in a story or novel. None of these factors introduce any crude distortions into the language, and yet they convey perfectly the spirit of the language of the given milieu.

Folk language, contemporary folk language, is before all else spoken language, the language of dialogue. And the fundamental feature of spoken language—whether folk or not—is the absence of periods and multiple subordinate clauses. It consists almost entirely of independent sentences, or independent sentences with a single subordinate clause. . . .[2]

The writer not only uses language, he also creates it; he creates its rules, its forms, and its vocabulary. He must therefore be fully aware of his responsibility in the choice of words. He must choose words capable of enriching the language, words that will purify it rather than litter it.

The prime source and creator of language is the people. We must study folklore. We must listen carefully to folk speech.

---

[2] This is followed by a page of brilliant analysis which, unfortunately, had to be omitted since it deals specifically with Russian forms.

Here we may find such unexpected images, such apt and witty epithets, such expressive words as will never occur to city people brought up on newspapers, to intellectuals whose language has been corrupted by newspapers. All these gems must be dug up, and not in big cities, but in the depths of the Russian heartland —in the provinces. (We must not, however, forget Pushkin's dictum that the best Russian may be learned from the old women of Moscow, her bakers of communion bread.) Generally, the truest and purest Russian survives only in the central Russian provinces and, I will add, in the Russian north—in the Olonetsk and Archangel regions. Only here can you learn the Russian language, only here can you draw on resources that can truly enrich literary Russian.

In the western Russian provinces, the Russian language has been corrupted by Byelorussian and Polish influences; in the provinces of southern Russia, by admixtures of Polish, Ukrainian and Yiddish. The use of southern and western provincialisms in dialogue is, of course, entirely legitimate. But it would be a gross error to introduce them into the text, into the author's comments or descriptions of landscape. This fault is especially pronounced in the works of southern writers, since the worst adulteration of the language has occurred in the south and particularly in Odessa.

In addition to the living sources capable of enriching the Russian language, there are also literary ones. These include above all folk poetry, epics, tales and songs. In order to utilize these, we must, of course, use primary materials, such as the texts recorded by the Russian Geographic Society of the Academy of Science, rather than anthologies and reworked versions. And, finally, we shall not go wrong if we go still further upstream, to the very origins of Russian, in our search for verbal gems; if we study old Slavonic texts, apocrypha, hymnals, and lives of the saints—especially those of the Old Believers. If you compare the Church Slavonic literature of the Old Believers with the Orthodox texts, you will discover the enormous difference between them. And this difference is not in favor of the Orthodox books, because during the reign of Peter the Great ecclesiastical books, and particularly the lives of saints, were revised, censored, and badly mutilated. The deletions include accounts of a number of delightfully absurd miracles—a tribute to the nascent spirit of positivism. Numerous erotic episodes were excised because the temptations and falls of the saints were often couched in primitive and direct language. Many old, vivid expressions were also deleted and replaced by newer ones.

A great many writers have used the sources I have mentioned for the enrichment of their language. Among the old writers, Leskov commanded an extraordinarily rich vocabulary; he made use, on the one hand, of Church Slavonic sources and, on the other, of folklore and provincialisms (in the good sense of the word). Melnikov-Pechersky used the published texts of the Old Believers and provincialisms. Lev Tolstoy and Chekhov had an excellent knowledge of folklore. Not long ago I reread Tolstoy's plays and was struck by the wealth and genuine folk character of language in such of his plays, for example, as *The Power of Darkness*. It is a wonder that no one has yet made any studies of Tolstoy from this point of view. Among the new writers, Gorky has a good knowledge of folklore. But in his early years, at least, he made little use of this knowledge, and when he did, it was with insufficient skill. His dialogue, with all those "wise" aphorisms dispensed by his heroes, often sounded false. It was only in his third period that Gorky made excellent use of his wealth of knowledge in this area, as in his "Yeralash." Remizov is a great and unquestioned master of language. He makes use of living folklore as well, but his basic specialty is digging out gems from old books, especially those of the Old Believers.

In speaking of the younger generation of writers, the critics have often commented—I trust, not without reason—on the knowledge of folklore evidenced in my works. I have drawn almost solely on living folklore, which I have heard in the Tambov, Kostroma, and northern regions. Shmelyov and Trenyov also have a good knowledge of folklore, although they are sometimes guilty of jarring southern provincialisms. Among the poets, we may single out Nikolay Kluyev for his remarkable knowledge and mastery of language; he uses strong and genuine northern Russian, drawing on north Russian folklore and the sacred verse of the Old Believers.

These writers may serve as secondary sources for the study of language. But secondary sources should be used only to enter into the spirit of the language, to learn to love the language and to use it. Drawing materials from secondary sources will not do.

You will achieve originality and make the reader feel that you speak your own language only if you draw directly upon primary sources.

A few words must be said here about the technical methods to be followed in using provincialisms and old Russian words. Some writers, totally devoid of taste, generously interlard their text with provincialisms or, even worse, with foreign words, explaining them in notes at the bottom of the page. It is quite obvious that such footnotes distract the reader, divert his attention, and break the spell of the work. They are absolutely inadmissible. On the other hand, it is equally inadmissible to litter the text with words which are entirely incomprehensible to the reader. What is the solution? The solution lies in presenting an entirely new and unfamiliar word in such a way that the reader will understand its general sense, if not its exact meaning. Sometimes this may be difficult, and then another method may be used: next to the unfamiliar word you add a clarifying apposition or a better-known synonym. You will thus make sure the reader understands you, without vitiating the effect and without the pedantic device of the footnote.

Up to now we have spoken about various sources for the enrichment of the language. In addition to these outside sources, however, the writer has still another one, closer home: himself. What I want to say is that the writer has the right to create new words—so-called neologisms. There is no doubt that the primary sources of language which we draw upon as a matter of course were also enriched in the same manner—by the creation of neologisms. Among the people, we often encounter men who are never at a loss for words, men with an innate talent for language. And just as the man endowed with musical talent will naturally create new melodies, so the man with linguistic talent will create new words. And if these new words are apt and expressive, they remain fixed in the memory of the listeners and gradually acquire the rights of citizenship. The use of neologisms is the natural path of the development and enrichment of language. Indeed, it is the only path. And the writer must not be denied the right to create them.

However, the only viable neologisms are those which are in harmony with the laws and spirit of the language, those which are created by the subconscious rather than invented. Neologisms produced in the laboratory jar never last long. In most cases, when you encounter a truly apt neologism, it is difficult to establish its novelty; it always seems to you that you have heard or seen the word before, it sounds so natural.

The language of speech is another problem. Paradoxical as it may seem, the question of spoken language in literary prose is essentially a social question. If we glance back, we shall see that the closer society was to a feudal order, the greater and sharper was the distinction between literary and spoken language. In the Middle Ages, for instance, the written language was Latin. Or take a more recent example: the struggle in the early years of the nineteenth century to bring literary Russian closer to the language of speech—the struggle between Shishkov, chairman of the Academy, and Karamzin—between the "Conversations of Lovers of the Russian Language" and "Arzamas,"[3] whose members included Zhukovsky, Batyushkov, and Vyazemsky.

The "Arzamas" group won. But then the usual story repeated itself: revolutionaries who defeat the old immediately become conservatives and guardians of "standards." The victors themselves become a reactionary element which hinders further development. The same thing happened here. The language of speech once again left literary language far behind; a new cleavage was formed between literary and spoken Russian. And the struggle to bring the two together still goes on. New Admiral Shishkovs have appeared, defending the inviolability of Turgenev's language in literary prose as fervently as the old Shishkov defended the language of Lomonosov and Derzhavin, accepting no neologisms, fighting against the enrichment of literary language with folk expressions and turns of phrase.

I consider this fusion of spoken and written language a vital phenomenon, paralleling the general historical tendency toward the democratization of all life. In short, my thesis is this: in contemporary literary prose the language must be as close as possible to the direct, spontaneous language of living speech. Spoken language should be used not only in dialogue—this has long be-

[3] Literary societies which existed in Saint Petersburg in the second decade of the nineteenth century, the former conservative and defending the classical tradition, the latter romantic and favoring the introduction of the language of speech into literature.

come axiomatic—but also in the narrative, in descriptions of landscape, surroundings, characters. This, of course, does not apply in cases where the writer is seeking to recreate a past epoch and must make use of stylization.

This thesis is, essentially, the logical corollary of a principle I discussed earlier. If a story or a novel is to be regarded as theater and the writer as an actor, it follows that he must behave as an actor does during a performance: he must speak, and the audience must hear him all the time, see his gestures and his facial expression. When I say "he," I do not mean the author. In an epic work the author must be invisible. The audience does not see the actor Kachalov, it sees Hamlet, Stavrogin, Brand, Ivan Karamazov. So here, too: the reader must hear and see the author in the role, with the makeup necessary to reproduce the spirit of the milieu protrayed.

Have any of you wondered: Why dwell so much on spoken language? It seems simple enough. We all speak—spontaneously, without any oratorical devices. But that is just the point: we all know how to speak, but very few know how to write the speech down just as we speak—simply, fluently, dynamically. There is an anecdote about a lawyer who came to his dentist and began to describe his toothache with the words "Gentlemen of the jury!" Well, most writers seem to regard themselves as lawyers and orators rather than as actors, and they write with oratorical turns of phrase. The usual, hackneyed narrative style is like a corseted woman. I've had occasion to meet elderly society ladies who were uncomfortable without a corset: they felt constrained by the absence of the constraint—the corset. The usual narrative form is just such a corset, and it is high time to discard it.

The main feature of nonoratorical, nonliterary, uncorseted language is its great dynamism. It has no complex periods, no multiple dependent clauses. In speech, subordinate clauses usually become independent sentences. You will not say "In view of the bad weather, I stayed home all day," but "The weather was bad and I stayed home all day." You will not say, "After the clock, which was standing on the mantel, struck nine, we went home." You will say, "The clock on the mantel struck nine and we went home." Participles are rarely encountered in living speech. "Having dined, drunk my coffee, and lit my cigar, I settled down to read a novel." This is the stock language of the narrative form. If you use spoken forms, you will say: "I dined, drank my coffee, lit a cigar, and settled down to read a novel." In spoken language, you use particles such as "well" and "now." This is similar to folk usage; the only difference is that folk speech uses them more frequently and has a greater variety of them.

When words express intense emotion or passion, this verbal clothing is never neatly buttoned all the way in living speech, it is always careless, often fragmentary. In such dramatic scenes, speech is characterized by incomplete sentences, by omission of such parts of speech as subjects and predicates; it is feverish, broken.

It might seem unnecessary to point out that dialogue must be couched in living, conversational language. If I do so, it is only because our writers, even modern ones, frequently write dialogue in corseted, pomaded, oratorical language. This is especially true of writers who work with previously conceived themes, who build their plots by the deductive method. Among these we might name Artsybashev, Vinnichenko, and (occasionally) Gorky.

In addition to gray, newspaper language, which reads like a bad translation, we often find them guilty of still another fault—lengthy monologues. As you know, the monologue was in great vogue in old drama but is entirely out of fashion in the new. Nor has it any place in the new literary prose. A monologue is always best developed in action, interspersed with other material.

Another requirement of dialogue demands great skill on the part of the author. But if the device succeeds, it is extremely effective and provides enormous artistic economy. I am referring to the individualization of each character's speech. Each character, or at any rate each principal character, should speak his own, individual language. Artistic economy is achieved by this method because it obviates the need to remind the reader of the specific characteristics of the heroes: their individualized speech itself serves this purpose. And artistic economy is an imperative in literary prose: the fewer words you use and the more you say with them, the greater the effect, and—all other conditions being equal—the greater the artistic "efficiency."

What I have said about oral language will, I hope, make the difference between the language of dialogue and the usual literary language clear enough. But what determines this difference? It is determined by the difference in the time elapsing between the moment when an idea occurs to the mind and its external manifestation, its embodiment in words. If you are writing an article, for example, there is considerable time at your disposal; your ideas can arrange themselves into complex sentences and periods. When you speak, there is less time: this is why spoken language is more dynamic, shorter than literary language; it frequently omits elements that are not absolutely essential, it leaves things half said. And, finally, if you do not voice your ideas aloud, you have still less—infinitely less—time than when you speak. If we analyze the language of thought, mental language, we shall find that its basic characteristic is even greater brevity than we observe in speech. Obviously, there is no room here for any complex forms or subordinate clauses. Indeed, if you try to follow the language of thought in your own mind, you will not find even the simplest sentences—only shreds, fragments of simple sentences. Only the most essential elements of a sentence are used: sometimes only a verb or only an epithet, an object.

Fixing these fleeting shadows of words, phrases, syllogisms on paper is extremely difficult, and few succeed in it. Because it is so difficult, we may permit a lessening of dynamism in conveying the language of thought, we may express mental language in the language of speech. But if the language of thought is expressed in descriptive, narrative form, the result will almost always be limp and unconvincing, it will not reach the reader. Even without distinct awareness of this, the reader will inevitably sense the disparity between the form and the substance—the heavy, empty narrative form and the airiest, lightest, most fugitive substance—thought.

Reproduction of interior, mental language is a must in conveying the characters' thoughts at tense, critical moments. If you succeed in capturing this language, the artistic effect will always be very great. At first glance this assertion may seem paradoxical: why should fragments of sentences, scattered as after an explosion, have greater effect on the reader than the same thoughts and images arranged in regular, steadily marching ranks? But if you think for a moment about the psychological aspect of the problem, the answer will become clear. In reading such tense passages written in ordinary narrative prose, you have probably caught yourself skipping, discarding fragments of phrases, or even entire phrases, instinctively leaving only the most essential signposts of ideas. When you use "mental" language at moments of great tension, you meet the reader's natural, instinctive need. You do not compel him to skim, even if half-consciously, through what will drop out of his awareness in any case; you effect an economy in the reader's attention. Within a shorter time, you give him more impressions. The result is, once again, artistic economy. This is first.

Secondly, by reproducing this embryonic language of thought, you give the reader's mind only the initial impulse, compelling him to connect these scattered signposts of ideas with the links of association, to supply the lacking elements himself. The sketching in of road signs puts the reader, as it were, in your power, does not allow him to deviate; at the same time, the unfilled spaces between them leave him free for partial creative activity. In short, you make the reader a participant in the creative process, and the results achieved by one's own creative effort, rather than another's, are always sharper and more vivid.

Texture and pattern. The same principle of joint creative effort by author and reader underlies a number of other technical methods in literary prose, especially the newest. And, I would add, in the new art generally. Compare the thorough elaboration of all details by the academicians and the approach of the new painters. In the new works you have mere contours, a seeming incompleteness—the same invitation to the viewer to fill in what is missing by using his own creative imagination. This method of omission of psychological lines, of an incomplete psychological pattern, of supplying little more than hints can also be used in literary prose. There are numerous devices along this line, the first among them being the unfinished sentence. You may often observe this in yourself: when you are thinking of something frightening, or dear to you, or totally absorbing at the given moment, thought often lapses suddenly, without naming the chief object. "And what if. . . ." "So. . . ." Unfinished sentences are used even more frequently in dialogue. I am not referring to the usual, mechanical interruptions of one character's speech by another's reply, but of sentences deliberately left incomplete because the reader can complete them himself.

The same principle underlies the method that I would call the method of misleading denials. You, speaking as the author, may deny something that logically follows from the entire preceding construction, or you may suggest an obviously false conclusion, compelling the reader to invest greater energy in drawing the correct conclusion; this debate with the author fixes the idea in the reader's mind all the more effectively. Ironic assertions and denials belong, essentially, to the same category.

Besides unfinished phrases, false assertions, and retractions, there is also the method of omitted associations. This method illustrates most vividly the principle of joint creative effort by author and reader. It consists in the deliberate omission of the central idea, instead of which the author expresses secondary, tangential thoughts. But these tangential thoughts are not accidental; they are carefully chosen to lead the reader inescapably to filling in the omitted central idea. The author merely hints at this idea, which is offered, not on the page, not in the lines, but somewhere between the lines. By this method, the author creates, as it were, only the spirit of the idea, without materializing it in words. The creative process is thus carried from the three-dimensional world into a world of higher dimensions. Naturally, this method is appropriate and will produce the desired effect only when the author is dealing with a highly sophisticated audience, capable of responding to subtleties in a work of art.

At this point we can also draw an additional conclusion: to guide the reader to the omitted association, we must often make him recall a certain object or person encountered earlier. And this brings us to still another method, closely linked with the preceding one. I would call this the method of reminiscence. In dealing with characters, it is usually employed quite automatically. Even a relatively inexperienced writer will not confront the reader with a new character at a moment of high tension. The characters involved in the action at such moments are already known to the reader; he has already encountered them at some point of the story before. This requirement was set forth earlier, when I said that we must do all we can to avoid episodic characters in our works. The demand for a vital, organic connection between character and plot is absolutely essential with regard to all the more or less important personages in the story or novel. But now I want to extend this thesis to inanimate objects as well. If such objects are more or less important in the story, they must flash before the reader once, and twice, and three times in the course of the work. So that, when they appear at a moment of heightened action, they must come to the reader's mind as already familiar, as a living reality, known and remembered.

In addition to the main purpose—greater vividness and palpability, a sharper presence in the reader's imagination—the method of reminiscence achieves yet another purpose, that of artistic economy.

Thus the methods based on the principle of joint creative effort are incomplete phrases, false denials and assertions, omitted associations, allusions, and reminiscences. In addition, there is also the method of the reflected image. Chekhov writes: "He was met by a lady, tall and bony, with slightly graying hair and black eyebrows, evidently non-Russian. . . . At dinner they served meatless soup, cold veal with carrots, and chocolate. Everything was sweetish and insipid, but the table glittered with gold forks, bottles of soy sauce, an extraordinary ornate cruet stand, a gold pepper box."

All these are the methods of Impressionism. As we see, the new trends in literature closely parallel the new trends in painting.
1919–20

BACKSTAGE

In every sleeping car compartment there is a little ivory handle: turn it to the right, and there is full light; to the left, darkness; set it in the middle, and a blue light goes on. Everything is visible in this light, but it does not interfere with your falling asleep, it does not keep you awake. When I am asleep and dreaming, the handle of consciousness is turned left. When I write, it is set in the middle: consciousness burns with a blue light. I see a dream on paper. My imagination works as it does during sleep, it moves along the same path of associations. But this dream is cautiously (the blue light) guided by consciousness. As in a dream, you need but think it is a dream, you need but turn on full consciousness, and the dream disappears. There is nothing worse than insomnia, when the switch is broken and, no matter how you set it, you don't succeed in turning off full consciousness. The white, sober light persistently glares into your eyes. I suffered an attack of such literary insomnia about ten years ago, when I was giving a course of lectures on "The Technique of Fiction" at the Studio of the House of the Arts. For the first time, I was compelled to take a look backstage, into my own work processes, and for several months after that I could not write. Everything would seem to be in order, the sheet of clean white paper was ready, and I would be drifting off into sleep, when suddenly— a start, and I would waken, and everything would be lost, because I had begun to observe, with my conscious mind, the mechanics of sleep, the rhythms, assonances, images; I had caught sight of the cables, pulleys, and traps behind the scenes.

This insomnia ended only when I learned to forget, while working, that I knew how I wrote. I cannot fall asleep when I hear a conversation nearby. I need the door of my room to be tightly shut, I need to be alone. And this is equally essential for falling asleep into a story, a novel, a play. There is a little girl downstairs, in the apartment below. I have never seen her, yet I have seen her and known her for a long time (a skimpy whitish pigtail, freckles, mousy eyes). In the mornings, when I sit down at my desk, she sits down at her piano and plays—the same exercise for the past year and a half. If there is indeed such a thing as an "astral chronicle," as the theosophists assert, it must have borne for a long time an imprint of my ruthless revenge upon this girl. I have killed her many times over.

The most difficult thing is to begin, to cast off from the shore of reality into dream. The dream is still gossamer, fugitive, unclear. It eludes capture. Everything interferes—not only the freckled brat below, but also my own breath, the sensation in my hand as it holds the pencil, a crooked line. And now comes the stage of cigarette after cigarette, until the daytime world is veiled in a blue mist (the switch handle is in the middle). Then, as page follows page, the dream becomes ever stronger, the motor of the imagination turns ever more rapidly, the pulse quickens, the ears burn. And, finally, one day the real thing comes—when the dream becomes obsessive, when you go about hypnotized by it, when you think about it in the street, at meetings, in the bathtub, at a concert, in bed. Then you know the piece is launched, that it will turn out well, and you work gaily, with delight, with intoxication. In the morning you hurry to finish your strong tea, and you draw on the first line with the same appetite as you do on your first cigarette. This appetite will now last you, not the usual three, but five or six hours, until the late Petersburg dinner. But no matter how well the work is going, how fast the wheels are turning in my head, in the evening I switch off the current and stop the machine. Otherwise—I have learned it from experience—I shall not fall asleep till morning, and that means the loss of the next day.

Chemists know the meaning of the term "saturated solution." A glass seems to be filled with colorless, familiar, ordinary water, but you need only drop into it one more grain of salt and the solution comes alive. Diamond shapes, needles, tetrahedrons—

and after a few seconds, instead of colorless water, you have the gleaming facets of crystals. Sometimes we, too, are in a state of saturated solution, and then a chance visual impression, a fragment of a sentence heard in a railway car, a two-line item in a newspaper may be enough to crystalize several printed pages.

On one occasion I went from Petersburg (it was still Petersburg then) to Tambov Province, to the luxuriant, black-earth town of Lebedyan, to the same street, overgrown with mallow, where I had run about as a schoolboy. A week later I was returning—via Moscow, along the Pavelets road. I awoke as the train stopped at a small station not far from Moscow and raised the blind. Before my window—as though framed by it—the physiognomy of the station gendarme slowly floated by: a heavy forehead pulled low over the tiny, bearlike eyes, a grim square jaw. I caught the name of the station: Barybino. Those moments marked the birth of Anfim Baryba and *A Provincial Tale*.

In Lebedyan, I remember, I had a call from a local fellow writer—a postal official. He told me that he had eight pounds of poems at home, and in the meantime, he read me one, which began with these lines:

> How pleasant to stroll in the month of May,
> With the bloom of geranium odors laden,
> And at the same time with one hand play
> With a young and beauteous maiden
> Who arrived here from Syzran, far away.

These five lines did not let me rest until they finally became transformed into the story "Alatyr," with its central figure, the poet Kostya Yedytkin.

In 1915 I was in the Russian north—in Kem, Solovki, Soroki. I returned to Petersburg seemingly ready, filled to the brim, and immediately began to write, but nothing came of it: the final grain of salt, necessary for the beginning of crystalization, was still lacking. It was only two years later that this grain was added to the solution: in a railway car I overheard a conversation about bear hunting, and someone said that the only way to escape from a bear is to feign death. This gave me the end of the story "The North," and then the rest of the story unfolded from end to beginning (this method—the reverse unfolding of the plot—is most frequent with me).

One winter night in 1919 I was on watch duty in our yard. My partner—a frozen, half-starved professor—complained about the lack of firewood: "Sometimes I am even tempted to steal some wood! But the trouble is that I cannot do it, I'd rather die than steal." On the following day I sat down to write "The Cave."

I have a clear recollection of the birth of the story "In Old Russia." This was an example of "artificial insemination," when the sperm is provided by the work of another artist (most of the time we are androgynous). The other artist in this case was the painter B. M. Kustodiev. The Akvilon publishing house sent me a series of his drawings of "Russian types," with the request that I write an article about them. I did not feel like writing an article—I had just finished an article about Yury Annenkov (for his book *Portraits*). I laid out Kustodiev's drawings on the table: a nun, a beauty in a window, a merchant in bottle-shaped boots, a young fellow from a store. I looked at them for an hour, two hours—and suddenly they came alive, and instead of an article, a story began to write itself, with characters who walked out of Kustodiev's pictures.

All these are instances of "saturated solution," when the entire preliminary work is done subconsciously and the tale or the story begins almost spontaneously, like a dream. But a work can also originate in another way—in a process analogous to falling asleep deliberately, when one becomes one's own hypnotist.

This method is slower and more difficult. First comes an abstract thesis, the idea of the work; it lives in the mind, on the upper floors, for a long time and persistently refuses to move down, to grow flesh and skin. The pregnancy lasts until it seems endless (if I am not mistaken, the unfortunate elephant females carry for two years!). One is obliged to maintain a strict diet, to read only books belonging within a circle of definite ideas or definite epochs. I remember that, for *The Flea,* this period lasted about four months. My diet was as follows: Russian folk comedies and tales, plays by Gozzi, some things by Goldoni, the billboards of old show booths, old Russian popular prints, Rovinsky's books. The work on the play itself, from the first to the last line, took only five weeks.

In order to immerse myself in Attila's period (for the play *Attila*), I needed almost two years. I had to read dozens of Russian, French, and English volumes and produce three versions of the play. And quite regardless of the fact that the play never reached the stage, all this turned out to be only preparatory work for the novel.

The paper is cut, the indelible pencil sharpened, cigarettes are prepared, and I sit down at my desk. I know only the conclusion or only one of the scenes or only one of the characters, and I need five or ten of them. And so, the first page usually witnesses the incarnation of the characters I need. I make sketches for their portraits, until I can see clearly how each one walks, smiles, eats, speaks. As soon as they come alive to me, they will begin to act unerringly on their own, or, to be more exact, they will begin to err, but only as each of them can and must err. I may try to reeducate them, I may try to build their lives according to plan, but if they are alive, they will inevitably overturn all the plans I may devise for them. And often I do not know until the last page how my story (their stories) will end. At times I do not know the conclusion even when I know it, when the whole work starts from the end.

This was true of the novella *The Islanders.* An Englishman of my acquaintance told me that there are people in London who live by a very peculiar profession—catching lovers in parks. I saw a scene of such a hunt as a suitable ending. The entire complicated plot of the novella grew out of this ending. And then— to my surprise—it turned out that the novella ended quite differently from the original plan. The hero—Campbell—refused to be the scoundrel I had meant him to be. It is worth noting that the first version of the ending, which was eliminated from the text of the novella, later took on independent life in the form of the story "The Fisher of Men."

There was a notice on the door of the editorial office: Visiting Hours from 2:00 to 4:00 P.M. I was late—it was half-past four—and therefore I entered in a state of embarrassment which was aggravated by the reception I was given. At the desk sat Ivanov-Razumnik and another man, a dark, shaggy-haired gypsy with flashing white teeth. As soon as I identified myself, the gypsy jumped up: "A-ah, so that's you? Thank you kindly! That was quite a thrashing you gave my aunt!" "What aunt? Where?" "Why, Chebotarikha, in *A Provincial Tale,* that's where!"

The gypsy turned out to be Prishvin, we turned out to be from the same province, and Chebotarikha turned out to be Prishvin's aunt.

I had seen this aunt many times as a child, she was firmly fixed in my memory, and I had to expel her from myself into a story. I knew nothing about her life. All her adventures were pure fiction, invented by me, but she did own a tannery, and her portrait in *A Provincial Tale* was drawn from nature. I left her real name almost without change. No matter how I tried, I could not call her anything else—just as I cannot call Prishvin anything but Mikhal Mikhalych. Incidentally, this is a rule: names and surnames become a part of fictional characters as inalienably as they do in the case of living people. And understandably so: if a name is felt and selected rightly, its very sound will suggest the individual's characteristics.

The case with Prishvin's aunt is perhaps the only one in my experience. As a rule, I write without models. If people from the outside world occasionally find their way into my world, they are usually altered so radically that I alone know whose shadow rests on them. But since the door backstage is open today, I will reveal the sources of several of these shadows, especially since there are so few of them.

I remember when I read "Alatyr" to A. M. Remizov one day, he listened, drawing devils on a slip of paper. I do not know to this day whether he realized that the Alatyr expert in demonology, Father Pyotr, author of "The Life and Nourishment of Devils," was a relative of his.

The eternal student Senya, who dies on the barricades in the story "The Ne'er-Do-Well," is still alive and well. He is an old fellow student, Ya. P. G——v. Neither his outward appearance nor the actual events of his life will be found in the story; nevertheless, he is the man who provided its basic tonality.

Later on he became the founder of a sect of book worshipers. During the early, hungry revolutionary years he visited me frequently, always carrying a basketful of books bought for his last money, for money from the sale of trousers to a Tartar in the market. And, in stage makeup which transformed him beyond recognition, he emerged upon the boards once more in the role of "Mamay of 1917" in the short story "Mamay."

Again, to return to my schooldays: it was a spring day, on the eve of Easter; I entered the courtyard of the house where Colonel Kniper lived and stood petrified with astonishment. In the middle of the yard there was a trough resting on a trestle; near the trough, the colonel himself, with rolled-up sleeves, and his orderly, puttering busily around him. It turned out that Colonel Kniper was beating fifty egg whites in the trough, to be made into *Baumkuchen* for the Easter table. This scene lay dormant in me for fifteen years. And only fifteen years later it sprouted, like a seed, and grew into the gourmet General Azancheyev in the novella *At the World's End.*

A strange thing happened with this novella. After its publication, I have met two or three former far eastern officers, who assured me that they knew the living people depicted in the novella, that their real names were such and such, and that the action occurred in such and such a place. Yet I have never traveled to eastern Russia beyond the Urals; all those "living people" (with the exception of one-tenth of Azancheyev) lived only in my imagination, and of the entire novella, only the chapter about "the Lancepoop Club" was based on a story I had heard from someone. "In what regiment did you serve?" I was asked. "None. I have never served in the army at all." "All right, all right! You can't put that over on me!"

It turns out, then, that it is possible to "put things over"—to build a world and the people living in it even without firsthand experience. The fauna and flora of a writer's desk are far richer than we think. They have not been studied enough.

And so the needed characters finally come, in one way or another. They are here, but they are still naked, they must be clothed in words.

A word has color and sound. From now on, painting and music go side by side.

From the very first page, the writer must determine the basic pattern of the entire musical weave; he must hear the rhythm of the entire work. But one seldom succeeds in hearing it at once. It is almost always necessary to rewrite the first page several times (the novella *At the World's End,* for example, had four different beginnings; *The Islanders* had two; "Alatyr," six). This is understandable. In the solution of the rhythmic problem, the prose writer is in a far more difficult position than the poet. The rhythmics of verse have long been analyzed; they have their own code of laws, and their own set penalties. But no one has yet been brought to trial for rhythmic crimes in prose. In analyzing prose rhythm, even Andrey Bely, the subtlest student of verbal music, made a mistake: he applied a verse foot to prose (hence his sickness—chronic anapaestitis).

To me, it is entirely clear that the relation between the rhythmics of verse and prose is the same as that between arithmetic and integral calculus. In arithmetic we sum up individual items; in integral calculus we deal with sums, series. The prose foot is measured, not by the distance between stressed *syllables,* but by the distance between (logically) stressed *words.* And in prose, just as in integral calculus, we deal not with constant quantities (as in verse and arithmetic) but with variable ones. In prose, the foot is always a variable quantity, it is always being either slowed or accelerated. This, of course, is not fortuitous: it is determined by the emotional and semantic accelerations and retardations in the text.

Let us take two examples: "and the silence became still deeper, more bitterly cold"—retardation; "suddenly a car veered out"— acceleration, surprise (a series of unstressed and therefore rapidly spoken syllables).

When these phrases were written, mathematics were, of course, only the blue light; the rhythm was chosen by the subconscious, but it was chosen correctly. I need only have written "quiet was" instead of 'silence became," and the retardation would have been spoiled. I could have written "suddenly an automobile appeared," and the element of suddenness would have been weakened.

Vowels also determine the solution of another problem, as dynamic as rhythm. They determine what Bely calls the "breath" of the phrase. We have inhalation in the rise of vowels: *oo-o-e-ä-ў-ee;* exhalation—in their fall, from *ee* to the closed, muted *oo.* I have learned to hear this breath quite recently, but ever since then it has been painful for me to read a phrase expressing a rising mood and yet built on falling vowels, or a phrase stretched horizontally by repeating *a*'s, when the meaning demands that it drop to the bottom like a stone. . . .[1]

---

[1] Because the sounds and their emotional associations are very different in Russian and English, some of the examples given by Zamyatin in this and the following two paragraphs had to be omitted in translation.

Consonants are the static element, the earth, substance. If, for example, I not only see but also hear a landscape, it is instrumented on consonants. "Fog, close as cotton, and the strange sound of muffled footsteps—as though someone were persistently following behind you . . ." This phrase (from *The Islanders*) is colored by dark, unresonant sounds—*f, t, th, st.* . . .

On consonants I also build the external picture of my characters. This is consistently followed in *The Islanders,* where each person has his own leitmotiv, which invariably accompanies his appearance on the scene. . . .

And what of painting? Has it been forgotten? No, the writer must hear and see simultaneously as he works. And if there are sound leitmotivs, there must also be visual ones. In the same novella, *The Islanders,* the basic visual image for Campbell is a tractor; for Lady Campbell, worms (lips); for Mrs. Dewly, pince-nez; for the lawyer O'Kelly, his double, a pug. In "The North," there is a constant juxtaposition of Kortoma and a smug, gleaming samovar, Kortomikha and a discarded glove. In "The Flood" Sofya is symbolized by a bird, Ganka by a cat.

Each of these visual leitmotivs is similar to a focus of rays in optics: it is the intersecting point of all the images connected with the given character. I rarely use individual, chance images; these are only sparks, which live for a brief moment, and then are extinguished, forgotten. A chance image is the result of inability to concentrate, to truly see, to believe. If I firmly believe in the image, it will inevitably give rise to an entire system of related images, it will spread its roots through paragraphs and pages. In a short story, the image may become integral and spread throughout the piece, from beginning to end. The six-story, fiery-eyed house on the dark, deserted street, echoing with shots in 1919, presented itself to me one night as a ship in the ocean. I believed in the image completely—and the integral image of the ship determined the entire system of images in the story "Mamay."

The same was true of "The Cave." A more complex instance is "The Flood." Here the integral image of the flood is followed through on two planes. The actual flood in Petersburg is reflected in the spiritual flood, and all the basic images of the story flow into their common channel.

"Not a single secondary detail, not a single superfluous line: nothing but the essence, the extract, the synthesis, revealed to the eye within one-hundredth of a second, when all sensations are gathered into focus, sharpened, condensed. Today's reader and viewer will know how to complete the picture, fill in the words—and what he fills in will be etched far more vividly within him, will much more firmly become an organic part of him. This is the way to the common creative action by the artist and the reader or viewer."

I wrote this several years ago about Yury Annenkov, about his drawings. I wrote this not about Annenkov but about us, about myself, about verbal pictures, as I think they should be.

There was a time when I acutely felt that I had lost one hand, that I needed a third hand. This was in England, when I first drove a car: I had to work the steering wheel, shift gears, manage the accelerator, and blow the horn, all at the same time. I had a similar feeling many years ago, when I began to write: it seemed utterly impossible at the same time to direct the movement of the plot, the emotions of the characters, their dialogues, the instrumentation, the images, the rhythms. Later I learned that two hands are quite sufficient for driving a car. This happened when most of the complex movements became a matter of reflex, were carried out without conscious effort. The same thing happens sooner or later at the desk.

The image of the automobile driver that I employed is, of course, incorrect, imprecise. Such an image is permissible only backstage; on stage, in a story or novel, I would surely have crossed it out. The image is incorrect because a good driver will guide his car unerringly—even in London—from the Strand to Euston Road. But I, after reaching Euston on paper, will return to the Strand and will take the same road a second time—and it is, perhaps, only on the third trip that I will bring my passengers to their destination. A work that would seem to be finished is not yet finished to me. I invariably begin to rewrite it from the beginning, from the first line, and, if I am still dissatisfied, I rewrite it once again (the short story "The Land Surveyor" was rewritten about five times). This is equally true of a novel, a story, a novella, or a play. And even of an article: to me, an article is the same as a story. I think that it is easiest for me to write a play. In a play, the writer is not overwhelmed by a multitude of possibilities; the language is limited to dialogue.

The slow process of rewriting is very useful: there is time to examine all the details, to change them before the work cools off and hardens, and to throw out all that is superfluous. These "superfluous" elements may be good in themselves, but when they are not essential, when the work can live without them, they are mercilessly eliminated. Would it not be absurd to allow an unnecessary lever to remain in a machine simply because it glitters? In the human organism there is nothing superfluous except the appendix, and doctors remove it at the first opportunity. Most frequently, such appendixes are descriptions, landscapes which do not serve as levers transmitting the psychic movements of the characters. The operation for their removal is as painful as any other; nevertheless, it is essential.

My manuscripts are deceptive; there are very few corrections, paste-ins, deletions, and everything seems to flow along easily. But this is only seeming. All the difficulties are dealt with behind the scenes. I try every scene ten times mentally before setting it down on paper. I never leave behind unfinished phrases, scenes, or situations. Tomorrow, I may not like what I wrote today, and I will start again from the beginning, but today it must look finished to me; otherwise I cannot go on.

I almost never make any extensive, radical changes in the piece after it is written. I have already become convinced of the truth of my characters, I see them, they are alive, and all that has been written about them is already their past; the past cannot be altered—it happened. Sometimes I succeed in forgetting —crossing out—some details of this past. In recollections, one can improve, embellish a point here and there, but that is all. Revisions of a finished manuscript are such recollections. The revisions are usually confined to changes in epithets or images, the order of words, the music. Every new edition means new revisions; the age of a piece will not save it from changes. Last summer, when I was preparing the material for my *Collected Works,* every piece was gone over again with sandpaper and pumice. Most of the changes were made in *The Flea, At the World's End,* and "Alatyr" (in the latter, for example, all the margins were decorated with transposition marks).

Incidentally, this was an opportunity to glance back at the

road traversed in the past fifteen years and to compare my writing then and now. And it turned out that all the complexities I had passed through had been only a road to simplicity ("The Yawl," "The Flood"). Simplicity of form is legitimate for our epoch, but the right to this simplicity must be earned. Some kinds of simplicity are worse than theft—they express a disrespect for the reader: "Why waste time and fuss? They'll swallow it as it is."

I spend a great deal of time on my work, probably more than the reader would require. But this is necessary for the critic, the most demanding and carping critic I know—myself. I can never deceive this critic, and until he says that everything possible has been done, I cannot put the final period to the work.

If there is any other opinion I respect, it is the opinion of my fellow writers—those who, in my judgment, know how a novel, a story, or a play is made. They have made them themselves, and made them well. No other criticism exists for me, and I cannot understand how it could exist. Imagine a brash young man, who has never drawn a single blueprint for a ship, coming to a plant or a shipyard and teaching the engineers and the workers how a ship must be built. Such a young man would be thrown off the premises without delay.

Our softheartedness keeps us from doing this, although such young men often disturb us in our work as much as flies in summer.

1930

Евгений Замятин

ALEXANDER BLOK

The year is 1918. A tiny editorial office—empty, hastily set up, temporary—two or three chairs, stacks of books fresh from the printer in the corner. We are still unaccustomed to wearing hats and coats indoors. A friendly-hostile conversation with one of the editors of a left socialist–revolutionary journal.

A knock at the door, and Blok is in the room. His present face, the face of a knight, and a ridiculous, flat American cap. And the cap suggests the thought that there are two Bloks—the real one, and another, superimposed, like this flat American cap. His face is tired, darkened by some harsh wind, locked.

There is a hurried, whispered editorial conference in the corner near the books—and for a moment I am alone with Blok.

"Today?" (his answer). "How can anyone write? I struggle to keep body and soul together. It's very difficult . . ."

And suddenly, through the metal, from under the steel visor—a smile, altogether childish, pale blue.

"I thought you'd surely have a beard down to here, like a country doctor. And you're an Englishman instead. A Moscow Englishman."

This was my first meeting with Blok. The brief conversation, the smile, the cap.

For three years after that we were all locked up together in a steel projectile and, cooped up in darkness, whistled through space, no one knew where. In those last seconds-years before death, we had to do something, to settle down to some sort of a life in the hurtling missile. And so extravagant plans were hatched in the projectile: World Literature,[1] the Union of Literary Workers, the Writers' Union, a theater. And all the writers, all those who had survived, were constantly bumping into each other in the cramped space—Gorky and Merezhkovsky, Blok and Kuprin, Muyzhel and Gumilyov, Chukovsky and Volynsky.

At first—the buzzing, crowded waiting room of World Literature on Nevsky Prospekt. And Blok, passing through, shaking hands, and speaking in his special, clearly articulated, firm way, so that every syllable was heard: "Nikolay Stepanovich!" "Fyodor Dmitrievich!" "Alexey Maximovich!"

In those days Gorky was in love with Blok—he always had to be in love with someone or something for an hour. "This is a man! Yes!" At the meetings of World Literature, Gorky listened to Blok as he listened to no one else.

It was still unclear to us that we were holding our meetings inside a speeding steel shell, and Blok had evidently not yet grown tired of trudging from meeting to meeting. But at that time he was not yet the hopeless and weary Blok of later days, and Gorky was not the only one to be captivated by him.

One spring evening there was a meeting in a private apartment. Gorky, Batyushkov, Braun, Gumilyov, Remizov, Gizetti, Oldenburg, Chukovsky, Volynsky, Ivanov-Razumnik, Levinson, Tikhonov, and others—many people—and one Blok, talking about the crisis of humanism.

I remember distinctly Blok on a raised platform, at a lectern —although I know that there could be no platform there. Nevertheless, Blok stood on an elevation, apart from the rest. And I remember there was immediately a wall between him and the rest, and behind the wall, barbarian music of conflagrations, smoke, raging elements—audible to him, and to no one else.

And later, in the adjoining room: the dying fire in the fireplace; Blok by the fire, the wings of his eyebrows meeting, searching for something intently in the dying fire. And heated discussion past midnight, and Blok's tired, indifferent reply from afar, from behind the wall.

I believe that this whole question—the crisis of humanism— had somehow sprung from Heine: Blok was editing Heine for

---

[1] A publishing house organized at Gorky's initiative and functioning under the People's Commissariat of Education.

World Literature. He worked with extraordinary care and per-
severance. I recall some ordinary conversation about money, and
Blok's words: "Payment? What payment can there be? Yesterday I translated twelve lines in two hours. And it was warm in
my room, the stove was burning. Translation, as it should be
done, is very difficult."

He did everything "as it should be done." And yet he felt, and
never for a moment ceased feeling, that it was "not it, not the
real thing."

I can see him in a meeting room, by the window, with Gumilyov. A depressing, rosy, cold sky. Gumilyov cheerful as ever, full
of promising plans and schemes. And Blok, looking past him,
into the window: "Why do they pay us not to do what we
should be doing?"

And outside, the wind-emptied, rosy, cold sky.

Cooped up, in the dark, inside the hurtling whistling steel projectile, we hurried to meetings, one meeting overlapping another.
The Union of Literary Workers decided to devote itself inside
the missile to the publication of fine literature. An editorial board
was formed, consisting of Blok, Gorky, Kuprin, Shishkov, Slyoz-
kin, Muyzhel, Merezhkovsky, Chukovsky, and myself. Manuscripts poured in. Blok had to report on the poems, and I remember one of his reports, sharp and polished. As always at
meetings, he did not speak, but read, and the manuscript of the
report survived. One of the poets impaled on the point of this
report asked me to obtain the text from Blok. At the next meeting, Blok said to me: "I did not bring it. What for? It may be
very important for him to write poems. Let him write."

We decided to publish a journal. It was to be called *Tomorrow,* and I recall I was asked to write something in the nature of
a manifesto. I wrote about the circle of yesterday, today, and
tomorrow and said that literature is always about tomorrow and
in the name of tomorrow, and that this determines its attitude
toward yesterday and toward today. Hence, I concluded, literature is always heresy and rebellion.

Later, on the way to the next meeting, I had a brief conversation with Blok about it. For a moment, I remember, behind that
slow, metallic, locked face, I caught a glimpse of a man who
was painfully and with great difficulty tearing something away
from himself. This was my first conversation with Blok—with-

out walls. I remember the end of it. I said, "You have gone very far from what you were a year ago. You are changing." The answer was: "Yes, I feel it myself."

Petersburg—swept out, emptied; boarded-up stores; houses pulled down bit by bit for firewood; brick skeletons of stoves. Frayed cuffs; collars turned up; vests; sweaters; and, in a sweater, Blok. Fevered efforts to outstrip want, and ever new, transient, precarious plans, new meetings, hurrying from meeting to meeting.

And then, late at night, after three or even four meetings, we gathered in one of the small backrooms of World Literature. A dining table, a lamp under a green shade; faces in the shadow. To the left of the door, a warm tile stove bench, and on it and around it Blok, Gumilyov, Chukovsky, Lerner, myself. And round little Grzhebin, rolling from corner to corner like a top.

It is difficult to repair plumbing or build a house, but it is very easy to build the Tower of Babel. And we were building the Tower of Babel: we planned to publish a Pantheon of Russian Literature—from Fonvizin to our days. One hundred volumes!

We believed, perhaps with a faint smile—but we believed, or wanted to believe. And Blok believed most of all. As ever, and as in everything he did, he approached this "as it should be" approached.

In the motley, shimmering heap, it was necessary to discern some order, to catch the rhythm. And Blok revealed such a sharpness of eye, such a keenness of ear that no one else could keep pace with him. We decided to build the tower by his plan. Grzhebin's Publishing House has somewhere in its files the list prepared by Blok. And in Blok's notes, found after his death, there is an entry: "November, 1919. Preparation of a list of one hundred volumes." If the Tower of Babel is ever built, it will be one of the monuments to Blok, to the thoroughness and care with which he made his choices.

In the frozen, hungry, typhus-ridden Petersburg, there raged an epidemic of cultural and educational activities. Since literature is not education, all poets and writers became lecturers. And in place of money there was a strange new unit of exchange—the ration, obtained by abandoning poems and novels for lectures.

Blok had a difficult time during that period; he was incapable of such an exchange. I remember he used to say: "I envy you all: you can speak, you are lecturing somewhere. I cannot do it. I can only read what I have written."

Nevertheless, the epidemic swept him along as well. We formed a Section on Historical Plays. It was another Tower of Babel. The plan was to show the entire world history in a cycle of plays—no more and no less. The author of the idea was Gorky, and the group chained to the table in the meeting room consisted of the same people: Blok, Gumilyov, Chukovsky, Oldenburg, and myself. Two others on the committee were Shchuko and Lavrentiev.

Blok, I recall, did not have too much faith in this project from the first. He said, "You can't make art carry science on its back."

Yet he worked, as always, with utter absorption. After all, this was not lecturing, it was not a substitute for creative work. We had all become accustomed to substitutes: we ate pancakes of potato peel and drank water instead of wine. And Blok persistently tried to turn water into wine.

One of the first meetings was held in the majestic office of the Theater Department, where we sat in luxurious leather chairs.

Blok read his outline for a historical play. I don't know whether the outline has been preserved, but I know that the play was never written. It dealt with Blok's beloved Middle Ages: knights and ladies, pages and minstrels. And I recall how the theatrical powers that be shrugged their shoulders lightly when it was read. Blok put the outline away somewhere.

Several plays had already been submitted to the section. Everyone was asking Blok, "When will you give us yours, Alexander Alexandrovich?" And he replied: "How can I? Everybody is being evicted from our apartment house. I run around all the time trying to get permission to stay. Yesterday we went to Smolny with a letter from Gorky. Tomorrow I have to go to the district office." Or: "Oh, the play! I've been puttying the windows all morning. Tomorrow I'll have to do two more rooms. It's slow work, I don't know how to do it."

Finally, the battle of the apartment was won, the windows were puttied. Blok began to think about the play. "I'm not sure yet whether I ought to take the battle with the Tartars on Kulikovo Field—I feel very close to it—or Tristan and Isolde."

He said that he had already made some sketches for "Tristan," when suddenly he turned out a play from Egyptian life, *Ramses,* perhaps the last thing he wrote. It was read. Some comments were made on *Ramses.* Blok joked: "I've only adapted Maspero. I really had nothing to do with it."

The section was promised its own theater. But there was no firewood for heating it. Our plays were turned over to the People's House, and from the People's House to the theater on Vasilievsky Island.[2] Ramses—on Vasilievsky Island! I learned about this by chance and told Blok. He said, with a smile that was far from gay: "I'd rather it was not produced at all."

And the section vetoed the production of *Ramses* and our other plays. Our Tower of Babel was collapsing.

The spring of 1921—and one of the last meetings of the section. The window was open, letting in the clanking of streetcars and the voices of boys on the sidewalk. And no one knew why, but suddenly everything seemed funny. Neither Gumilyov nor Blok nor I had any cigarettes. Gumilyov filched someone's cigarettes and was distributing them under the table. And the shadow on Blok's temple disappeared, and his lips trembled with silent, schoolboy's laughter. And every word in the preposterous play— a play was being read—seemed funny, and he infected everyone else with his laughter.

This was one of the few occasions during those years when I saw Blok young. And perhaps it was the last time I saw Blok.

Afterwards we walked together to Nevsky Prospekt. I remember clearly, as though it was carved out, a cloud to the left of the Nikolayevsky Station creeping up on the sun, but the sun was still there, spraying light.

"I have a strong desire to write," said Blok. "This almost never happens nowadays. Perhaps I'll really take a rest and sit down to it."

On Sadovaya we waited for the streetcar—it was a long time in coming. The cloud crept over the sun, covered it, and hung like a slab over us. And for some reason we began to speak of winter, of the winter that turned Petersburg into a mass of caves. We spoke of our becoming like animals, aware of summer, sun,

---

[2] An outlying section of Saint Petersburg.

winter. He told me that since his illness it was difficult for him to walk.

Overhead the cloud, the slab. Again I saw the familiar, faintly visible shadow on his temple. And I thought: No, he will not take a rest, he will not sit down. This is only a momentary flash of sunlight.

My almost daily meetings with Blok throughout those last three years were hurried, brief—like meetings in a railway car. And the period when we were closest to each other and least hurried was the summer of 1920. I worked together with him on the text and the production of *King Lear* at the Bolshoi Dramatic Theater.

I remember the rehearsals in the dark, empty, resonant hall. At the director's little table before the stage, or in the first row, on my right—Blok's medallion profile. On the stage, the same entrance, for the fifth, the sixth time on end; for the fifth and the sixth time, actors fell, killed. And I saw Blok twitch his head impatiently—as though his collar was too tight—at every false word or gesture.

At the end of each scene, a dark figure climbed over the footlights and down a little ladder, toward Blok: "Well, Alexander Alexandrovich, how was it? Not too bad?"

I had the feeling that the dark, empty hall was filled for them with a single viewer, Alexander Alexandrovich. The most rebellious obeyed his quiet, slow words. "Alexander Alexandrovich is our conscience," I was told once, I believe, by the director Lavrentiev. I heard the same phrase afterwards from many people in the theater, as if it were an established formula.

The final rehearsals, with sets and costumes, lasted until two and three o'clock in the morning. Blok always stayed to the end, and the later it was, the more he seemed to come to life, the more he spoke. A nocturnal bird. "Doesn't it tire you?" I asked him. The answer was: "No—I love the theater, the stage, the darkened hall. I am a very theatrical person, you know."

At one of the final rehearsals, late at night, it was suddenly decided to eliminate the scene in which Gloucester's eyes are plucked out. We could not bear to watch it. Blok felt that the scene should be retained. "Our age is no different from the sixteenth century. We can very easily look at the cruelest things."

After the morning rehearsals we often walked together toward Mokhovaya. Of our forgotten, obliterated conversations, only scattered fragments remain, cast up on the shore by the waves. But if you examine them closely, you see that they all speak of the same thing.

I can see it clearly. Hanging onto the straps, we stand in the crowded streetcar. People jostle each other, step on each other's toes. And in the midst of this crush, the last words of a strange conversation. "Does it ever happen to you that you look at yourself from the outside—you are definitely on the outside, at the other end of the room, and you see yourself—and you are not yourself but a stranger?"

The answer—after a pause—with eyes very far away: "Yes, it has happened—three times in my life. Nowadays it never happens any more. Nowadays nothing ever happens to me"—with a trace of bitterness at the corners of his mouth.

On another occasion, we were walking along Basseynaya— I don't remember where we were going. Blok, wearing his usual cap. And a bare fragment of a sentence, unconnected with anything: "There is no air. I cannot breathe. Perhaps I am sick."

And—it may have been on the same day, or some other day— a long conversation, and his bitter, harsh words about deadness and lies. Then, frowning, stubbornly—perhaps to himself rather than to me: "And yet there is a grain of truth—of every genuine truth—in all of this. A hating love—this is perhaps the most exact description of my feeling toward Russia."

At one of the meetings, I had an English magazine with me, in which I found a review of a translation of Blok's "The Twelve." The review was entitled "A Bolshevik Poem." I showed it to Blok. He smiled wryly.

After that, we talked about Bolshevism. "Bolshevism and revolution," said Blok, "are not to be found either in Moscow or in Petersburg. True Bolshevism—pious, Russian—lives somewhere deep in Russia's heartland, perhaps in the villages. Yes, that's probably where it is."

He always spoke slowly, in cool, metallic tones. And it was only once or twice that I heard the edge, the sting in that metal —and I saw that he was drawing in the reins, curbing himself.

Once he spoke like that about Marxism. The other time was

after he had read Struve's *Russkaya mysl* [Russian thought],
published abroad. I seldom heard him use such harsh words:
"What do they know, out there? Simply barking like dogs." And
he wrote an extremely trenchant article about it for the *Literary
Gazette* of the Writers' Union. The *Gazette* never appeared. This
was in April of 1921, before his last trip to Moscow.

Blok was wholly of the Neva, the mists of white nights, the
Bronze Horseman. The motley Moscow, earthly, full-bodied,
like a merchant's wife, was alien to him, and he was alien to
Moscow. His readings in Moscow, in May of 1921, demonstrated this.

His last, sad triumph was in Petersburg, on a white April night.

I remember him saying that the authorities had not permitted
his evening; there were charges of speculation, of admission prices
which exceeded the set norm. Finally, permission was granted.
The huge theater (the Bolshoi) was filled to the very top. In
the dim light there was a rustling—women's faces, many faces,
turned to the stage. Chukovsky talked about Blok, in a tired
voice. And then, lit from below, from the footlights, Blok, with
a pale, tired face. For a moment he hesitated, his eyes choosing
a place to stand. Then he took his place at the side of the lectern. And, in the silence, his poems about Russia. His voice was
muted, as if already coming from far away, monotonous. And
only at the end, after many ovations, it momentarily rose higher,
grew firmer—the last flight.

There seemed to me a mournful, sad, tender solemnity in this
evening, Blok's last one. I remember a voice behind me, in the
hall: "They seem to be holding a wake!"

And, indeed, it was a wake, the city's wake for Blok. For
Petersburg, Blok had gone directly from the stage of the Dramatic Theater beyond that blue, serrated wall that is patrolled
by death. On that white April night Petersburg saw Blok for the
last time.

At our meetings, everyone had his customary seat. And now,
Blok's chair, at the end of the table, by the window, stood empty:
Blok was ill. During the previous winter, his chair had also been
vacant for a month. But after a month in bed, Blok had returned,
seemingly the same. And indeed, there was nothing unusual in

Alexander Blok in death

his illness—acute rheumatism, from living in an unheated house. Few people in Petersburg escaped it. No one suspected that this ordinary illness had already numbered his heartbeats. And everyone was taken unawares by the news that Blok's condition was serious, and that his only hope was in going to a sanatorium abroad without delay.

No one saw him during the three months of his illness: people disturbed him, even the customary things around him disturbed him, he did not want to talk to anyone, he wanted to be alone. And yet he could not break away from his hated-beloved Russia. He consistently refused to go to a sanatorium in Finland until he realized that staying meant death. But even then he would not sign any petitions or papers. The letters to Moscow, requesting permission for Blok to go abroad were written (in June) by the Executive Board of the Writers' Union.

Gorky was in Moscow. He went from office to office with papers and appeals. The news that reached us said he had obtained promises, that Blok would be allowed to go, soon. Blok tossed in agony: there was no air, he could not breathe. The people who had visited his home said it was painful to sit in the next room and hear him gasping.

We attended meetings, stood in queues, rode precariously on the footboards of streetcars. Blok tossed in agony. Gorky went from official to official. And, finally, on August 3 or 4, the permission finally arrived from Moscow: Blok could go abroad.

A windy, rainy morning. Sunday, eleven o'clock, August 7. The telephone rang. It was from Alkonost—from Alyansky:[3] Alexander Alexandrovich was dead.

I remember the shock, the pain, the rage—at everything and everyone, at myself. We were to blame, all of us. We wrote, spoke—we should have shouted, we should have banged our fists —to save Blok.

I could not bear it and telephoned Gorky: "Blok is dead. None of us can be forgiven for it."

A blue, hot day, August 10. Blue smoke of incense in the crowded little room. The long face of a stranger with a prickly

[3] S. M. Alyansky was the founder and owner of the private publishing house Alkonost, which published most of Blok's works. It existed in Saint Petersburg from 1918 to 1923.

moustache and a pointed beard—a face resembling Don Quixote's. And his death was easier to bear, because this was not Blok, and it was not Blok who would be buried today.

The coffin was carried down the narrow, curving, dirty stairway and across the yard. A crowd had gathered at the gates outside. The same people who had waited on that white April night at the entrance of the Dramatic Theater for Blok to come out—all that was left of the literary community in Petersburg. And only now it became clear how few remained.

The church at the Smolensk Cemetery was full. A slanting ray of sunlight across the cupola above, slowly climbing down. An unknown girl made her way through the crowd to the coffin, kissed the yellow hand, and walked away.

And, finally—under the sun, along narrow avenues, we carried that alien, heavy thing that remained of Blok. And silently, as silently as he had lived throughout those last years, the earth received him.

1924

FYODOR SOLOGUB

The incident took place in General Betrishchev's study.[1] It was there that Pavel Ivanovich Chichikov said: "No, try to love us black. Anyone will love us white." This dictum was served up so cleverly, so impressively, that General Betrishchev accepted it as an axiom. But transpose it from Chichikov's flat world, from the world of dead souls, into a world where tragic souls are burning, and you will see that this generally recognized axiom is turned upside down. You will find that loving with a black or gray little love is given to everyone (among the Chichikovs), and it is only the few who have strength enough for the difficult paths of another kind of love. One of these few is Fyodor Sologub.

I remember, in the summer of 1920, Blok and I were going somewhere by streetcar down Liteyny Prospekt. Holding onto the straps in the jolting car, Blok said to me: "Today I love Russia with a hating love—this is, perhaps, the closest definition." Blok's words "a hating love" are also the closest definition of the love that Sologub is sick with. Lightning will flash only when one of the poles has a positive, the other, a negative charge. This love is like lightning: at one of its poles there is inevitably a minus sign, sharp and irreconcilable.

The memory of Blok did not occur by chance. Sologub and Blok belong to the same order. In each, if you listen closely, you will hear the same overtones. Through the roar and the clamor of life, both continually hear the same voice—the voice of the

---

[1] The reference is to a scene in Gogol's *Dead Souls*.

Fair Lady. Blok may call her the Unknown One, and Sologub, Dulcinea, but she is one and the same, and neither will ever reconcile himself to the Lady becoming Darya, simply Darya, yawning with relish at supper, in a bathrobe, with paper curlers in her hair. Darya, or Aldonsa—the name makes no difference, she has thousands of names, but never the one, Dulcinea—is ample–bodied and rosy-cheeked. She is not a bad woman, she is not black, merely blackish, or perhaps gray; she may even be almost white. And any Chichikov, any Sancho Panza, will be delighted to accept her—because they are wise, they know that even the sun has spots, they know that to accept a human being and life with "the good and the bad" and the "almost," to love them black or gray, is far more practical, simpler, more comfortable, more sensible.

But the eccentric Don Quixote and the eccentric Sologub will turn away from Aldonsa at once, because they possess some innate reagent which tells them unerringly when the wine of Aldonsa-life contains even a single milligram of "the good and the bad," a single drop of "almost." And both Don Quixote and Sologub will throw such wine out the window. Not because they do not love the wine of life, but because they love it more than anyone else, because they love it too much: they want either the purest or none at all, everything or nothing. And this determines the road traveled by those who have been granted the magnificent, tormenting gift of intransigent love.

This road is the tragic road of Ahasuerus, the road to Damascus taken by Sologub's knight Romualdo de Turenne, the road of those eternally hungering souls about whom the pious sing on Thursday of Holy Week. The roses, the palms, the fountains and cupolas of the city in the desert may tell thousands of people that this is indeed Damascus. Don Quixote and Sologub and his knight Romualdo will leave Damascus to go further; their path will lead them on into the endless desert until their bones come to rest in it. It is their great and difficult destiny not to be satisfied with any Damascus that may be achieved. To them every achievement, every embodiment destroys the true Damascus. To them there is nothing more terrible than walls, than settling down in one place. And it is precisely here that they are at the opposite pole from the millions of Chichikovs and Sancho Panzas or whatever other names they may have. The Chichikovs can live only within walls, in the secure, the solved, the found, the answered. Romualdó and Sologub can live only when there is something beyond, still undiscovered, still unanswered. The Chichikovs dread infinity above all else; to Sologub, to the romantic, infinity is his own true element. Millions of Chichikovs are undoubtedly frantic with joy because Einstein, lost in sophisms, has calculated that the universe is finite and that its radius is so many billion miles. But Sologub would be unable to live in this universe if he did not know that the calculations are mere sophistry. It would be too confining for him—because, no matter when, its end can be reached.

I have until now consistently juxtaposed these two names: Don Quixote of La Mancha and Fyodor Sologub. This has been done frequently ever since Sologub came out to the tourney with a shield on which he had written in his own hand the name of his lady, Dulcinea. And yet Sologub was mistaken, I was mistaken, everyone else was mistaken. The parallelism of the lines of Don Quixote and Sologub is only seeming: at a certain point their lines intersect, to diverge broadly. And the angle of this divergence is so great that at the end of his road Don Quixote ceases being Don Quixote. Many have heard his last words: "Why no, Good Sirs, do not call me the Knight of La Mancha. I am simply Alonzo the Good." No one will ever hear such words from Sologub.

Sologub's love is the color of white-hot lightning, flashing between two poles, fusing the plus and the minus with fire. Don Quixote's love is the color of a cloud floating off into infinite distance. Don Quixote's love is gentle and good-humored; he never killed anyone. Sologub's love is merciless; Sologub kills.

But the weapon that Sologub kills with is the stiletto which medieval knights called *misericordia* (mercy); it was used—for humane reasons, because of love of man—to finish off those who were mortally wounded. Just so—because of love of man —Sologub kills all his favorite heroes with the misericordia, to spare them the bitterness of discovering Aldonsa in Dulcinea. In the "Poisoned Garden" the Youth and the Beauty die, of course, after embracing for the first time. The knight Romualdo de Turenne dies, of course, on the way to Damascus. And Vera, of "The Snake Charmer," unquestionably must die when she is only a step away from her Damascus. And Seryozha, in the story

Fyodor Sologub

"The Stars," "throws himself eagerly, joyously, from the earth to the lambent stars"—in order to die. And the radiant Raya appears to Mitya in the story "Consolation" to tell him, "Don't be afraid," when he leaps from the fourth floor. Thus, Sologub, invariably, with everyone he loves. Such is the merciful cruelty of Sologub's love of man.

But man is man only when he answers exactly to his biological designation—when he is *Homo erectus,* when he has already risen from all fours and knows how to look up, into infinity. With those who are still on all fours, who still root around in the earth with their snouts, with the Sancho Panzas—ruddy, plump, contented, finite—with these Sologub is merciless; he punishes them with the sentence of life, they never die in his world, they cannot die. Take a look at *The Petty Demon;* over its vast length, nobody dies; everyone there is immortal. People always speak of the immortality of great men, of heroes. This, of course, is an error. The hero is indissolubly linked with tragedy, with death. Only the philistine is indestructible, deathless. And for him, for the deathless one, Sologub reserves a weapon different from the misericordia—a merciless weapon, the whip.

The whip has not yet been given its full due as an instrument of human progress. I know of no more potent means than the whip for raising man from all fours, for making him stop kneeling down before anything or anyone. I am not speaking, of course, of whips woven of leather thongs; I am speaking of whips woven of words, the whips of the Gogols, Swifts, Molières, Frances, the whips of irony, sarcasm, satire. And Sologub wields such a whip perhaps even more skillfully than the stiletto of misericordia. Read the two books of his fairy tales, and you will see that they are still as sharp as they were twenty years ago. Read *The Petty Demon,* and you will see that Peredonov is doomed to immortality, doomed to wandering through the world forever, scribbling denunciations and "assuring all the leading citizens of the town of his own trustworthiness."

Flowers must be tended if they are to grow. Mold grows everywhere by itself. The philistine is like mold. For a moment it seemed that he had been thoroughly burnt out by the revolution; but now he is crawling out, smirking, once again from under the still warm ashes—cowardly, limited, dull, self-satisfied, all-knowing. And the whip of satire must be cracked over him once again—we must have a new *Petty Demon*.

The patent for the knout has, not without good reason, been recorded by history in Russia's name—but only of the knout made of leather. Irony, satire have been imported into Russian literature from the West. And, although there is no more fertile soil for satire than our black earth, we have thus far raised only three or four full-grown plants, and one of these is, of course, Sologub. The reason for this is that in Russia the Sancho Panzas have always been too weak-nerved to have sufficient courage to listen calmly to satire. I do not know whether the edict of Peter I, which stated that "For composing satire, its author shall be put to the cruelest torture," has ever been repealed. But even this is not the main thing. The truth is simply that the Russian writer, with few exceptions, has always had too much Russian soft-heartedness, has always been too easy-going. In this respect, Sologub is fortunately not Russian: he can, when the need arises, turn into steel, gleaming and merciless.

And not only is his satire European; his entire style is tempered in the European forge and bends like steel. Without the slightest trace of strain or fracture he withstands the 180-degree bend from the stoniest, heaviest everyday life to the fantastic; from the land permeated with the smell of vodka and cabbage soup to the land of the *olla*.[2] The fine and difficult art of bringing together within a single formula both the solid and the gaseous states of the literary material, the everyday and the fantastic, has long been known to European masters. Among Russian prose writers the secret of this alloy is truly known, perhaps, to only two, Gogol and Sologub.

The word has been tamed by Sologub to such an extent that he even permits himself to play with this dangerous element, bending the traditionally straight style of Russian prose. In *The Petty Demon* and *Deathly Charms,* as well as in many of his stories, he deliberately mixes the strongest extract of everyday language with the elevated and refined diction of the romantic. In "The Steward Vanka and the Page Jean," these dissonances are sharpened even more and are further complicated by a charming play with deliberate anachronisms. In the "Fairy

---

[2] A Spanish stew, Don Quixote's favorite dish.

Tales" we find a new twist—play with hyperbolized folklore. In his entire prose output, Sologub takes a sharp turn off the main-traveled roads of naturalism, in content, in language, in psychology. And if we take a close look at the stylistic experimentation of the newest Russian prose, its struggle against the traditions of naturalism, its efforts to build a footbridge to the West, we shall see the shadow of Sologub. With Sologub, a new chapter begins in Russian prose.

If, along with the European sharpness and refinement, Sologub had also assimilated the European's mechanical, bankrupt soul, he would not be the Sologub who is so close to us. But under his severe and restrained European clothing, Sologub has preserved the stormy, reckless Russian soul. This love, which demands all or nothing, this absurd, incurable, beautiful sickness is not limited to Sologub, to Don Quixote, to Blok (and this is the sickness Blok died of)—it is our Russian sickness, *morbus rossica*. It is the sickness that afflicts the better part of our intelligentsia—and, happily, will always afflict it. Happily, because a country where there are no longer any intransigent, eternally dissatisfied, forever restless romantics, where only the healthy remain, only the Sancho Panzas and the Chichikovs, such a country is doomed sooner or later to snore under the quilt of philistinism. Perhaps only the vast Russian steppes—but recently the domain of galloping Scythians who did not know the meaning of home or of settled existence—could have given birth to this Russian sickness. And, despite his outward Europeanism, Sologub belongs to the Russian steppes; in spirit, he is far more Russian than many of his contemporaries, such as Balmont or Bryusov. Cruel time will blot out many names; Sologub's name will remain in Russian literature.

1924

CHEKHOV

The revolution is often likened to a blizzard—that hoary, frenzied, truly Russian outbreak of elemental forces. Go out into the garden in the morning after a blizzard, and you will not see a single familiar path, a single familiar object. Everything is white, new, there are snowdrifts everywhere, and you don't know what is beneath them—perhaps a well, perhaps a bench, perhaps a bush. Just so, all roads are blanketed and snowdrifts are piled up everywhere after these past ten years of Russian blizzard. And one of these snowdrifts has covered Chekhov.

Talk about Chekhov with a reader of the newest, latest generation, and most of the time you will hear: "Chekhov? Whining, pessimism, superfluous people." or "Chekhov? Completely irrelevant to the new literature, revolution, society." This means that Chekhov is not known, people have ceased to see him, all paths to him are blanketed with snow. And it means that it is time to take a shovel, clear away the snowdrift, and show Chekhov, show his biography. Not his external biography—that has been dealt with quite enough, but the biography of his spirit, the line of his inner development.

"Just as I will lie in the grave alone, so, in essence, I also live alone." We do not know what this brief entry from Chekhov's notebook, published after his death, refers to. It may be assumed that he wrote it about himself: and it was, indeed, true of him; he lived alone all his life. He had many warm acquaintances, but friends to whom he could throw the doors to himself wide open —such friends he did not have. There was a special kind of chastity, of modesty, in him, which compelled him to conceal

224

everything that stirred him deeply, truly. This is why it is difficult in Chekhov's case to trace what I have called the "biography of the spirit." And it is only from "circumstantial evidence," by considering certain scarcely noticeable events of his external biography, by listening carefully to the words of his characters, that we can discover the nature of his faith and his social views.

Chekhov had lost the God of the church when still a very young man. This was attributable to a large extent to the fact that Anton Pavlovich (and his brothers) had been brought up "in the fear of God." The obligatory performance of prayer and ritual duties produced the opposite effect to what his parents had sought to achieve. Later, as an adult, Chekhov wrote: "I have no religion now. When my two brothers and I sang in church "May it be rectified," everyone looked at us with tears of emotion and envied our parents, but we felt like little prisoners at forced labor."

Having lost his church religion, Chekhov took a long time to find another. For many years he lived without any God, without any faith. He spent the first period of his literary activity, up to the mid-eighties, "leaping like a calf let out into the open, laughing and making others laugh" (from Chekhov's letters). And it was not until the late 1880s that he experienced a sharp change and began for the first time to think seriously about life, its meaning, and death. For the first time, his writings acquire the sharp tang of bitterness, longing, dissatisfaction. Already in "Happiness" and "The Steppe" the thought of death occasionally darkens the sunny expanse like the shadow of a flying bird, and then "life seems desperate and terrible." In "A Dull Story" this light, flickering shadow grows into a black, hopeless, oppressive cloud.

And it was not only physical death that Chekhov had begun to see; he also saw another kind of death, slow and perhaps even more agonizing. He saw thousands buried alive in the bog of commonplace and trivial daily existence. With the skill of an experienced physician who, from the slightest, almost imperceptible symptoms, discovers a mortal disease in the patient, Chekhov finds banality where at first glance life seems to be serene and happy ("The Teacher of Literature," "My Life," "Ionych," and later "The Bride"). In "The Black Monk" he makes a clear decision: death is preferable to ordinary, dim existence.

And if Chekhov had ceased writing during those years, his critics, who leap out at the first mention of his name with the labels of "pessimistic," "whining," and "obsessed with superfluous people," would have been right. However, in the nineties we see a new shift in the path of his inner development, for it was then that Chekhov emerged from his former indifference to social questions. The Chekhov who wrote as "Chekhonte" in *Budilnik* [Alarm clock] and *Strekoza* [Dragonfly] had gone to work without a moment's hesitation for the reactionary *Novoye vremya* [New times]. But now Chekhov says about Burenin and Zhitel, journalists working for *Novoye vremya,* "They simply disgust me; in my convictions, I am 7,375 versts from Zhitel and Company" and "After reading Zhitel, Burenin and the rest of those judges of mankind, I am left with the taste of rust in my mouth, and my day is spoiled" (from Chekhov's letters). In the end, Chekhov discontinued his work for *Novoye vremya.*

The journey to Sakhalin undertaken by Chekhov in 1890–91 was not a journey in search of literary material. It was prompted by social concerns, and Chekhov's book, *Sakhalin,* written after his return, brought very real results—a whole series of improvements in the lot of the convicts in Sakhalin. Chekhov's decision to live in the village and his move to Melikhovo was also caused not only—or, perhaps, not so much—by his illness, as by other reasons. "If I am a doctor, I need patients and hospitals; if I am a writer, I must live among the people, not on Malaya Dimitrovka. I need at least some small fragment of social and political life," he wrote at the time to one of his friends. And, finally, in 1902, after the revocation of Gorky's election to the Academy of Arts and Sciences, Chekhov, together with Korolenko,[1] resigned his title as academician. By this action, Chekhov definitely entered the ranks of the "unreliables," and it becomes quite clear with whom he would have allied himself had he lived until 1905.

At the same time, in his stories and novellas, Chekhov dealt more and more frequently with themes of a social nature. This began with "A Fit," in which he posed the problem of prostitution with unprecedented sharpness and forthrightness. In "A Murder," "Peasants," and "The Ravine," he revealed a new approach to the peasant question. At one time, he was carried away

[1] V. G. Korolenko (1853–1921), a highly popular liberal writer and journalist.

by Tolstoyan ideas ("My Life"). He came to give increasingly
more thought generally to the injustice of a social order in which
some live in ignorance and poverty, and others in wealth. "The
arrogance and idleness of the strong, the ignorance and brutelike
existence of the weak, intolerable poverty all around, crowded
living, degeneracy, drunkenness, hypocrisy, lies. . . . Yet, in every
house and in the street we see only peace and quiet. Among those
who live in the city, no one cries out in indignation. . . . The only
protest is in mute statistics: so many people gone insane; so many
pails of vodka consumed; so many children dead from malnutri-
tion. . . . And, evidently, such a state of affairs is necessary; evidently, the happy are feeling good only because the unhappy
carry their load unprotestingly." Thus, Chekhov in his story
"Gooseberries." The hero of another story, "The House with a
Mezzanine," even points out the way to a cure for the social ills:
"If all of us, city and village people, all without exception, agreed
to share the labor expended by mankind for the satisfaction of
physical needs, then each of us would have to work no more
than two or three hours a day. Imagine all of us, rich and poor,
working only three hours a day, and free the rest of the time. . . .
We would all devote this leisure to the sciences and the arts. Just
as the peasants communally mend the road, so all of us together,
communally, would look for the truth and the meaning of life.
And—I am sure of that—this truth would be discovered very
soon, man would free himself of this constant, tormenting, oppressive fear of death—perhaps even of death itself."

So Chekhov wrote in 1895. What a difference from the hope-
lessness of "The Steppe," when life seemed "desperate and terrible." By complex ways, by looking deep into the dark well of
the human soul, full of filth, somewhere at the very bottom of it
Chekhov at last found his faith. And this faith turned out to be
faith in man, in the power of human progress. And man became
his God. "We are the highest beings, and if we truly realized the
full power of human genius, we would become as gods!" "Believing in God is easy. The inquisitors also believed in him, and
so did Biron and Arakcheyev.[2] No, you must find faith in man,"
wrote Chekhov. And the nearer he came to the end of his life,

[2] Biron, favorite of Empress Anne (reigned 1730–40); Count A. A.
Arkacheyev (1769–1834), extreme reactionary, minister of war under
Alexander I; both notorious for their ruthlessness.

the stronger grew his faith in "the great and brilliant future" of man, in the "kingdom of eternal truth" ("The Black Monk"). "Oh, if only it came soon, this new, bright life, when we shall be able to look directly and boldly in the eyes of our fate, and know ourselves right, gay and free," he wrote ("The Bride") a short time before his death in 1903.

As before, the quiet glow of twilight lies over everything he wrote during his last years. But this is not the old twilight: it is not the evening twilight which is followed by night; it is the twilight before sunrise, and through it, in the distance, the dawn comes up ever more brightly.

It would be a crude mistake to conclude from what has been said that Chekhov was a tendentious writer. He was further from tendentious sermonizing than any other Russian writer. "Tendentiousness is based on people's inability to rise above specifics." "The artist must be only a dispassionate witness." "I am not a liberal, not a conservative, not a gradualist. . . . I want to be a free artist." These ideas are found in many of his letters. In life, Chekhov was a doctor, but in his novellas, stories, and plays there is not a single political prescription. He could justly say of himself, in Hertzen's words: "We are not the doctors, we are the pain."

Chekhov looked at life without glasses—and it is precisely this that helped him to become a genuine Realist. As an "impartial witness" he lived through the end of the nineteenth and the beginning of the twentieth centuries, and everything written by Chekhov is as valuable a document for the study of Russian life during this period as Nestor's chronicle is for the study of the beginnings of old Russia.

This, then, is what we uncover when we remove the snowdrift piled up over Chekhov in recent years. We uncover a man profoundly agitated by social problems; a writer whose social ideals are the same as those we live by; a philosophy of the divinity of man, of fervent faith in man—the faith which moves mountains. And all of this brings Chekhov close to Russia's recent blizzard years, all of it makes Chekhov one of the harbingers of these years.

If we take an attentive look at Chekhov as an artist, a master, we shall, again, find a close kinship with the literary art of our epoch.

In Chekhov's stories everything is real, everything has dimensions, everything can be seen and felt, everything is here, on earth. None of his stories has anything fantastic, mysterious, otherworldly. Even if we meet a fiery-eyed poodle that terrifies us into thoughts of the devil, it turns out, of course, to be simply a friend's lost dog ("Fear"); if we encounter the ghost of the Black Monk, Kovrin, who speaks to the ghost, knows all the time that it is merely an apparition, a hallucination, a symptom of illness. For the most evanescent, most elusive movements of the spirit, Chekhov finds a realistic image, with weight and dimension. Listening to a beautiful woman's singing is "like the taste of a cold, fresh melon" ("All of Life"); a writer's injured vanity is "a box of dishes which are easy to unpack, but impossible to put back into place as they were" ("Difficult People"); the constant mockery of the Petersburg native is "like the shield of the savage" ("The Story of an Unknown Man"); a man embittered by contempt is "rusted" (ibid.).

Something else, too, is revealed by the examples, chosen at random: Chekhov's images are original and bold. "The district elder and the district clerk were so thoroughly permeated by lies that the very skin on their faces was the skin of rogues and swindlers" ("In the Ravine"). "Pimfov's face became still flabbier—another moment, and it would melt in the heat and trickle down into his vest" ("The Thinker"). Before Chekhov, no one would have dared to write like that. And here Chekhov comes before us as an innovator: he was the first to use the methods of Impressionism.

Also new was the extraordinary terseness and brevity of Chekhov's stories, qualities he brought to their utmost limits. He was the first to legitimize in Russian literature the short story form which had long existed in the West. The greatest master of the short story, Maupassant, undoubtedly influenced Chekhov. No wonder he had such admiration for Maupassant's art and dreamed of translating him "as he ought to be translated."

In his plays, especially the last plays, Chekhov also made a clear and conscious attempt to create new literary forms. He deliberately deviated from the generally accepted canons of playwriting. After finishing *The Seagull,* he wrote: "I have finished the play. I began *forte* and finished *pianissimo*—against all rules." "I am writing a play . . . violating stage conventions outrageously. . . . Little action, five poods of love," he wrote in another letter.

His plays are examples of "psychological drama," where external, scenic effects are usually absent, and the conflict takes place under the surface of life, in the human soul.

Innovator and great artist, Chekhov has undoubtedly influenced a number of later Russian writers. Among Chekhov's pupils are Bunin, Shmelyov, Trenyov, and other writers of the younger generation. All of them form a single group, a single constellation—of Realists.

Seamen set their course by the constellations; and it is by the literary groupings in which more or less related writers are united that we must find our way in the wide sea of Russian literature. But in order to find a constellation, the eye must first select some particularly large and bright star. Such a star in the Realist constellation is Chekhov.

And, of course, the line that leads from Chekhov to present-day Realism is a straight line—the shortest distance.

1925

MEETINGS WITH KUSTODIEV

Properly speaking, this essay should have a different title: "Meetings with Boris Mikhailovich and with Kustodiev." Precisely that —not with one, but with two. For I met them at different times, and each of them—the painter Kustodiev and the man Boris Mikhailovich—lives in my memory as a separate individual.

With the painter Kustodiev I became acquainted a long time ago, not in Leningrad, but still in Petersburg, at one of the "World of Art" exhibitions. At this exhibition my eye was suddenly caught by one of Kustodiev's paintings, and I could not move away from it. I stood and stood before it; I not only saw it, but began to hear it, and hastily jotted down the words I heard in the margins of the catalog. Soon all the margins were filled. I do not know the title of that painting, but I remember it: winter, snow, trees, snowdrifts, sleighs, ruddy-cheeked Russian gaiety—Kustodiev's colorful old Russia. Perhaps I was so struck by the painting because I was living with the same colors at that time: I was writing my novella *A Provincial Tale*. True, Kustodiev saw the old Russia with different eyes, far milder and kinder than mine. But there was only one old Russia, it united us, and, sooner or later, we inevitably had to meet.

This meeting, when I got to know and love not only Kustodiev, but also Boris Mikhailovich, took place much later, after about ten years, when Petersburg no longer existed, when it had become Petrograd-Leningrad, when Kustodiev's opulent old Russia lay dead. And now that it was dead, I had no desire to speak of it as one had been able to speak about the living. Kicking a dead lion was an easy victory that did not tempt me. And so it came about that Kustodiev's old Russia and mine could now be painted on canvas and on paper in the same colors. It so happened that I met the artist Kustodiev in our joint book, *In Old Russia*. And this was also the beginning of my friendship with the man Boris Mikhailovich.

In the fall of 1922, the Akvilon Publishing House sent me a series of Kustodiev's "Russian Types," with the request that I write an article about them. What was I to write about? Kustodiev's painting technique? Others could do it better. I wrote no article, but did something else: I simply spread out before me all those Kustodiev beauties, coachmen, merchants, innkeepers, nuns. I looked at them as I had once looked at his painting at the exhibition, and the story "In Old Russia" somehow wrote itself.

I finished it, and two days later received a telephone call from Akvilon that Kustodiev would like me to visit him in the evening. Interpreting "evening" in the usual Petersburg manner, I called on Boris Mikhailovich late, about 10:00 P.M., and had my first glimpse of the ordeal—I can think of no other word to describe it—that was his life during those last years.

A small room, a bedroom, and on the right, in the bed by the wall—Boris Mikhailovich. I remember that bed very well; it had a rail stretched from head to foot at the height of about a meter, and I wondered about it. My manuscript lay on the little table by the bedside. Boris Mikhailovich wanted to talk to me about some passages in the text. He stretched his hand, and suddenly I saw: he raised himself a little on his elbow and grasped the rail; then, clenching his teeth and fighting down the pain, he ducked his head, as if to ward off a blow from behind. Afterwards, I saw this movement many times, and eventually became used to it, as we become used to everything. But then, I remember, I felt ashamed of being healthy while he was convulsed with pain, clutching the rail; I felt ashamed that I would soon get up and go, and he could not get up. This shame prevented me from hearing what he said about our book; I understood nothing and left as quickly as I could.

I went away with the impression, What a frail, exhausted, pain-racked man.

Several days later I was there again, and this time I thought, What vitality, what astonishing strength of spirit this man possesses.

I was taken to his studio. The day was bright and frosty, and, whether from the sun or from Kustodiev's paintings, the studio was gay: opulent bodies glowed on the walls, crosses burned with gold, green summer grass carpeted the earth—everything was alive with joy, blood, running sap. And the man who had filled all those canvases with the rich sap of life was sitting in a wheel-chair (near the potbellied stove customary in those years), with dead feet wrapped in a blanket, and speaking jestingly: "Feet— what are they but a luxury? But now my hand is beginning to hurt—that's something to be resented."

Many things are revealed to us only in contrasts, in the juxta-position of opposites. And it was only in that room, when I first saw the artist and his paintings, the artist and the man, that I realized what enormous creative will was needed to paint all those canvases sitting thus in a wheelchair, gripped with pain. I understood that Boris Mikhailovich was stronger and tougher than any of us. And also that his life was a martyrdom, and he himself was a consecrated man, a zealot, such as his beloved old Russia had known in olden times. With the sole difference that his feat was not for the salvation of the soul, but for the sake of art. Illarion the Hermit, Afanasy the Sitter, Nil the Stylite, and—in our own day—yet another anchorite and sitter. But this hermit did not curse the earth, the body, the joy of life; he cele-brated them with his colors.

As we know from all the lives of the saints, every true anchorite and saint was occasionally visited and tempted by the devil. It fell to me to become such a devil to Boris Mikhailovich—and the result of the temptation was Kustodiev's only published series of erotic drawings—his illustrations to my story "The Healing of the Novice Erasmus." This book, published by the Petropolis Publishing House in Berlin, was our second joint work.

The artist's task in this case was extremely difficult. What was required, of course, was not the crude, overt eroticism of the kind found in Somov's well-known works; the illustrations had to provide in images what was given in the text only in allusions, between the lines. And this seemingly insoluble task was solved by Kustodiev with extraordinary grace and tact, and—I must add—with a great sense of humor.

I do not know how Kustodiev had managed to retain this sense of humor, to carry it unimpaired through his pain-racked life.

And yet the man Boris Mikhailovich possessed it in even more generous measure than the painter Kustodiev. He loved jests, wit, laughter. His laughter as we sat together at the table was at times so young and merry that we who were healthy could only envy him.[1]

I saw Boris Mikhailovich in high spirits many times, I saw him tired and ill, but I never saw him dejected or discouraged. Perhaps the reason for this was that his hands were always occupied on the drawing board attached to his chair, there was always some work before him. And I remember he often said that work was his best medicine.

But at times work became a sickness rather than a medicine, afflicting the artist Kustodiev, not the man Boris Mikhailovich. "I am doing all sorts of nauseating semicommissions, trying to get together some money for a trip, and they don't pay me," he wrote me in the summer of 1926. And during the earlier years of our friendship, in 1923 and 1924, he suffered even more from this affliction. To live and feed the stove, he had to put aside his own, his real work and undertake all those "semicommissions." At such times his pencils would suddenly begin to break, his erasers would disappear, everything would go wrong, everything was irritating. I remember one day when a book cover design he had made for the publishing house Zemlya i Fabrika [Land and factory] was returned to him; it had been judged unsuitable to the required "ideological purpose" and had to be done afresh. This was the only occasion during all the years of our acquaintance when I saw Kustodiev lose his usual self-control, when I saw him truly angry.

In the early winter of 1923, Boris Mikhailovich decided to paint my portrait, and for two weeks I came for a sitting almost every morning. When I arrived, the studio still seemed to be pervaded by the silence of the previous night, the stove crackled faintly; outside, the bells of the Vvedensky Church were ringing.

---

[1] I can imagine, for example, how he would have laughed over the article in *Izvestia,* in which the Moscow critic Friche contrasts the virtuous Kustodiev with iniquitous me, never suspecting, in his innocence, that Kustodiev illustrated my story "The Healing of the Novice Erasmus," or that "In Old Russia" was written as the text to Kustodiev's paintings.

What a pity that Boris Mikhailovich was denied this opportunity for another hearty laugh.—AUTHOR'S NOTE.

Boris Mikhailovich held out his hand to me carefully, his fingers bent: it hurt, and he moved it with caution. After greeting me, he would immediately slip his hand into the breast of his jacket to warm it. And suddenly he would bring out a kitten, then another. He was very fond of animals. Then, skillfully maneuvering the wheels of his chair, he would find the proper position and take up his pencil. His lips were still smiling, still finishing a sentence, but his eyes changed at once; they became as sharp as the eyes of a hunter taking aim. At first he would usually work silently. Later, when, as he put it, his "pencil warmed up," we would begin to talk.

Never again, it seems to me, were we able to talk as we had during those winter mornings. We spoke of everything—people, books, countries, the theater, Russia, the Bolsheviks. Sometimes I recalled something funny and told him, and then he would put down his pencil and laugh, doubling up, so that the laughter would not hurt. But most of the time we would be telling one another about our past travels. To the Christian hermits, compelled to continence, temptation naturally assumed the shape of a woman. To Kustodiev, compelled to live within four walls, temptation naturally took the shape of travel. Sometimes he would dream aloud: "Ah, if I could get to Paris, just once more —or no, better to London, and sit somewhere high up, on the roof of a ten-story building, where you can see everything—" Shut in for many years, suffering from chronic visual deprivation, he was literally starved for new sights.

One day I found Boris Mikhailovich in his chair in an altogether unaccustomed place, in the corner by the window. Bending over slightly, he looked out into the street and was not in his usual hurry to begin work. I asked him about it. "There is late mass today, the people will be coming out of church soon, I must see them," he explained. And I understood: even this was rich food for his starved eyes.

But where, despite such poverty of external impressions, did Kustodiev find all the colorful wealth of material we see in his paintings? He evidently had an extraordinary visual memory, which held stored up in its depths inexhaustible reserves of every kind.

During those weeks, as the portrait was being painted, the

pages of Kustodiev's life opened before me from day to day, and I saw more and more clearly the enormous spiritual strength of this man.

It seemed to me that Boris Mikhailovich felt worse that winter than ever before. He was particularly tormented by spasms. A table with a removable plywood top had been attached to his chair. One day, in the throes of a spasm, his legs jumped up and overturned this top, scattering his paint and pencils. After that, it was necessary to tie his legs to the chair with leather straps while he worked. This, of course, did nothing to lessen the pain.

I remember frequently seeing Boris Mikhailovich's face changing strangely: the right side of the face flushed crimson, while the left side remained pale. And then the same, familiar movement of the head, drawn into the shoulders and bent forward, as though to ward off a blow from behind.

It was physically painful to see this. But no matter how many times I asked Boris Mikhailovich to put down his work and take a short rest, he never agreed. By some incredible effort of will, he would master the pain and go on—doing both what he wanted, what he felt was his real, his own work, and also what he had to do in order to live, to eat, to heat his stove.

There was one thing that frightened him, that he did not dare to think about—the pains in his right hand. He was beginning to find it difficult at times to hold a pencil or brush in his hand, but he mentioned it to me only once or twice. It threatened to rob him of the very meaning of his life; it was like taking faith in God away from a Christian martyr.

One thing remained—to try an operation (the third one), and Boris Mikhailovich went to Moscow to have it done. This extremely complicated operation—removal of a tumor of the spine —was performed by the famous German surgeon Professor Foerster, who had also treated Lenin. The operation lasted four and a half hours. It was performed under local anesthesia, which wore off after the first two and a half hours; the second half of the operation was done virtually without anesthesia. What super-human stamina was needed to endure it!

His desire to live and to work was so great that Boris Mikhailovich endured it and was able to continue his heroic existence for a few more years. After the operation, I saw him in better spirits, for the excruciating spasms were gone. Once he even told me that feeling was returning to his feet. But he never spoke about it again. The operation merely provided some relief; it did not end his ordeal or return him to a normal life.

The winter of 1924–25 bound us with even closer ties. It saw the appearance of our new joint work—the production of *The Flea* at the Second Moscow Art Theater.

The theater understandably wanted to have an artist who was close at hand, a Muscovite. They tried Krymov, but his sketches were not acceptable. Yet the rehearsals were already in full swing, and it was time to make the sets. One morning the director of *The Flea,* Dicky, and I were sitting together in the dark empty lobby, talking—no, not talking, being silent—about this. Both of us had a single name in our minds—Kustodiev—and both spoke it aloud in unison. We sent Kustodiev a telegram. He wired that he agreed and was immediately going to work on the sketches.

He worked on *The Flea* with great enthusiasm. And understandably so: in this play, the colors of his beloved old Russia could burn most vividly. And, I believe I can safely say that it was one of his most successful works in the theater, perhaps the most successful.

Once again I visited Boris Mikhailovich every two or three days. He showed me what he had done, we devised new details, developed new and amusing ideas. Working with him was a real delight. A great, accomplished master, he was utterly free of any petty vanity; he willingly listened to suggestions and more than once changed what he had already done. All he wanted was a truly successful production, and he contributed all he could to this end, sparing no effort.

Soon the sketches were ready and dispatched to Moscow. A day later came Dicky's enthusiastic response. Now the theater was certain of success.

Kustodiev was constantly compelled to tear himself away from the work on *The Flea* to carry out a variety of boring commissions—book jackets, illustrations. He was extremely fatigued, but nevertheless decided that he must go to Moscow for the premiere. On February 7 or 8 he was already there. He was installed in the theater itself, in the office, next to the lobby. I remember the special tenderness that all the actors lavished on him. A veritable pilgrimage began to the office; people came singly or in groups. The work of the production, feverish now on the eve of the dress rehearsal, went on, and Boris Mikhailovich was caught up in its contagion. His chair would be wheeled into the dark, empty theater, lit only by the lamp on the director's table, and placed in the aisle. Boris Mikhailovich himself checked the sets, the light, the makeup, the costumes.

And, at last, the same wheelchair, but this time in the brightly lit theater. The sets for each act were greeted with applause. The theater won a triumph, and a large share of this triumph must, of course, be attributed to Kustodiev.

Most important of all, it seems to me, was the fact that in his work for this production Kustodiev not only won a triumph with the audience, but also a victory over himself. This was perhaps his first major work in which he completely abandoned his usual realistic manner and showed himself a great master in a realm that had seemed quite alien to him—the realm of the grotesque. But even here he remained true to his constant theme—old Russia.

In the spring of 1924 the former Alexandrinsky Theater made plans to produce *The Flea.* It was thought at first that if the theater engaged Kustodiev again, the production might turn out to be too similar to that in Moscow. Other artists were considered, but their sketches and models seemed all wrong.

Boris Mikhailovich could not imagine a production of *The Flea,* which he had come to know and love so well, without his participation. "I'll do it again, differently, if only for myself," he said to me. And, indeed, he made new sketches for sets and costumes. Of course, Kustodiev remained Kustodiev in them, but his rich imagination succeeded in finding another—equally successful—solution to the problem.

These sketches were used in the production of *The Flea* at the Bolshoi Dramatic Theater in Leningrad during the winter of 1926–27.

After the Leningrad premiere of *The Flea,* the mock society which we called the Physical-Geocentric Association (abbreviated to *Figa*) organized—a flea party! For this party I wrote a parody "The Life of the Flea," with humorous references to the author of the play, its artist, the actors, and the critics. After reading "The Life," Boris Mikhailovich jestingly threatened me: "Very well, I'll get even with you, remember."

When I saw Kustodiev next time, he had already begun his "revenge": he showed me his first two drawings for "The Life of the Flea." Mock pious, these drawings were made in the same manner—that of old Russian woodcuts—as the illustrations to "The Healing of the Novice Erasmus" but were even more graceful, sharper, lighter, and more laconic. This was, perhaps, because Kustodiev did them gaily, playing, for his own amusement.

Of the twelve drawings he planned, he was able to finish only seven. His "revenge" was never completed.

The Leningrad production of *The Flea* and the little book "The Life of the Flea" proved to be our last joint works.

My friendship with Boris Mikhailovich was especially close during the summer of 1926.

As soon as the wheels began to clatter outside on the dry pavement, as they always did in spring, Boris Mikhailovich began, as usual, to dream of travel. And, as always, there was no money for any distant journeys. "Where can I go, so that my capital will suffice? But I want real country, not a dacha near Petersburg."

I planned to spend the summer in my native town of Lebedyan, in Tambov Province, in the very heart of the central Russian black-earth belt. I invited Kustodiev to come there too, although, frankly speaking, I had no hope that anything would come of it except talk. It was a difficult journey—two nights on the train, one of them in a car with hard seats. But when I told him about the rye fields, the churches on the mountainside, the orchards heavy with ripening apples, Boris Mikhailovich caught fire and decided that he must see it all at any cost.

I left for Lebedyan earlier. Boris Mikhailovich and his family did not come until some six weeks later, in early August. I had already found lodgings for him—two rooms with a balcony in a white one-story house, with windows facing the street, which was thickly overgrown with grass. Outside the balcony wandered a white-headed calf, tied to a peg. Geese waddled importantly. On market days the geese scattered before the rattling peasant carts, women in vivid colors walked to market from neighboring villages. One end of the street led to a pale-blue belltower dating back to the reign of the empress Elizabeth in the eighteenth century and leaning like the Tower of Pisa. The other end opened on a limitless expanse of fields. This was "the real thing," genuine old Russia.

I lived in the next street, five minutes' walk from the Kustodievs. Every day, either my wife and I visited Boris Mikhailovich or he was wheeled in his chair to our garden. Sometimes we all went out into the fields, or to the banks of the Don. And I saw how greedily Boris Mikhailovich devoured everything with his starved eyes, how he rejoiced in the distances, in rainbows, faces, summer rain, ripe, ruddy apples.

That summer the fruit was especially fine in the garden of the house we lived in. We often saved a branch of apples for Boris Mikhailovich and wheeled him to it in his chair, to give him the pleasure of plucking them himself. "Yes, yes, this is just what I wanted—to pick apples myself," he would say. And, crunching an apple, he would sketch and sketch: he was particularly fond of the view from above, from our garden, across the Don.

I had seldom seen Boris Mikhailovich so gay, talkative, and full of jokes as he was all through that month. But by the end of August the weather turned cold and rainy, and Boris Mikhailovich began to complain of feeling chilly. Soon he returned home, to Leningrad. I saw him again the following winter at rehearsals of *The Flea* at the Bolshoi Dramatic Theater. By the time next summer came, Boris Mikhailovich was dead.

And so closed the circle of my meetings with Kustodiev: from the book *In Old Russia* to the living old Russia of Lebedyan. He spent his last summer with what he loved most. And this was not by chance. *Rus*—old Russia—was essentially the sole theme of all his works; he was never unfaithful to it, and it never failed him—and never will.

Some time after Kustodiev's death I happened to speak about him with one of our leading painters. He confessed to me: "You know, when he was alive, I did not really like Boris Mikhailovich's work too much. But now that he is gone, I see how much he was needed. There is no one to fill his place—it will always remain unfilled."

He was right. For Kustodiev was a unique, inimitable artist—and his remarkable, heroic life was equally unique.

1928

ANDREY BELY

The head bent over the desk is covered with a dark velvet cap. Around the cap, an aureole of fine, flying gray hair. On the desk, thick, open volumes on atomic physics, the theory of probability. Who it this? A professor of mathematics?

But strangely, the mathematician is lecturing at the Petersburg House of the Arts. Quick, flying movements of the hands, tracing curves in the air. You listen, and you find that these are the curves of rising and falling vowels. This is a brilliant lecture on the theory of versification.

Another view: the same man with hammer and chisel in hand on scaffolding in the dim cupola of a temple. He is carving out a pattern. The temple is the famous Goetheanum in Basel, built with the participation of the most dedicated adherents of anthroposophy.

And after the silence of the Goetheanum, suddenly the frenzied hubbub of a Berlin cafe, the imps of jazz squealing as they fly out of the throat of the trumpet, out of the saxophone. The man who had worked on the anthroposophic temple, his tie twisted, a slightly bewildered smile on his face, is dancing the fox-trot.

Mathematics, poetry, anthroposophy, fox-trot—these are some of the sharpest angles that make up the fantastic image of Andrey Bely, one of the most original Russian writers, who has just ended his earthly journey: he died in Moscow on a blue, snowy January day.

What he had written was as extraordinary and fantastic as his life. This is why even his novels—not to speak of his numerous

241

theoretical works—have always been read principally by the intellectual elite. He was above all "a writer's writer," a master, an inventor whose inventions have been used by many Russian novelists of the younger generations. None of the many recent anthologies of contemporary Russian literature which have appeared in various European languages fails to mention Andrey Bely.

But here we see again one of those paradoxes that abound in his biography, both personal and literary: the books of this master, the theoretician of an entire literary school, remain untranslated, and live only in their Russian incarnation.[1] I am not certain, however, whether one can properly say that they are written in Russian, so unusual is Bely's syntax, so full of neologisms his diction. The language of his books is Bely's language, just as the language of *Ulysses* is not English, but Joyce's language.

And yet another paradox. This most typical Russian writer, a direct descendant of Gogol and Dostoyevsky, has served in Russian literature as a conductor of purely French influences. Bely was one of the founders and the only serious theoretician of the Russian Symbolist school. With all the uniqueness of this literary tendency, which is closely interwoven with religious questions among the Russian intelligentsia, its ties with French Symbolism —with the names of Mallarmé, Baudelaire, and Huysmans—are beyond dispute. This alone should be enough to draw the attention of the French reader, and particularly the literary reader, to the original figure of Andrey Bely.

The fragmentary, intersecting lines with which I have sketched the contour of his portrait were dictated by the style of Bely's personality itself. He always left one with an impression of impetuosity, flight, feverish excitement. For those whose eye is accustomed to more academic lines, to dates and names, we shall supplement the sketch with a few facts to fill in the contour.

Bely's youth was dominated by two seemingly disparate, but essentially related elements—mathematics and music. The former was in his blood: he was the son of a well-known Russian professor of mathematics and studied mathematics at the same Moscow university where his father taught. Perhaps Bely would also have gone on to teach, if he had not suddenly begun to feel

[1] Some of his works have since been translated, notably his novel *Petersburg.*

the aesthetics of formulas in an entirely new way: mathematics became *audible* (this is how he expressed it himself), it transmuted itself into music. And this muse, it seemed, had captured him completely, when suddenly the erstwhile mathematician and musician   Boris Bugayev (his real name) became the poet Andrey Bely. His very first book of poems brought him into the most advanced literary circles of the time and established his close kinship with Blok, Bryusov and Merezhkovsky.

This was at the beginning of the twentieth century, during the years bordering on 1905, when the huge, rusty body of Russia shifted from its familiar, time-hallowed orbit, when the search for the new began in all the strata of Russian society. Bely was the son of this epoch, one of those restless Russian spirits, akin to Dostoyevsky's heroes, who never content themselves with that which has already been achieved. Very soon it was not enough for him to be a fashionable poet, even one of the leaders of a new literary school. He looked for an answer to the most tormenting "eternal" questions. He searched for them everywhere— at meetings of the Petersburg "Religious-Philosophical Society"; in smoke-filled rooms where students argued heatedly all night until the morning hours; in the prayer rooms of Russian sectarians and at clandestine socialist meetings; in tearooms and taverns, where some Russian pilgrim with a cross on his staff would discourse quietly to the accompaniment of the shouts of tipsy coachmen.

This motley vortex could no longer be fitted into the spare lines of a poem, and Bely went on to the novel. During those years he wrote two of his best known books, *The Silver Dove* and *Petersburg*. The former introduces the reader to the weird atmosphere ruling the life of a sect known as the Flagellants and tells the story of a refined intellectual, a poet who stumbles into this milieu and is destroyed by his encounter with the dark forces of the Russian village. As Bely himself wrote later, he took a look in this novel at "Rasputin in his initial stages" (Rasputin had indeed, as we know, emerged from the Flagellant sect). In the latter novel, Bely shows the tsarist Petersburg as a city already doomed but still beautiful with a dying, spectral loveliness. One of the masters of this Petersburg, Senator Ableukhov, is condemned to death by the revolutionaries with whom his son, a student, is connected. The plot of the novel is built around this sharp conflict. In this book, Bely's best work, Petersburg finds its true portrayer for the first time since Gogol and Dostoyevsky.

Bely spent the prerevolutionary years (1912–16) in restless wanderings in Africa and Europe. His meeting with the leader of the anthroposophists, Dr. Rudolph Steiner, proved decisive for Bely. But anthroposophy to him was not the quiet haven it is for many weary souls—to him it was merely a port of departure into the infinite spaces of cosmic philosophy and new artistic experiments. The most interesting of these was the novel *Kotik Letayev,* perhaps the only attempt in world literature to embody anthroposophic ideas in a work of art. A child's psyche is chosen as the screen that is to reflect these ideas—at the age when the first glimmerings of consciousness stir within the child, when the child steps out of the world of shadowy recollections of his pre-natal existence, the world of four dimensions, into the solid, three-dimensional world which wounds him painfully.

In postrevolutionary Russia, with its new religion of material-ism, anthroposophy was out of place, and in 1921 Bely went abroad once more. This was to him a period of "temptation in the desert": the woman he loved left him to be near Dr. Steiner; the poet remained alone in the stone vacuum of Berlin. From the anthroposophic heights he plunged down—into fox-trot, into wine. But he was not smashed, he had strength enough to rise and start life again, returning to Russia.

The hair around the cupola of his head, covered with the velvet cap, was now gray, but he was full of the same impetuous flight, the same youthful ardor. I recall one evening in Petersburg when Bely dropped in to see me "for a few moments." He was in a hurry, he had to deliver a lecture that evening. But then the con-versation touched upon a topic especially close to his heart—the crisis of culture. His eyes lit up, he squatted down and stood up, illustrating his theory of the "parallel epochs," the "spiral move-ment" of history. He spoke uninterruptedly. It was a brilliant lecture, delivered before a single listener. The others vainly waited for him in the lecture hall that evening. It was only when mid-night struck that Bely suddenly recalled himself from his flight of enthusiasm and clapped his hands in consternation.

This lecture was a chapter of his large work on the philosophy of history, on which he had been working continuously through-out the preceding years. As though already sensing the nearness of his end, he hurried in this book to sum up the results of all his restless intellectual wanderings. To my knowledge, this work remained unfinished.

The other works of his final years—the volume of memoirs, *At the Turn of the Century,* and the two novels, *Moscow* and *Masks*—were also summations. We no longer find here the fantastic, four-dimensional world of *Kotik Letayev* and *Petersburg.* These novels are built on real, partly autobiographical, material from the life of the Moscow intelligentsia during the crucial years of change in the early twentieth century. The clearly satirical approach taken by the author was a concession to the spirit of the time, which demanded disparagement of the past. But Bely's tireless formal experimentation, this time chiefly in the lexical area, continued in these last novels as well. Until the very end, he remained the "Russian Joyce."

Paris, 1934

MAXIM GORKY

They lived together, Gorky and Peshkov. Fate bound them intimately, indissolubly. They resembled one another closely, and yet they were not entirely alike. Sometimes they argued and quarreled, then they made peace and walked through life side by side. Their paths diverged only recently: in June, 1936, Alexey Peshkov died; Maxim Gorky continues to live. The man with the very ordinary Russian worker's face and the modest name of Peshkov had chosen for himself the pen name Gorky.[1]

I knew them both. But I see no need to speak about the writer Gorky. His books speak about him best of all. I should like here to recall the man with the great heart and the great biography.

There are many remarkable writers who have no biography, who pass through life only as brilliant observers. One of these, for example, was a contemporary of Gorky and one of the subtlest masters of the Russian word, Anton Chekhov. Gorky could never remain a mere observer; he always plunged into the very thick of events, he wanted to act. He was endowed with such great energy that the pages of a book confined it: it brimmed over into life. His life is itself a book, an absorbing novel.

The background against which this novel opens is extraordinarily picturesque and, I would say, symbolic.

High, serrated walls of an ancient kremlin on a steep river bank, golden crosses, and the cupolas of innumerable churches. Lower down, by the water, endless warehouses, barns, wharves, stores. Every year this was the site of a famous Russian fair,

[1] "Bitter." A romantic gesture in the spirit of the time, but rather amusing, since Gorky was not a bitter man.

where merchants went on Homeric sprees and made millions, where the long frock coats of Russian merchants mingled with Asian robes. And, finally, on the opposite bank a piece of Europe, a forest of factory chimneys, fiery maws of blast furnaces, iron bodies of ships.

This city, Nizhni Novgorod, where sixteenth- and twentieth-century Russia lived side by side, was Gorky's home town. The river on whose banks he grew up is the Volga, which produced such legendary Russian rebels as Razin and Pugachev, the Volga about which so many songs were fashioned by Russian boatmen. Gorky's first and chiefest links are to the Volga: his grandfather was a hauler here.

This was a Russian American, a self-made man. He had begun as a barge hauler and ended as an owner of three brick factories and several houses. It was in the home of this close-fisted and stern man that Gorky spent his childhood—a very short one. At the age of eight, the boy was already apprenticed to a shoemaker, thrown into the muddy river of life to swim as best he could. Such was the system of upbringing chosen by his grandfather.

After that came a dizzying succession of places of action, adventures and occupations, in close parallel with the lives of Jack London and, perhaps, even of François Villon, transported into twentieth-century Russia. Gorky was a cook's assistant on a ship, a salesman of icons (what irony!), a ragman, a baker, a stevedore, a fisherman. The Volga, the Caspian Sea, Astrakhan, the Zhigulev Mountains, the Mozdok steppes, Kazan. And later, the Don, the Ukraine, Bessarabia, the Danube, the Black Sea, the Crimea, Kuban, the mountains of the Caucasus. And all this on foot, in the company of homeless, picturesque tramps, with nights around fires on the steppe, in abandoned houses, under rowboats turned upside down. How many adventures, encounters, friendships, fights, nocturnal confessions! What material for the future writer, and what a school for the future revolutionary!

His initiation into the order of revolutionaries came at the hands of Russian students, for whom rebellion was at that time as sacred a tradition and as obligatory as their blue student's cap. This initiation took place in Kazan. There, too, Gorky met a certain professional revolutionary. This was followed by a chapter of classic "going to the people." Gorky went to a village and worked there as a salesman in a grocery store. But, of course, the roles of both "salesman" and "employer" were merely conspiratorial disguises permitting them to conduct propaganda among the peasants. The object of their propaganda, however, was evidently badly chosen: one dark night the peasants set fire to our conspirators' hut, and they barely managed to get out alive. This night may have sown the seeds of Gorky's antipathy toward the Russian village and the peasant, and turned him toward the city and the urban proletarian.

Several years later this romantic vagabond published a book of stories, revealing to the astonished reader not only a hitherto unknown world of tramps, but also an entire system of anarchist philosophy professed by these stepchildren of society. "Sign painter Alexey Peshkov," as he was identified in his passport, became Maxim Gorky. He immediately became one of the most popular writers in Russia, especially among left-wing youth circles and the intelligentsia.

Now, it would seem, he could forget hazardous adventures and quietly harvest his laurels. But his restless bargeman's blood was too fiery for that: not long after Gorky's book appeared, the revolutionary Peshkov was arrested by the gendarmes and sent to the "scene of his crime," Tiflis, where he was imprisoned in the Metekhsky tower. The imprisonment did not last long, Gorky was released—only to find himself soon afterward in a Nizhni Novgorod jail, and thence to be deported to a remote village.

These misadventures of Peshkov were an additional stimulus to the rapid growth of Gorky's fame among the rebellious intelligentsia. At the age of thirty-odd years, he was already elected a member of the Imperial Academy of Sciences. A revolutionary, a former tramp—and a member of the Imperial Academy? This was scandalous. The election was annuled by order of the emperor Nicholas II, who wrote across the Academy's report, "Most original!"

His Majesty showed undeniable foresight: several years later, during the first Russian revolution, in 1905, Gorky was imprisoned in the famous fortress of Peter and Paul. It would, of course, have been rather awkward to lock up an academician.

The following chapters of Gorky's life took place abroad. He became a political émigré, cut off from Russia and his native Volga, which he loved so much. He was able to return only shortly before the revolution of 1917.

During the war, I spent almost two years in England, where I was sent as an engineer, to supervise the construction of ice-breakers ordered by the Russian government. I returned to Petersburg only in the fall of 1917, and it was then that I met Gorky for the first time. It so happened that I met both Gorky and the Revolution at the same time. Therefore, the image of Gorky is bound in my memory with the new, postrevolutionary Russia.

A small, white room, the office of the editor of the journal *Letopis* [Annals]. An autumn evening in Petersburg. Occasional gunshots in the street. The editor is, evidently, accustomed to this accompaniment, and it does not interfere with the lively conversation.

This editor is Gorky, but the topic of the conversation is by no means literary. The question of my story has already been settled. Gorky liked it, and it has gone to type. But the icebreakers I had built, and technology, and my lectures on naval architecture—"Damn it! I swear I envy you. And I will die a mathematical illiterate. A shame, what a shame!"

A self-taught man who had spent only six months in primary school, Gorky never stopped studying all his life and was widely informed. But toward subjects he did not know, he always had a touching, childishly respectful attitude. I have observed this in him many times.

The shots outside the window came nearer. I recalled the German zeppelin and airplane raids over England and spoke about the methods used there to fight the raids. This, again, was new to Gorky—something he did not know, and, surely, had to know. But his secretary had more than once looked in on us with letters and galley proofs. "Look, if you can wait a little, let's go and have dinner at my place, eh?" Gorky suggested.

He lived on the top floor of a huge house. A short distance away, to the right, could be seen from the window the gray walls and golden spire of the fortress of Peter and Paul.

There were two hosts: Gorky and his second wife, M. F. Andreyeva, a former actress of the Moscow Art Theater. But there were ten or twelve guests around the table. Some of them, as I learned later, not without astonishment, had been living in Gorky's home as "guests" for a number of years—as had once been the custom in the homes of Russian landed gentry.

When Gorky was with a new acquaintance who had in some way aroused his interest, he could be as captivating as a woman. All he needed to do was launch into the story of some of his adventures and encounters. He was an excellent raconteur; the people he spoke about came alive and joined us at the table—they could be seen and heard. Some of these people I met later in Gorky's book, and it seemed to me that Peshkov had told about them even more vividly that evening than Gorky did in his book.

Three or four weeks later the scattered gunshots which had accompanied my first meeting with Gorky turned into the chattering of machine guns and the deep booming of cannon. Fighting was going on in the streets of Petersburg—it was the October Revolution. The huge ship of Russia had been torn from the shore by the storm and carried off into the unknown. No one, including the new captains, knew whether the ship would be dashed to splinters or reach some unfamiliar continent.

One morning, sitting in Gorky's book-filled office, I told him about an idea for a fantastic novel which had come to me during those days. The scene of action was to be a stratoplane on an interplanetary flight. Not far from the goal, there was to be a catastrophe—the interplanetary plane would begin to fall precipitately. But the fall was to last a year and a half. At first, naturally, my heroes were panic-stricken. But how would they behave afterwards? "I'll tell you how," Gorky said, his moustache twitching slyly. "A week later they will be calmly shaving, writing books, and generally behaving as if they had at least twenty more years to live. And, by God, that's as it should be. We must believe that we won't be shattered, otherwise we're lost."

And he believed it.

The writer Gorky was sacrificed: for several years he became a kind of unofficial minister of culture, organizer of public works for the derailed, starving intelligentsia. These works were like the building of a Tower of Babel; they were planned for decades ahead: a publishing house, World Literature, to publish the classics of all times and all nations in Russian translation; a Committee for Historical Plays, to dramatize no more and no less than all the major events of world history; the House of the Arts,

to unite artists of every kind; the House of Scientists, to unite
all scientists and scholars.

In the capital, which was already without bread, light, or streetcars, in the atmosphere of collapse and catastrophe, these ideas
seemed utopian at best. But Gorky believed in them ("we must
believe") and managed to infect the skeptical Petersburg intellectuals with his faith. Academicians, poets, professors, translators,
playwrights—all of them began to work in the institutions created
by Gorky, with ever-increasing enthusiasm.

I found myself on the leading committees of three or four of
these institutions, in all of which Gorky invariably served as
president. I met him very often at that time, and I wondered
more than once how many hours this man had in a single day.
Always coughing into his smoke-yellowed moustache, half his
lungs destroyed by tuberculosis, where did he find the strength
for all that he was doing? One day I asked him about it. With a
mysterious air, he led me to a sideboard, took out a small dark
vial, and explained that it contained the essence of a wonder-
working Chinese root called ginseng. It had been brought to him
by an admirer from Manchuria. But, I am sure, it would be more
accurate to say that the wonder drug was really his faith.

Something else remains in my memory: the calmness and confidence with which he presided over meetings of professors and
academicians. It would never have occurred to an outside observer that this man who cited names and dates with such ease
(he had an extraordinary memory) was a self-educated former
tramp. The only thing that distinguished him from the rest was
his peculiar pronunciation (to put it mildly) of foreign words
and names; he did not know a single foreign language.

One of Gorky's ideas at that time was to publish a hundred
volumes of the best works by Russian writers, beginning with
Chekhov. I mention this relatively modest undertaking because
it gave me the opportunity to witness a rather curious situation—
Gorky as a critic of Gorky.

There was no lack of flatterers around Gorky in those days.
At a meeting of the editors of "100 Volumes," one of them
launched into an enthusiastic enumeration of Gorky's works, gar-
nishing each title with a plentiful sauce of compliments. Gorky

1920   ю. Анненкоb.

Maxim Gorky

looked down, angrily pulling at his moustache. When the speaker named his famous poem in prose, "Song of the Stormy Petrel"—an early work—Gorky interrupted him: "You must be joking. I cannot even think of this piece without embarrassment—it is a very weak poem." When several of Gorky's plays were named, again with compliments, he broke in once more: "Excuse me, gentlemen, but the author you are discussing is a poor playwright. With the exception of one play, *The Lower Depths,* everything else, in my opinion, is worthless."

Much later I witnessed another incident of the same kind, but this time altogether humorous. A rather brash young man, belonging to one of the "proletarian" groups, was visiting Gorky. When asked what he was working on, the guest replied that he had begun a three-volume novel but abandoned it: "In our dynamic age only idiots write three-volume novels." Gorky responded with utmost calm: "Yes. They're saying, you know, that Gorky is also writing the third volume of his *Klim Samgin.*"

The young writer was ready to sink through the earth. But in Gorky's jesting tone there was also a painful awareness of his failure with this last, enormous novel.

Perhaps the best thing written by Gorky after the revolution were his remarkable recollections about Lev Tolstoy. To me, this work is particularly memorable; it opened before me a door to Gorky's inner world, those spiritual apartments to which we are reluctant to admit strangers.

At one of the literary evenings in Petersburg, the "main attraction" was the appearance of Gorky, who was to read his still unpublished recollections of Tolstoy. Tall, lean, somewhat stooped, he stood on the stage. The glasses he put on for the reading aged him suddenly by ten years. From my place in the first row I could see every movement he made. As he was coming to the end of his reading, something strange came over him: it seemed that he could no longer see through his glasses. He began to stumble and halt. Then he pulled off his glasses. And we saw tears rolling down his face. He sobbed aloud, muttered "Forgive me," and walked out into the next room. This was not the writer and old revolutionary, Gorky, but simply a man unable to speak calmly about another man's death.

I know that Gorky the man is remembered by many people

with gratitude, in Russia and particularly in Petersburg. Dozens of people are indebted to him for their lives and their freedom.

Everyone knew that Gorky and Lenin were close friends, and that Gorky was closely acquainted with the other revolutionary leaders. And at the time when the revolution had adopted the methods of terror, the last point of appeal, the last hope of many, was Gorky. Wives and mothers of arrested men came to him. He wrote letters, argued over the telephone, and, in the most serious cases, took trips to Moscow himself, to see Lenin. Many times his attempts at intervention failed. Once I asked Gorky to help an acquaintance who had fallen into the hands of Cheka. On his return from Moscow, Gorky told me, puffing angrily at his cigarette, that Lenin had reprimanded him. "It's time you knew," said Lenin, "that politics is generally a dirty business, and you had better stay out of it."

But Gorky could not stay out.

It is my impression that the policy of terror during those years was one of the main causes of Gorky's temporary break with the Bolsheviks and his departure abroad.

A short time before his departure, as I was returning from Moscow to Petersburg, I met Gorky on the same train. It was late at night, and everyone in our compartment was asleep. We stood together in the corridor for a long time, watching the sparks flying outside the black window, and talking about the great Russian poet Gumilyov, who had been shot several months before. Gumilyov was alien to Gorky both in his literary and in his political views. Nevertheless, Gorky had done everything possible to save him. He told me that he had already succeeded in obtaining a promise in Moscow to spare Gumilyov's life, but the Petersburg authorities had somehow learned of it and hastened to carry out the sentence at once. I had never seen Gorky so upset as he was that night.

A year and a half later, when I was spending the summer in a remote Russian village, I came across an issue of a provincial Communist newspaper with a bold headline, "Gorky Is Dead!" The headline proved to be the prank of some journalist "wit": the article dealt with the "political death" of Gorky, who had just published abroad a protest in connection with the trial in Moscow of a group of Socialist Revolutionaries.

This was the culminating point of Gorky's quarrel with the Bolsheviks. And not only with them, but also with himself, because unquestionably, in addition to being "Peshkov," a man with an almost femininely soft heart, he was also a Bolshevik.

When the Revolution went on from the period of ruthless destruction to the building of a new life, Gorky returned to Russia. The things that caused his departure had evidently been forgotten. When I tried to take a look inside him and find out what "Peshkov" thought (or, rather, felt) now, I received this answer: "*They* have very great goals. And this justifies everything to me."

In a recent article about the new Russian novel (in *Marianne*), I called Gorky "le papa de la littérature soviétique." A curious typographical error turned "papa" into "pape." By a strange coincidence, this error repeated almost precisely what Gorky used to say about himself in jest: he called himself a "literary chief priest."

It seems to me that this jest is the most accurate description of Gorky's position in Soviet literature. There were, of course, many writers who came to Gorky to "kiss the papal slipper." Gorky was bored with such pious pilgrims and hurried to get rid of them. "Stares at me as if I were some idiot in a bemedaled uniform," he commented angrily about one of these visitors. But the majority of writers came to him not as to a man with literary medals or a literary authority, but simply as to a man—they came not to Gorky, but to Peshkov.

I witnessed the beginning and development of Gorky's friendship with a group of young Petersburg writers called the Serapion Brethren, with which I was also closely connected. This group originated in the Petersburg House of the Arts, where Gorky had succeeded, in the early revolutionary period, in organizing a kind of literary university (I was one of the lecturers there). When several talented writers emerged from among the students of this university, Gorky felt like a happy father; he fussed over them like a hen over her chicks. And a very touching relationship continued between them and Gorky even later, when the chicks grew up and became virtually the classics of the new Soviet prose.

It is very interesting that, in a literary sense, this entire group of writers was more "left" than Gorky. It sought new forms—

and it certainly did not seek them in Gorky's realism. Their attitude toward Gorky was therefore all the more revealing: it was truly love for the man.

For this group, as for all Soviet writers who were not Communists but only Fellow Travelers, the years between 1927 and 1932 were the most difficult period. Soviet literature had fallen under the command—it is difficult to describe it by any other word—of the organization of "proletarian writers" (in the Soviet code language, the RAPP). Their principal talent was their party card and their purely military decisiveness. These energetic young men took upon themselves the task of immediate "reeducation" of all the other writers. Naturally, nothing good came of this. Some of the writers subject to "reeducation" became silent; the works of others betrayed obvious false notes which jarred even the least demanding ear. Anecdotes about the censorship multiplied, and dissatisfaction grew among the Fellow Travelers.

I spoke about this many times during my meetings with Gorky. He smoked silently, biting his moustache. At times he stopped me, saying: "Wait a moment. I must make a note about this incident."

The meaning of these notes did not become clear to me until much later, in 1932. In April of that year, a genuine literary revolution occurred, surprising everyone: by government decree, the activity of the RAPP was declared to "hamper the development of Soviet literature," and the organization was disbanded. The only man to whom this did not come as a surprise was Gorky: I am convinced that it was he who had prepared this action, and he had done it like a highly skilled diplomat.

At that time he no longer lived in Petersburg but had moved to Moscow. In the city proper, the house of the millionnaire Ryabushinsky was placed at his disposal. But Gorky stayed there infrequently, spending most of his time at a summer home about one hundred kilometers from Moscow. Stalin's summer home was nearby, and he took to visiting his "neighbor" Gorky with increasing frequency. The "neighbors," one with his invariable pipe, the other with a cigarette, closeted themselves for hours, talking over a bottle of wine.

I believe that it will not be inaccurate to say that the correction of many "excesses" in the policy of the Soviet government, and the gradual softening of the dictatorship's rule resulted from these friendly talks. Gorky's role in this will surely be recognized at some time in the future.

I shall not expand here on the reasons why and how I had come to see that it was best for me to go abroad for a time. In those years, it was not easy for a writer with my reputation as a "heretic" to obtain a passport for foreign travel. I asked Gorky to intervene in my behalf. He begged me to wait until spring (of 1931). "You will see, everything will change." In the spring nothing changed, and Gorky, rather reluctantly, agreed to secure permission for me to go abroad.

One day Gorky's secretary telephoned to say that Gorky wished me to have dinner with him in the evening at his country home. I remember clearly that extraordinarily hot day and the rainstorm—a tropical downpour—in Moscow. Gorky's car sped through a wall of water, bringing me and several other invited guests to dinner at his home.

It was a "literary" dinner, and close to twenty people sat around the table. At first Gorky was silent, visibly tired. Everybody drank wine, but his glass contained water—he was not allowed to drink wine. After a while, he rebelled, poured himself a glass of wine, then another and another, and became the old Gorky.

The storm ended, and I walked out onto the large stone terrace. Gorky followed me immediately and said to me: "The affair of your passport is settled. But if you wish, you can return the passport and stay." I said that I would go. Gorky frowned and went back to his other guests in the dining room.

It was late. Some of the guests remained overnight; others, including myself, were returning to Moscow. In parting, Gorky asked: "When shall we meet again? If not in Moscow, then perhaps in Italy? If I go there, you must come to see me! In any case, until we meet again, eh?"

This was the last time I saw Gorky.

I had, however, still one more meeting with Gorky, a purely literary one, and at a distance. This happened quite recently. About six weeks before his death, a film company in Paris decided to do a film of Gorky's famous play *The Lower Depths* from my scenario. Gorky was informed of this, and wrote that he was pleased at my participation in the project, that he would like to see the adaptation of his play and would wait to receive the manuscript.

The manuscript was never sent: by the time it was ready for mailing, Gorky was dead.

1936

H. G. WELLS

I

The laciest, most Gothic of cathedrals are, after all, made of stone. The most marvelous, most fantastic fairy tales of any country are, after all, made of the earth, the trees, the animals of that country. In woodland tales, there is the wood goblin, shaggy and gnarled as a pine, hooting like a forest echo. In tales of the steppes, there is the magical white camel, flying like storm-driven sand. In tales of the Arctic regions, there is the shaman-whale and the polar bear with a body of mammoth tusks. But imagine a country where the only fertile soil is asphalt, where nothing grows but dense forests of factory chimneys, where the animal herds are of a single breed, automobiles, and the only fragrance in the spring is that of gasoline. This place of stone, asphalt, iron, gasoline, and machines is present-day, twentieth-century London, and, naturally, it was bound to produce its own iron, automobile goblins, and its own mechanical, chemical fairy tales. Such urban tales exist: they are told by Herbert George Wells. They are his fantastic novels.

The city, the huge modern city, full of the roar, din, and buzzing of propellers, electric wires, wheels, advertisements, is everywhere in H. G. Wells. The present-day city, with its uncrowned king, the machine—as an explicit or implicit function—is an invariable component of every fantastic novel written by Wells, of every equation in his myths; and this is precisely what his myths are—logical equations.

Wells began with the mechanism, the machine. His first novel, *The Time Machine,* is the modern city version of the tale of the flying carpet, and the fairy-tale tribes of morlocks and eloi are, of course, the two warring classes of the modern city, extrapolated, with their typical characteristics heightened to the point of the grotesque. *A Story of the Days to Come* is a look at the present city through the monstrously enlarging telescope of irony. Everything here rushes with fabulous speed—machines, machines, machines, airplanes, turbine wheels, deafening gramophones, flickering fiery advertisements. In *When the Sleeper Awakes,* once again airplanes, electric lines, searchlights, armies of workers, syndicates. In *The War in the Air,* again airplanes, swarms of airplanes and dirigibles, herds of dreadnoughts. In *The War of the Worlds,* London, London trains, automobiles, crowds, and that product of asphalt, the most typical city goblin —the Martian, a steel, hinge-jointed, mechanical goblin, with a mechanical siren, to call and to hoot in a manner befitting one who performs the duties of a goblin. In *The World Set Free,* we see the city version of the legendary bursting grass,[1] but this bursting grass is not found in a clearing in the woods on Midsummer night; it is found in the laboratory, and is called atomic energy. In *The Invisible Man,* there is chemistry again—the present-day, urban, chemical invisible cap. Even when Wells seems for a moment to be untrue to himself and takes you from the city to the woods, the fields, or a farm, you hear the hum of machines and smell the odors of chemical reactions. In *The First Men in the Moon,* you find yourself on an isolated farm in Kent, but you discover dynamos in the cellar, a gasometer in the arbor, and workshops and laboratories in all the outbuildings. In *The Food of the Gods,* a little house in the forest turns out to be a laboratory of experimental physiology. No matter how much he may wish to get away from asphalt, Wells still remains on asphalt, among machines, in the laboratory. The modern chemical-mechanical city, enmeshed in wire and cables, is the very foundation of H. G. Wells, and all he writes is woven on this foundation, with all its fanciful and, at first glance, paradoxical and contradictory patterns.

The motifs of the Wellsian urban fairy tales are essentially the same as those encountered in all other fairy tales: the invisible cap, the flying carpet, the bursting grass, the self-setting table-

---

[1] In Russian folklore a magical plant that blooms briefly on Midsummer night and is believed to open all locks and reveal hidden treasure.

cloth, dragons, giants, gnomes, mermaids, and man-eating monsters. But the difference between his tales and, let us say,ours, is the difference between the psychology of a Poshekhonian[2] and that of a Londoner: our Russian Poshekhonian sits down at the window and waits until the invisible cap and the flying carpet come to him magically, "at the pike's behest"; the Londoner does not rely on "the pike's behest," he relies on himself. He sits down at the drawing board, takes the slide rule, and calculates a flying carpet. He goes to the laboratory, fires the electric furnace and invents the bursting grass. The Poshekhonian reconciles himself to his wonders happening twenty-seven lands and forty kingdoms away. The Londoner wants his wonders today, right now, right here. And therefore he chooses the trustiest road to his fairy tales —a road paved with astronomic, physical, and chemical formulas, a road rolled flat and solid by the cast-iron laws of the exact sciences. This may seem paradoxical at first—exact science and fairy tale, precision and fantasy. But it is so, and must be so. For a myth is always, openly or implicitly, connected with religion, and the religion of the modern city is precise science. Hence, the natural link between the newest urban myth, urban fairy tale, and science. And I do not know whether there is a single major branch of the exact sciences that has not been reflected in Wells's fantastic novels. Mathematics, astronomy, astrophysics, physics, chemistry, medicine, physiology, bacteriology, mechanics, electrotechnology, aviation. Almost all of Wells's fairy tales are built upon brilliant and most unexpected scientific paradoxes. All his myths are as logical as mathematical equations. And this is why we, modern men, we, skeptics, are conquered by these logical fantasies, this is why they command our attention and win our belief.

Wells brings the reader into an atmosphere of the miraculous, of the fairy tale, with extraordinary cunning. Carefully, gradually, he leads you up from one logical step to the next. The transition from step to step is quite imperceptible; trustingly, without realizing it, you mount higher and higher. And suddenly, you look back and gasp, but it is too late: you already believe what had seemed, from the title, absolutely impossible, totally absurd. Take any of Wells's fantasies at random, let us say, *The In-*

[2] The reference is to *Old Times in Poshekhonie,* M. Y. Saltykov-Shchedrin's satirical stories about the Russian province.

visible Man. What nonsense! How can we, who live in the twentieth century, believe in such a child's fairy tale as an invisible man?

But wait: what is invisibility? Invisibility is nothing more than the simplest, most realistic phenomenon, subject to the laws of physics, the laws of optics. And it depends on the capacity to absorb or reflect light rays. A piece of glass is transparent; the same piece of glass in water is invisible. And if we grind the glass into powder, the powder will be white, it will be opaque, it will be clearly visible. Consequently, the same substance may be either visible or invisible; everything depends on the condition of its surface. You will say: yes, but man is living substance. What of that? Among the creatures in the seas are jellyfish, almost invisible; some of the marine larvae are entirely transparent. You may say: Yes, but those are larvae, and this is man—two very different things. But do you know that, already today, medicine uses transparent or partly transparent anatomic preparations of the human body for purposes of study and instruction? I can even name you the man who developed this method; he is a German, Professor Spalterholtz. And if we can make one hand transparent, we can make two hands transparent; and if we can do it with two hands, we can do it with the entire body. And if science has succeeded in achieving this transparency in a dead body, perhaps it will succeed in achieving it in a living body as well? After all, transparency, visibility, a living organism—these are not in any way mutually incompatible concepts; we have seen that. And hence . . . And you are already thinking: "Who knows, perhaps, it may well be so." And you are already enmeshed, you are hitched to the steel locomotive of logic, and it will carry you along the rails of the fantastic wherever Wells may choose.

In the same way, in *The Island of Dr. Moreau,* Wells will compel your belief in a surgeon who transforms animals into men by skillful operations. He will compel your belief in the sleeper who awakes one hundred years later; in Cavorite, a substance that shields you from the earth's gravity, and in the possibility— already quite obvious—of making a perfectly easy journey to the moon in an apparatus constructed of this Cavorite; in the invention of Herakleophorbia, which increases the growth of humans, plants, and animals to giant dimensions. He will compel your belief in the possibility of traveling not only in space, but also in time; in a war with the Martians; in a siren who walked out of the sea onto the beach of a seaside resort; in the country of the blind; in a new accelerator; in Mr. Plattner's adventure in the fourth dimension. He will compel you to believe that any of his fantasies is not a fantasy, but reality—if not today, then tomorrow.

And, indeed, in our era, an era of the most improbable, most incredible scientific miracles, how can one say that this or that is impossible? Thirty years ago people would have laughed at anyone who seriously spoke of the possibility of flying from London to Paris, from Paris to Rome, from New York to Australia. Thirty years ago, only fairy tales could speak of the things we read about in our newspapers today—about a wireless telephone, about someone speaking into some sort of a transmitter in London and being clearly audible in New York. Thirty years ago no one would have believed that you can see through opaque objects; today every schoolboy knows about X rays. And who knows, perhaps in another thirty years, or in ten, or in five, we shall look as calmly at a machine departing for the moon as we now look at an airplane, barely visible, a dark speck in the sky.

The Wellsian fantasies are perhaps fantastic only today, and will become ordinary, everyday matters tomorrow. Indeed, many of Wells's fantasies have already been realized, since Wells has the strange gift of seeing the future through the opaque curtain of the present day. But, on the other hand, it is not quite so: his foreknowledge is not any stranger than a differential equation which allows us to know beforehand where a shell fired at a given speed will land; it is no stranger than the astronomer's prediction of a solar eclipse on such and such a date, at such and such an hour. There is no mysticism here, only logic; but this logic is bolder and is applied at greater range than usual.

Let us transport ourselves into the old London, the London of twenty-five years ago. It seems such a short time ago, and yet these twenty-five years are a century: dignified coachmen in top hats, with long whips, sit on their high boxes in the back. Horses, their hooves clop-clopping on the stone, draw clattering trams up and down the street. A jackdaw lazily flaps its wings in the sky. The sky is cloudless. It is the blessed reign of Queen Victoria; everything is firmly set in the world, and continually hardening, hardening, hardening. There will never again be any wars, revolutions, disasters. And Wells is, perhaps, the only one to see, through all that quiet and serenity, the violent, madly rushing life we know today.

At that time, when the first automobiles were just beginning to crawl along the streets, when they existed only to amuse the street urchins, Wells was already describing with amazing accuracy, in his book *Anticipations,* today's rushing London street, crowded with taxis, buses, trucks—a street where there is as little opportunity to see a horse as there is to see a gentleman in a silk hat in a Russian street today.

In the sky, too, Wells saw something altogether different. Only the most reckless dreamers thought of airplanes at that time. Somewhere in America Hiram Maxim's contraption, the ancestor of the modern airplane, was clumsily making running starts on rails. But Wells, in his novel *When the Sleeper Awakes,* already heard, high in the sky, the hum of passenger and military planes; he already saw battles between aerial squadrons, and airfields everywhere.

This was in 1893. And in 1908, when no one seriously entertained any thought of a European war, he discerned in the seemingly unclouded sky unprecedented, monstrous storm clouds. In that year he wrote his *War in the Air.* Here are a few lines from it, pregnant with prophecy:

> Everywhere went the airships dropping bombs . . . And everywhere below were economic catastrophe, starving workless people, rioting and social disorder . . . towns and cities with the food supply interrupted and their streets congested with starving unemployed . . . crises in administration and states of siege . . . provisional Governments and Councils of Defence and insurrectionary committees taking charge of the rearming of the population. . . . Money vanished into vaults, into holes, into walls of houses, into ten million hiding places. Money vanished, and at its disappearance trade and industry came to an end. The economic world staggered and fell dead. . . . It was like the water vanishing out of the blood of a living creature, it was a sudden, universal coagulation of intercourse. . . . Every organized government in the world was as shattered and broken as a heap of china beaten with a stick. . . . Every-

where there are ruins and unburied dead, and shrunken, yellow-faced survivors in a mortal apathy. . . . It is a universal dissolution.

And, amid the crashing din of the collapsing old civilization, details so familiar to us: aerial battles, airplanes, zeppelins, night raids, panic, lights put out, sky criss-crossed with searchlights, the gradual disappearance of books and newspapers; instead of newspapers, absurd, contradictory rumors; and, in the end, people lapsed back into savagery, huddling in dark, ruined buildings, expending all their energies in the primitive struggle with hunger and cold. All this is told by a man who seems already to have lived through our era. In 1908 this novel was fantastic; today it has become a realistic story of daily life.

The picture of the coming world war and the unprecedented world change connected with it evidently haunted Wells continually, for he returns to this theme time and again. Take his wonderful tale, *The War of the Worlds,* written in 1898. If you read it now, after the World War and the Revolution, how many familiar voices you will hear from behind the fairy-tale masks. Here is a battle with Martians. The Martians have outstripped man in technology, and their missiles "smashed on striking the ground— they did not explode—and disengaged an enormous volume of heavy, inky vapor, coiling and pouring upward in a huge and ebony cloud, a gaseous hill that sank and spread itself slowly over the surrounding country. And the touch of that vapor, the inhaling of its pungent wisps, was death to all that breathes."

Where is this from?—a fantastic novel written twenty years ago, or a newspaper of 1915–16, when the Germans first released their poison gases?

And again a world war, in the novel *In the Days of the Comet,* and the prophecy that this war will end in a radical transformation of human psychology, that it will end in a brotherly union of mankind. And once again, a world war, the last war, in the novel *The World Set Free.* Here we even find an exact indication of the warring alliances: the Central European powers attack the Slav Confederacy and France and England come out in defense of this confederacy.

In *The World Set Free* the whole self-devouring power of the old civilization is given in a single compact, concentrated symbol

—atomic energy. It is the energy which binds together with tremendous force the atoms of matter, the energy which makes the strongest steel of atomic steel particles, the energy which is slowly liberated during the mysterious transformation of radium into other elements.

The future envisioned by Wells for atomic energy parallels the history of the airplane: having mastered atomic energy, man uses it not only—or, to be more precise, not so much—for constructive, as for destructive ends. During the universal war described in *The World Set Free,* atomic bombs demolish entire cities and countries, annihilate the old civilization itself. And on its ruins, a new civilization is beginning to rise—on new foundations.

The task of construction is undertaken by a World Council, which creates a World Republic. The council abolishes parliamentarism in the form of parliaments in each individual country. After a short period of full control, in which it carries out initial organizational work, the council proclaims worldwide elections to a single world government. The council introduces a single monetary system for the whole world, develops a single world language, raises the level of development of the backward agricultural class, and reorganizes agriculture itself along collective lines. The council liberates the world from economic exploitation and at the same time "secures freedom of inquiry, freedom of criticism, free communication." The council itself gradually reduces its own power to naught, leading the world to a free life in which there are no governments, to an era which in Wells's fantastic world history is called "the Age of Efflorescence." The overwhelming majority of the citizens are artists of every kind; the overwhelming majority of the population is engaged in the highest form of human activity, the creative arts.

And, finally, in 1922, when the nations of Europe have gradually begun to heal the cruel wounds of the World War, Wells, in one of his latest novels, *Men like Gods,* leads the reader off into the happy land of Utopia where all men are brothers.

In all the Wellsian prophecies the reader has perhaps already caught a glimpse of yet another feature of his fantasy, a feature indissolubly bound with the city, that stone soil where Wells has all his roots. For, after all, the modern urban man is inevitably a *zoon politican,* a social animal: hence the social elements woven, almost without exception, into each of Wells's fantasies. Whatever tale he may be telling, however far it may at first glance seem to be from social questions, the reader will inescapably be brought to face these questions.

Take, for example, *The First Men in the Moon.* What could be further from the earth and from everything that happens here? You are rushing through space with the heroes of the novel in the Cavorite apparatus, you land on the moon, you travel in lunar valleys, you descend into lunar caverns. And suddenly, to your astonishment, you find that our own terrestrial social ills exist on the moon as well. The same division into classes, the rulers and the ruled. But here the workers have already turned into some sort of humpbacked spiders, and during periods when they do not work they are simply put to sleep and stacked in the lunar caverns like firewood, until they are needed again.

In *The Time Machine* we have hurtled with the author across a span of eighty thousand years—and again we find there our own two worlds: the underground world of the workers, and the aboveground world of the idle. Both classes have degenerated, one from exhausting labor, the other from exhausting idleness. And the class struggle has assumed cruel, brutish forms. In the year 80,000, the degenerate descendants of the exploited classes devour their "bourgeois" in simple animal fashion. In the grotesque images of the merciless mirror of Wellsian fantasy we once again recognize ourselves, our own time, the consequences of the same ills as those which plague the aged European civilization.

The "Sleeper" has slept two hundred years. Then he awakes— and what does he find? Again the same thing, the present city, the present social order, except that the abyss between white and black is infinitely deeper, and the workers, led by the awakened "Sleeper," rebel against capital. We open *A Story of the Days to Come*—the sharpest, most ironic of Wells's grotesques—and once again we see a magnificent parody on modern civilization. And, finally, *The War in the Air* and *The World Set Free,* with their detailed analysis of the era preceding the World War, an era when billions were spent on dreadnoughts, zeppelins, cannons, an era when mountains of explosives were accumulated in the cellars of the palace of the old civilization, while above them—strange as it may seem to us now—people lived, worked, and made merry without a thought or care. With extraordinary persuasion, Wells shows that the World War was only the natural conclusion of the syllogism of the old civilization. Louder than anywhere else, Wells calls upon people in these novels to bethink themselves before it is too late; he calls upon them to remember that they are not Englishmen, Frenchmen, or Germans, but men, and he urges them to rebuild life upon different principles.

We have not yet named these principles. But the reader has, no doubt, already guessed the word that has not been spoken aloud. These principles are, of course, the principles of socialism, and Wells is, of course, a socialist. This is beyond question. Yet if any political party should attempt to use Wells as a rubber stamp for its program, it would be much like attempting to affirm Orthodox Christianity by reference to Tolstoy or Rozanov.

I am not comparing Wells with Tolstoy. As artists, they are altogether different in magnitude. Yet Wells, too, is above all an artist. And every artist of importance creates his own world, with its own laws—creates it in his own shape and image, and no one else's. This is why it is difficult to fit the artist into a world that has already been created, a seven-day, fixed and solidified world: he will inevitably slip out of the set laws and paragraphs, he will be a heretic.

Wells, I repeat, is above all an artist, and this is why everything in his work is his own, and his socialism is also his own, Wellsian. In an autobiographical remark, he says that he has always been a socialist, but not a Marxian. Socialism to him is not a matter of strategy or class struggle. It is a plan for the reorganization of man's life, replacing disorder with order.

The purpose of social reconstruction, as he sees it, is to introduce into life an organizing principle—*ratio*—reason. Hence, Wells assigns a particularly important role in this reconstruction to the class of "capable men," and particularly to educated men, to scientists and technologists. He develops this theory in his *Anticipations*. His idea assumes a still more interesting—and, we must add, more heretical—color in *The New Utopia*, where leaders in the new life are called *samurai*, and where the new world is presented as a society built to a certain extent on aristocratic principles, a society led by a spiritual aristocracy.

There is yet another distinguishing feature in Wells's socialism, and it is, perhaps, more national than personal. Socialism to Wells is unquestionably a way toward curing the cancer which has eaten into the organism of the old world. But medicine knows two methods of fighting this disease: one is the knife, surgery; the other, slower one, is therapy. Wells prefers the latter.

The English, says Wells, are a parodoxical people, progressive and extremely conservative at the same time. They are constantly changing, but without any dramatic trappings. They have never known any sudden coups or revolutions. They have never "overthrown," "overturned," "destroyed," or "started everything from the beginning," as almost every other European nation has. Wells's banner is not reddened by blood. Human life, human blood are to Wells inviolate, because he is above all a humanist. It is precisely for this reason that he knows how to find such sharp, convincing words when he speaks of the classes condemned to hopeless toil and want, of man's hate for man, of the killing of man by man, of war and capital punishment. To Wells, no one is guilty; there is no evil will, there is only an evil way of life. Men may be pitied, they may be despised; but they must be loved— they may not be hated.

This idea found its most graphic expression in his novel, *In the Days of the Comet.* The hero of the novel is a young socialist worker, a simple man; he is convinced that there is a cruel, heartless plot against the poor. He is full of primitive hate, he is obsessed with thoughts of revenge upon the malicious plotters. But later the humanist Wells makes his hero confess: "You will consider those notions of my youth poor silly violent stuff, particularly if you are of the younger generation born since the Change." The Great Change itself, which had taken place under the influence of the marvelous "green vapor" brought by the comet that had collided with the earth, has made people organically incapable of hating and killing, has led them, organically and inevitably, to love. A similar idyllic transition from the Age of Confusion to happy utopia occurs in the novel, *Men like Gods.*

The same humanism is encountered in Wells's novel *War in the Air:* it will suffice to join the author in witnessing a scene like that of the execution of a member of the German air force, to see it with his eyes. This humanism is found again in *The Island of Dr. Moreau,* in which the doctor himself becomes the victim of one of his cruel experiments. And in *The Invisible Man,* where Wells cannot forgive his utopian genius for murdering people. And in *The Time Machine,* in that merciless caricature—the cannibal morlocks.

This is what reveals itself to us as we enter those fantastic edifices, Wells's fairy tales. We find there, side by side, mathematics and myths, physics and fantasy, blueprints and miracles, parody and prophecy, fairy tales and socialism. When we descend from the towers beyond the clouds to the lower floors, when we go on from Wells's fantastic novels to his realistic works—to the middle period of his creative life—we shall no longer find these strange juxtapositions. Here Wells is solidly on the ground, entirely in the firm world of three dimensions. And it was only in his last novels, written during the days when the three-dimensional world went spinning in the whirlwind of wars and revolutions, that Wells again detached himself from the ground, from daily reality. And in these novels we shall again find alloys of ideas that strike us at first glance as surprising and strange.

II

When I saw a flying airplane for the first time some twelve years ago and the airplane landed in a meadow and the flying man climbed out of his canvas wings and took off his strange, goggled mask, I was somehow disappointed. The flying man—small, clean-shaven, plump and ruddy-faced—turned out to be exactly like the rest of us; he could not get out his handkerchief with his chilled hands, and he wiped his nose with his fingers. Such a feeling—something akin to disappointment—will inevitably come to the reader when, after Wells's fantastic novels, he opens his realistic works. "Is this also Wells?" Yes, it is also Wells, but here he does not fly, he walks. On earth, this flying man has turned out to be not so very different from other English novelists. And if formerly we could, after reading two pages, say "This is Wells" without glancing at the signature, now we must take a look at the signature. And if formerly, in the field of science fiction and social fantasy, Wells was one, now he became "one of." True, one of the most significant and interesting English writers, but nevertheless "one of."

The reason for this is, undoubtedly, that Wells, like most of his English colleagues, devotes far more attention to plot than to language, style, the word—to all the things that we are accustomed to value in the latest Russian writers. He has not created his own Wellsian language, his own Wellsian manner of writing. And, indeed, there was no time for this, or he could not have managed to turn out the forty volumes he has written. His own, original, unique contribution is to be found in the plots of his fantastic novels. But as soon as he climbed out of the airplane, as soon as he turned to more usual plots, he lost a part of his originality.

The headlong, airplane flight of plot in the fantastic novels, where everything whizzes by—faces, events, ideas—this headlong flight makes it physically impossible for the reader to look closely at details, at the author's style. But the slow, unhurried movement of the novel of daily life provides an occasional opportunity to sit down and take a look at the storyteller's face, his clothes, his gestures, his smile. There seems to be something familiar in all that. But what? Another careful look, and it becomes clear—Dickens, Charles Dickens—he is Wells's famous ancestor. The same slow speech, perhaps too slow for today's reader; the same complex, lacy, Gothic periods; the same manner of giving a full, complete projection of the hero in all his dimensions, often from the moment of his appearance in the world; the same method of fixing the image of the character in the reader's memory by repetition of the salient trait; and, finally, as in Dickens, the ever-present smile. But Dickens's smile is gently humorous, it is the smile of a man who loves people, whatever they are, whatever their faults. Wells's smile is something different again: he loves man and at the same time hates him—for not being man enough, for being a caricature of man, a narrow philistine. Wells loves with a sharp, hating love, and that is why his smile is the smile of irony, and that is why his pen frequently turns into a lash, and the scars from this lash last a long time.

Even in his most innocently amusing and witty tales, seemingly written for a twelve-year-old reader, the more attentive eye will discern the same hating love. Take *The Food of the Gods*. The marvelous food produces chicks the size of horses, nettles as big as palms, rats more terrible than tigers, and, finally, giant humans as high as a church steeple. You read about a prince standing below, glancing up with horror through his monocle at his giant fiancée, fearful of looking ridiculous if he married her. This is amusing. You read about the tiny policeman who tries to arrest a giant and catches at him somewhere way below, at his leg; this is also amusing. You read of dozens of funny confrontations between giants and pigmies, and the searchlight of Wellsian irony lights up more and more sharply the puny little figure of the philistine pigmy who clings to his familiar, comfortable life in fear of the future, powerful giant man. And you begin to see more than the merely funny. Or take *The War of the Worlds:* there is a worldwide catastrophe, everything is collapsing, everything is perishing—and suddenly, in the midst of the crashing noise, you hear the voice of the pious curate, who laments the passing of the Sunday school.

This irony appears even more clearly in the web of Wells's realistic novels. Society ladies whose essential shape is held together by nothing more than their corset stays; fiercely moral old maids; wooden-headed school teachers; bishops who would dismiss Christ from his job for being poorly dressed and speaking words unsuited to a prince of the church; the stockbroker who is sincerely convinced that it was the Lord God himself who had inspired him to buy Pacific stocks. England may well be shocked to look into this cruel mirror of an angry love. And, it seems to me that nowhere does the Wellsian blade flash more keenly than in *Tono-Bungay,* perhaps the best of Wells's realistic novels. "I've met not simply the titled but the great. On one occasion— it is my brightest memory—I upset my champagne over the trousers of the greatest statesman in the empire." We read this in one of the first pages of the novel, and this irony winds its way through every page, through every adventure of the unforgettable Mr. Pondervo, that genius of advertising and charlatanry.

The world knows Wells the aviator, Wells the author of fantastic novels; these novels have been translated into every European language, they are even translated into Arabic and Chinese. And it is probably known to but a small minority of the wide reading public that Wells the author of fantastic novels is only one-half of Wells; he has written fourteen fantastic novels and fifteen realistic ones. His fantastic novels are: *The Time Machine, The Wonderful Visit, The Island of Dr. Moreau, The Invisible Man, The War of the Worlds, When the Sleeper Awakes, A Story of the Days to Come, The First Men in the Moon, The Sea Lady, The Food of the Gods, In the Days of the Comet, The War in the Air, The World Set Free, Men like Gods.* His realistic novels are: *The Wheels of Chance, Love and Mr. Lewisham, Kipps, The History of Mr. Polly, The New Machiavelli, Ann Veronica, Tono-Bungay, Marriage, Bealby, The Passionate Friends, The*
H. G. Wells

*Wife of Sir Isaac Harman, The Research Magnificent, Mr.
Britling Sees It Through, Joan and Peter,* and *The Secret Places
of the Heart.* Two of his novels, *The Soul of a Bishop* and *The
Undying Fire,* stand apart, opening a new path in Wells's
writing.[3]

If the reader has time enough to read all of the fifteen realistic
novels, if he has time enough to walk through this long row of
densely populated edifices, he will meet Mr. Wells himself in the
very first of them. Not abstractly, and not because every epic is
to a certain degree lyrical, but because in the earliest novels the
reader will find a part of Wells's autobiography. In his younger
days, Wells received too many blows at the hands of life, too
many and too painful to be forgotten. Messenger boy in a drapery
shop; then an assistant behind the counter, augmenting on sleepless nights the modest stock of knowledge he had brought out of
school; later, a student in a teachers' academy and schoolteacher
in an English small town. All these hard, strenuous, difficult years,
full of stubborn effort to improve himself, of struggle with
poverty, of enthusiasms, large plans, and disappointments—all
these years are imprinted in Wells's first three realistic novels,
The Wheels of Chance, Love and Mr. Lewisham, and *Kipps.*

In *The Wheels of Chance,* the assistant in the draper's shop,
Hoopdriver, is, of couse, Wells himself, just as Kipps in the novel
by that name is Wells, and just as the student in the teachers'
academy, Lewisham, in the novel *Love and Mr. Lewisham,* is
Wells. All these books are as autobiographical as Gorky's *My
Childhood* and *In the World* and Tolstoy's *Childhood, Boyhood,
and Youth.*

By the end of the 1890s, after the publication of *The Time
Machine* and *The War of the Worlds,* Wells, the former shop
assistant and former teacher, instantly became a popular writer.
The wheel of chance turned a hundred and eighty degrees, and
he comments on this in an autobiographical sketch.

---

[3] In addition to the twenty-nine novels enumerated above, four volumes
of fantastic tales and several children's books, Wells has also written a
number of sociopolitical, scientific, and philosophic books: *The Discovery
of the Future, Mankind in the Making, New Worlds for Old, An Englishman Looks at the World, What Is Coming, The Future of America, Socialism and the Family, First and Last Things, The Salvaging of Civilization,
God the Invisible King, Russia in the Shadows, Outline of History,* and
others (AUTHOR'S NOTE).

Ю. Анненков
петербург
Дом Искусств
1920.

In England, he says, as soon as a book wins some degree of success, its author becomes a prosperous man, able to travel whereever he chooses and associate with anyone he desires. He breaks out of the narrow circle to which he had been confined and suddenly begins to meet and associate with a vast number of people. Philosophers and scholars, soldiers and statesmen, artists and specialists of every kind, the wealthy and the aristocrats—the doors of all of them are open to him, and he can make any use of them he wishes.

Wells broke out of his narrow circle, his field of observation broadened enormously, and this immediately reflected itself in the mirror of his realistic novels. The personal, autobiographical element disappeared from them, and they became the field of action of crowds of people of the most divergent social positions —philosophers and scientists, soldiers and statesmen, artists, the wealthy, and the aristocrats. Wells did not forget his past, however, and even today he often rises to the upper floors, well lit and comfortable, merely to lead their happy and carefree inhabitants down into the cellars, to the hungry and the poor (*The Wife of Sir Isaac Harman, The Soul of a Bishop*).

Wells's novels of daily life become a sociological observatory, and his pen, like the pen of a seismograph, systematically records all the vibrations of the social world in England in the early years of the twentieth century. At the beginning of the 1900's, the ground of John Bull's islands is still extremely firm, and the records of the Wellsian seismograph trace the curves of small-scale, purely local vibrations; he deals with the problems of marriage and the family, of education, of women's suffrage (*Marriage, The Passionate Friends, The Wife of Sir Isaac Harman*). More general and fundamental social problems are still in a latent and static condition somewhere far beneath the surface, and are just as statically reflected in Wells's novels. But little by little the underground rumbling grows louder, the firm ground cracks to the very core, and the red, fiery lava of unprecedented wars and revolutions flows out of them. Beginning with *Mr. Britling Sees It Through,* this world-shaking earthquake becomes the sole theme of Wells's novels. Thus, gradually, these realistic novels abandon autobiography and become a chronicle of life in contemporary England.

If we now step aside for a moment and take a look at Wells's realistic novels from a distance, so that the eye, undistracted by details, will catch only the basic elements, we shall see that the architect who built those massive six-story edifices is the same Wells. As in his fantastic works, so in his realistic ones we find the same unceasing onslaught upon the aged European civilization; the same red glints of the special, Wellsian brand of socialism; the same humanism, the same "no one is to blame" as before; and the same gasoline and asphalt city, flickering with advertisements.

And suddenly, on the asphalt sidewalk, amidst gasoline incense, red flags, patent medicines, and men in derbies, you meet —God. The socialist, the mathematician, the chemist, the automobile driver, and the airplane pilot suddenly begins to speak of God. After the science fiction, after the most realistic of realities, there is suddenly a tract, *God the Invisible King;* a novel, *The Soul of a Bishop,* dealing with a religious experience of an Anglican priest; another novel, *The Undying Fire,* which is essentially not a novel at all, but a dispute about God; and the novel *Joan and Peter,* whose hero conducts dialogues with God.

At first it amazes you, it seems incredible. But after taking a second look, you recognize the same Wells, the eternal aviator. This seemingly unexpected turn to themes about God has taken place quite recently, during the recent days—years—after the outbreak of the World War and European revolutions. And this explains everything. It simply happened that all of life broke away from the anchor of reality and became fantastic; it simply happened that the most fantastic of Well's prophecies became facts; his science fiction tumbled down from the upper regions and became a daily reality. And, naturally, his restless imagination had to look for new fantastic material, had to fly still higher, still farther, to the very highest heavens—and there, in the distance, he envisioned the misty image of God. The apparently absurd war, the apparently unjustified deaths of millions of people raised tormenting questions in many minds: Why? What for? Isn't all of life simply meaningless chaos? And, of course, Wells could not escape these questions either.

He answers them, as was to be expected, in the negative: No, life is not meaningless; no, life, after all, has purpose and meaning. And we discover that long before, in 1902, Wells wrote in his *Anticipations:*

Either one must believe the Universe to be one and systematic, and held together by some omnipresent quality, or one must believe it to be a casual aggregation, an incoherent accumulation with no unity whatsoever. . . . All science and most modern religious systems presuppose the former; and to believe the former is, to any one not too anxious to quibble, to believe in God.

And thus, Wells builds a temple to his God, and next to it, on the same foundation, he erects his scientific laboratories, his socialist phalansteries. And now his seemingly surprising, seemingly incomprehensible turn to religious topics becomes understandable. With Wells this is, of course, the result of the terrestrialization, of the materialization of his former fantasies, and not "God-seeking" in the usual sense of the word.

The first of Well's novels about God is *The Soul of a Bishop*. In a preface which Wells wrote for a certain edition of his translated works, Wells calls this novel an ironic reflection of the changes which had occurred in the Anglican church under the impact of time. But in truth there is less irony here than anywhere else in his works, and the reader senses that the author is once again trying to answer the question: Has he any use for this rather prim and hypocritical English God? The novel, half-realistic and half-fantastic, clearly answers his question. The reader sees a most respectable bishop, wealthy, happy in his family life, brilliantly successful in his career. Everything seems to be fine, there seems to be nothing else to be desired. Yet something begins to gnaw at the bishop's soul—something tiny, almost invisible, like a speck of dust in the eye. And this speck of dust gives him no rest by day or by night; it finally grows into the tormenting question: Does that God whom the bishop serves really exist? And is that God really the Christ who had commanded that everything be given to the poor?

The bishop tries psychiatric treatment with several doctors in succession, and finally comes to a young doctor, one of those daring scientific revolutionaries who are so dear to Wells's heart. He begins to treat the bishop in a manner different from all the others: instead of trying to put out the flame in the bishop's soul, he fans it. He gives the bishop a marvelous elixir which raises his spirit to ecstasy, leading him away from our three-dimensional world to the world of higher dimensions. The bishop sees God with his own eyes, and speaks with him, once, then again, and then a third time. This God, he finds, is altogether different from the one he has been serving, and the bishop abandons the old God, leaves his wealth and his family. The bishop joins the ranks of religious and social heretics.

Wells's second novel about God is *The Undying Fire*. It opens with a grandiose and slightly grotesque picture:

> Two eternal beings, magnificently enhaloed, the one in a blinding excess of white radiance and the other in a bewildering extravagance of colors, converse amidst stupendous surroundings. These surroundings are by tradition palatial, but there is now also a marked cosmic tendency about them. They have no definite locality; they are above and comprehensive of the material universe.
>
> There is a quality in the scene as if a Futurist with a considerable knowledge of modern chemical and physical speculation and some obscure theological animus had repainted the designs of a pre-Raphaelite.

Enormous columns, curves and spirals. The sun and the planets flash and gleam through the depths of the floor of crystalline ether, sparkling with gold. Huge winged shadows fashioned of stars, planets, scrolls of the law, and flaming swords are continually chanting "Holy, Holy, Holy." One of the interlocutors is, of course, God, of whom—Wells adds—one is tempted to say that he is utterly bored to see everything that happens, for it is already and inevitably known to him. And God listens with the most lively interest to the words of the other participant in the dialogue—Satan.

After a certain disrespectful remark made by Satan, the archangel Michael wants to strike him down with his sword. But God stops the zealous archangel: what should we do without Satan?

And Satan says: "Without me, time and space would freeze to crystalline perfection. . . . It is I who trouble the waters. I trouble all things. I am the spirit of life. . . . Did I not launch man on the most marvellous adventures? It was I who gave him history."

Nevertheless, Satan feels that man is weak and foolish. Has he made any perceptible step forward these past ten thousand

years? Men are still endlessly murdering one another for no good
reason. And the end is in sight. Soon the entire human habitat
will cool and freeze over, and there will be an end to everything.
But no, God argues, in the end man will rule the world. For
"My spirit is in him."

Satan proposes to God that they finish their eternal chess game:
the game is becoming too cruel. All of mankind today is Job.
Would it not be more merciful to destroy everyone at once?

The dispute between the two mighty interlocutors now turns
to the question of Job, of who won and who lost in that contest.
God asserts that he had been the victor because, in spite of
all misfortunes, an unquenchable, undying fire remained alive
in man.

And God allows Satan to repeat his experiment with a new
Job. This new, modern Job is the English school teacher Mr.
Huss. He is showered with disasters: a message arrives that his
only son, a flier, has been killed in the fighting in France; a fire
ruins Mr. Huss and destroys his life's work, his cherished school;
and finally, he develops cancer. This may be his last day, for he
is to undergo an operation. Before the operation, he receives
three visitors: one of his former colleagues and two capitalists
who had invested their money in his school. The purpose of their
visit is to persuade him to give up his post as director of the
school.

The next two hundred pages are devoted to a two-hour discussion about God. Each of the participants in this discussion
has his own set ideas on religion. One has a portable, pocket-
sized, philistine God who does not prevent him, even during the
terrible days of the war, from living comfortably and pursuing
his business deals. The other is a dedicated believer in spiritual-
ism. The third is the doctor who is treating Mr. Huss, a consistent
materialist without any God whatsoever. And, finally, there is
the new Job, Mr. Huss, who obviously speaks for Wells himself.
The cruel absurdity of war has caused Wells to amend his previous thesis that the world is logical and rational, and therefore
must be governed by a higher intelligence, which he called "God."
Today, human life, so full of cruelty, diseases, misfortunes, and
poverty, is absurd, irrational, illogical. And yet, Wells feels, man
has the ability to conquer all of this. He will conquer it, he will
surely conquer it and build a beautiful life on earth. More than

that, he will break the crystal prison of our planet in space and will step off the earth into the invisible vistas of the universe. And since this is so, since this is inevitable, then there surely is a power leading man into this path, a power which Wells describes by the same term, "God."

This path, which man will follow, has not been traced by a blind, elemental process. No, the elements as such are irrational. Left to the elements, the world and man would go into decline. No, this path of the future is chosen by the higher, organizing intelligence, God, and it is his undying fire that burns in man. Such are the words of the new Job, worn out by misfortunes, in his final hours. And his faith in the powers of man—ergo, in God—is rewarded: the operation is successful, and a telegram arrives, informing Mr. Huss that his son was not dead, but taken prisoner by the Germans.

An echo of the same eternal, grandiose dispute between Satan and God can also be heard in Wells's latest novel, *Joan and Peter*. But here the colossal, cosmic chess game is placed inside a microcosm, man. This man is Peter, an English pilot during the last war. And it is not Satan, as in the earlier novel, but Peter who comes forward in the wig and robe of the accuser in the contest between mankind and God. Wounded and mutilated after an engagement with a German flier, the delirious Peter throws out a reproach to God: Why don't you manifest yourself? There is so much evil in the world. This appalling waste of lives in the war. How can you bear all this cruelty and filth?

And God replies: Why? You people don't like it? No, says Peter. Then change all this, says God. And the contemporary God goes on to enunciate a new, modern chapter in theology: "If I was the hot-tempered old autocrat some of you people pretend I am, I should have been tickling you up with a thunderbolt long ago. But I happen to have this democratic fad . . . and so I leave you to work out your own salvation. . . . I leave you alone." Why, for example—God goes on—don't you abolish your kings? You could. People could, but they don't want to badly enough.

And Peter sees more and more clearly that "the great old Experimenter" is right and wise: evil is as necessary in the cosmic organism as pain in the organism of man: it is a warning to hurry and try to cure the disease.

It does not matter that to some people this "Experimenter" is as concrete an individual as Peter himself, while to others he is even more abstract than the square root of one. The important thing is to teach men universal brotherhood. Isn't it ridiculous to fight to the death over how the word "brotherhood" is to be pronounced?

And so we learn from this novel yet another facet of the Wellsian God. And if we integrate this formula, it will become entirely obvious that in his religious constructions Wells still remains the same Wells. It will become obvious that his God is, of course, a London God, and that the finest incense to his God is, of course, the smell of chemical reactions and of the gasoline that fuels the airplane engine. For this God's omnipotence lies in the omnipotence of man, of man's intelligence, man's science. For this is not an Eastern God, in whose hands man is merely an obedient tool; it is a Western God, who demands of man activity and work above all. This God is familiar with the British constitution: he does not govern, he merely reigns. And the banners of this modern God are, naturally, neither gold, nor silver. They are red. This God is a socialist.

The compass-traced circumference of earthbound socialism and the hyperbola of religion, stretching into the misty distance —two such different, such incompatible notions. But Wells attempts to break the circle, to unbend it into a hyperbola, with one end resting on the earth, on science and positivism, and the other lost in the clouds. This art of passing without a scratch through the tightest paradoxes is already familiar to us: we have seen it in Wells's fairy tales, where he succeeded in fusing science and fantasy into a single entity.

Wells's realistic novel, *Joan and Peter,* is the most contemporary of all his works. It reflects England on the eve and during the war; it contains an echo of yesterday's and today's Russia. And, finally, it contains pages of great wit and artistry, written by a somehow renewed and rejuvenated Wells. Here, for example, are some lines from the beginning of the novel, telling about Peter and his earliest impressions of the universe:

> The theory of Ideals played almost as important a part in the early philosophy of Peter as it did in the philosophy of Plato. But Peter did not call them "Ideals," he called

them "toys." Toys were the simplified essences of things, pure, perfect and manageable: Real Things were troublesome, uncontrollable, overcomplicated and largely irrelevant. A Real Train, for example, was a poor, big, clumsy, limited thing that was obliged to go to Red Hill or Croydon or London. . . . A Toy Train was your very own; it took you wherever you wanted, to Fairyland or Russia or anywhere, at whatever pace you chose. Then there was a beautiful rag doll named "Pleeceman," who had a comic, almost luminous red nose, and smiled perpetually; you could hit Joan with him and make her squawk and yet be sure of not hurting her. . . . How inferior was the great formless lump of a real policeman. . . . Nobody could have lifted him by a leg and waved him about; and if you had shied him into a corner, instead of going just anyhow and still smiling, he would probably have been cross and revengeful.

And so, the entire original child's world comes alive before us—a world where things are animate creatures, and people are things. There was a comfortable and nourishing object, Peter's nurse, Mary, and next to her, "the brass-eyed monster with the triple belly who was called 'Chester-Drawers'; he shammed dead and watched you, and in the night he creaked about the room." There was the uncomfortable, overnoisy, irritating object called "Daddy," and next to him the live china pug Nobby, who protected Peter against chests, fathers, and everything frightening.

Imperceptibly, Peter goes on from his ideal, toy world into the world of reality, attends one school, another, a third, then Cambridge University. And, finally, the last stage of the education of Peter and Joan—the war, which taught them the most important, most profound things. *The Story of an Education* is the subtitle Wells gave his novel.

Not long before the war Wells visited Russia, and it is obvious that his impressions shaped his description of the Russian journey of Peter and his guardian Oswald.

This is how Wells saw Moscow:

> The great red walls of the Kremlin rising above the Moskva and the first glimpse of that barbaric caricature, the cathedral of St. Basil; . . . a dirty, evil-smelling little tramp with

his bundle and kettle, worshipping unabashed in the Uspensky cathedral; endless bearded priests, Tartar waiters with
purple sashes, a whole population in furs and so looking
absurdly wealthy to an English eye.

Then there is a description of the astonishing view of Moscow
from the Vorobyev Hills, blue snow, colored roofs, the golden
glitter of innumerable crosses. And, looking at Moscow from
above, Oswald—or, rather, Wells—says: "This isn't a city like
the cities of western Europe, Peter. This is something different.
. . . This is a Tartar camp, frozen. . . . A camp changed to wood
and brick and plaster."

Later, he says, "One understands Dostoyevsky better when
one sees this. One begins to realize this Holy Russia, as a sort
of epileptic genius among nations—like his Idiot, insisting on
moral truth, holding up the cross to mankind."

Yes, he continues, "Asia is advancing on Europe—with a new
idea." The Russians "seem to have the Christian idea. In a way
we Westerns don't. . . . Christianity to a Russian means Brotherhood. . . . And this city with its endless crosses is so in harmony
with Russian music, Russian art, Russian literature."

The cold, buttoned-up Petersburg seemed to the Englishman
much more like Europe, like England. He saw nothing Tartar,
nothing Asiatic here, until he found himself in the Russian parliament, the state Duma.

The final chapters of the novel are also linked to Russia.
Russia is on fire, and the sparks reach England. England has already gone through the cruel school of war; those who have been
in that school, including Peter, realize that the old life is no
longer possible. The old must be destroyed in order to build in
its place a world state, a League of Free Nations. The main thing
now is to work and work, without sparing oneself. "We've got
to live like fanatics. If a lot of us don't live like fanatics, this
staggering old world of ours won't recover. It will stagger and
then go flop. And a race of Bolshevik peasants will breed pigs
among the ruins."

This is how Wells sums up the views of the English intellectual
(the radically inclined, we must add) on present-day Russia.
And, of course, it is needless to speak of the gentlemen and

ladies who don't sleep nights because of those dreadful Bolsheviks. This part of society is represented by the caricature portrait of Lady Sydenham.

His own views on Communist Russia and the impressions he received during his recent visit there were developed in a series of articles in the *Sunday Express,* later published in book form under the title *Russia in the Shadows.* These articles provide extensive, although lightweight, material—as though glimpsed from a railway car window. But this does not belong within our present task of examining Wells the artist. I shall cite only one comment, which, it seems to me, could serve as an epigraph to those articles. I do not, says Wells, share the faith of the Communists; their Marx seems ridiculous to me, but I respect and appreciate their spirit; I understand it.

And the Wells portrayed in these pages could not have said anything else. The heretic who cannot tolerate any settled existence, any catechism, could not have said anything else about the catechism of Marxism. The restless aviator who hates the old earth, overgrown with the moss of traditions, could not have said anything else about an attempt to break away from this old earth.

To me, the word *airplane* contains all of our time. It also contains all of Wells, the most contemporary of contemporary writers. Mankind has stepped off the earth and, with a beating heart, has risen aloft. From the dizzying height immense distances spread before him. A single glance embraces entire nations and countries, the whole dried-out lump of dirt—the earth. The airplane speeds upward and kingdoms, kings, laws and creeds vanish from sight. Still higher, and the cupolas of some incredible tomorrow flash in the distance.

This new horizon, these new eyes of the aviator have come to many of us who have lived through the recent years. But Wells has had these eyes for a long time. Hence his prophetic visions of the future, his vast horizons of space and time.

Airplanes—flying steel—this is, of course, a paradox. And such paradoxes abound everywhere in Wells's works. Yet, paradoxical as it may seem, the airplane, all of it, to the last little screw, is logical through and through. Just so, to the last little screw, is Wells. The airplane is, of course, a miracle, mathematically calculated and fed on gasoline. And just such miracles are found in Wells. The airplane, daring what until now has been permitted only to angels, is, of course, the symbol of the revolution taking place in man. And it is this revolution that Wells is writing about all the time. I know of nothing more urban, more of today, more contemporary than the airplane. And I know of no English writer more of today, more contemporary than Wells.

THE GENEALOGICAL TREE OF H. G. WELLS

To the feudal aristocracy and the aristocracy of the spirit—geniuses and talents—"nobility" derives from diametrically opposite sources.

The glory of the feudal aristocrat is in being a link in the longest possible chain of ancestors. The glory of the aristocrat of the spirit is in having no ancestors—or having as few as possible. If an artist is his own ancestor, if he has only descendants, he enters history as a genius; if he has few ancestors, or is related to them distantly, he enters history as a talent. Wells very aptly remarks that writing is one of the present forms of adventure; the adventurers of the past would become writers today. The history of literature, like the history of every art and science, is a history of discoveries and inventions, a history of Columbuses and Vasco de Gamas, of Gutenbergs and Stephensons. There are few geniuses in history who discovered hitherto unknown or forgotten lands (the inhabitants of Atlantis may have known America). There are more talents, who improve or significantly change existing forms. And Wells unquestionably belongs to the latter.

But which Wells? There are two Wellses: one is an inhabitant of our three-dimensional world, the author of realistic novels; the other is a resident of a world of four dimensions, a traveler in time, the author of tales of science fiction and social fantasy.

The first Wells has discovered no new continents. He has many eminent relations. The second Wells is linked with his forebears only by distant kinship, and he has almost single-handedly created a new literary genre. And, of course, if it were not for the second Wells, the first would not have found a place among the brighter stars in the astronomical catalog of literature.

In English literature there are two main currents. One deals with the Englishman at home, in the isles of the United Kingdom;

the other, with the indefatigable sailor, the seeker of new lands, the dreamer and adventurer (an adventurer is always a dreamer). And the two Wellses—the realist and the fantasist—reflect these two trends.

The former trend reached its apex in Dickens, an apex still unsurpassed. And the first Wells, the sober realist and skeptic, indulging at times in good-humored, at other times in angry mockery, is clearly descended from Dickens. This is an instance of the direct blood kinship we mentioned earlier. And here Wells is only one of the branches growing out of the mighty trunk of Dickens. Other branches are Eliot, Meredith, Hardy, Shaw, Gissing, Bennett, Galsworthy.

The links between Wells, the author of social fantasies and science fiction, and the latter current of English literature are far more complex, subtle, and distant. Here he has no direct forebears, and will probably have many descendants.

Take Wells's sociofantastic novels—the first literary definition which comes to mind and which we have often heard is *utopia.* These novels have been described as social utopias. If this were true, then a long line of shadows would arise behind Wells, beginning with Sir Thomas More's *Utopia,* through Campanella's *The City of the Sun,* Cabet's *A Voyage to Icaria,* and all the way up to William Morris's *News from Nowhere.* But this genealogy would be incorrect, for Wells's sociofantastic novels are not utopias. His only utopia is his latest novel, *Men like Gods.*

There are two generic and invariable features that characterize utopias. One is the content: the authors of utopias paint what they consider to be ideal societies; translating this into the language of mathematics, we might say that utopias bear a $+$ sign. The other feature, organically growing out of the content, is to be found in the form: a utopia is always static; it is always descriptive, and has no, or almost no, plot dynamics.

In Wells's sociofantastic novels we shall hardly ever find these characteristics. To begin with, most of his social fantasies bear the $-$ sign, not the $+$ sign. His sociofantastic novels are almost solely instruments for exposing the defects of the existing social order, rather than building a picture of a future paradise. His *Story of the Days to Come* does not contain a single rosy or golden glint of paradise; it is painted, instead, in the murky colors of Goya. And we find the same Goya hues in *The Time Machine,*

The First Men in the Moon, The War in the Air, and *The World
Set Free.* Only *Men like Gods,* one of his weakest sociofantastic
novels, contains the sugary, pinkish colors of a utopia.

Generally, Wells's sociofantastic novels differ from utopias as
much as $+A$ differs from $-A$. They are not utopias. Most of
them are social tracts in the form of fantastic novels. Hence,
the roots of Wells's genealogical tree must be sought only in such
literary landmarks as Swift's *Gulliver's Travels,* Ludvig Holberg's
Niels Klim's Journey under the Ground, and Edward Bulwer-
Lytton's *The Coming Race.* But all that Wells has in common
with these writers is his approach to the theme—not the theme
itself, and not the literary methods employed. In fact, although
we sometimes find Wells using themes which had been developed
earlier by other writers (such as the theme of a journey to the
moon, encountered in Cyrano de Bergerac, Edgar Allan Poe, and
Jules Verne; or the theme of a sleeper who awakens after many
years, borrowed from numerous folk tales, first by Louis Mercier
at the end of the eighteenth century in his *Memoirs of the Year
2440,* then by Bellamy, Willbrandt, Edmond About, and others),
his approach to the theme is entirely different. All this leads us
to conclude that, in his sociofantastic novels, Wells created a
new, original variety of literary form.

Two elements lend Wells's fantasies their own unique character—the element of social satire and the element of science fiction invariably fused with it. This second element sometimes appears in Wells's writings in pure, isolated form, expressing itself
in his science fiction novels and short stories (*The Invisible Man,
The Island of Dr. Moreau,* "Aepyornis Island," "The New Accelerator," and others).

Of course, science fiction could enter the field of fine literature
only in the last decades, when truly fantastic potentialities unfolded before science and technology. This is why the virtually
sole example of science fiction in the literature of past centuries
is Francis Bacon's utopia, *The New Atlantis,* in its chapters which
describe the house of learning, "Solomon's House." In these
chapters Bacon brilliantly anticipates many of the modern con-
quests of science, which to the seventeenth century appeared as
pure fantasy. After that (if we disregard several pallid hints in
Cabet's *Voyage to Icaria*), true science fiction clothed in literary
form will be found only at the end of the nineteenth century. It

was that period—and this was not accidental, but entirely logical—that witnessed the almost simultaneous appearance of Kurd Lasswitz's *Pictures of the Future* and *Soap Bubbles,* (1879–90), Bellamy's *Looking Backward* (1887), Theodor Hertzka's *Freeland* (1889), and the works of William Morris, Flammarion, Jules Verne, and others.

In the works of these authors we find many details of a fantastic future akin to those envisaged by Wells: aerial carriages and perfected machines in Lasswitz; electric self-setting tablecloths in Hertzka, much like those seen in Wells's *A Story of the Days to Come.* But these parallels are due merely to the fact that Wells and the other writers necessarily drew their fantasies from the same realistic source—the same science, the same scientific logic. And, of course, none of the enumerated writers possessed such steely, artful, hypnotic logic as Wells, none had his rich and daring imagination. The only writers who could have given Wells literary impetus in his science fiction are Flammarion and Jules Verne. But even Jules Verne cannot be placed on the same plane with Wells (not to speak of Flammarion, who was not an artist at all). Only a child can be beguiled into belief by Jules Verne's fantasies; they can create the illusion of reality only in a child's unsophisticated mind. But the logical fantasies of Wells, most of them enhanced by a sharp seasoning of irony and social satire, will capture the mind of any reader.

This is further helped by the form of Wells's sociofantastic and science-fiction novels.

As we have pointed out, the elements of classic utopia are absent from Wells's works (with the sole exception of his novel *Men like Gods*). Static well-being, petrified paradisiac social equilibrium are logically bound with the content of a utopian work; hence the natural consequence in its form—a static plot and absence of a story line. In Wells's sociofantastic novels the plot is always dynamic, built on collisions, on conflict; the story is complex and entertaining. Wells invariably clothes his social fantasy and science fiction in the forms of a Robinsoniad, of the typical adventure novel so beloved in Anglo-Saxon literature. In this respect Wells carries on the traditions created by Daniel Defoe and continued by James Fenimore Cooper, Mayne Reade, Stevenson, Edgar Allan Poe, and by the contemporary writers—Haggard, Conan Doyle and Jack London. However, in adopting the form of the adventure novel, Wells deepened it, raised its intellectual value, and brought into it the elements of social philosophy and science. In his own field—though, of course, on a proportionately lesser scale—Wells may be likened to Dostoyevsky, who took the form of the cheap detective novel and infused it with brilliant psychological analysis.

An artist of considerable stature, a brilliant and subtle dialectician who has created models of an extraordinarily contemporary form—models of the urban myth, of socioscientific fantasy —Wells will unquestionably have literary successors and descendants. Wells is only a pioneer. The period of socioscientific fantasy in literature is only beginning. The entire fantastic history of Europe and of European science in recent years makes it possible to forecast this with certainty.

In modern English literature, Wells is followed by Conan Doyle, in some of his works (as, for example, in *The Lost World,* where the theme of Wells's story "Aepyornis Island" is developed in the form of a novel), and Robert Blatchford (in his novel *The Sorcery Shop*). The influence of Wells is felt unmistakably in Jack London's sociofantastic novel *The Iron Heel,* as well as in *Before Adam* (compare them with Wells's "A Story of the Stone Age"). In the most recent period, George Bernard Shaw and Upton Sinclair have entered the field of fantasy, with Shaw's *Back to Methuselah* and Sinclair's novel *They Call Me Carpenter* and his play *Hell.* It is Wells, too, who has probably given an impetus to the talented Polish writer Zulawski, author of a moonlight trilogy, *On the Silver Sphere, The Victor,* and *The Old Earth,* as well as the young Swedish writer Bergstedt, author of the sociofantastic satire, *Alexandersen.* The Frenchman Anatole France is working parallel to Wells in the field of the social pamphlet clothed in the artful form of ironic-fantastic novels—*The White Stone, Penguin Island,* and *The Revolt of the Angels.* The latter takes the same point of departure as Wells's *The Wonderful Visit*—angels among men. But France developed this theme far more profoundly, wittily and subtly than Wells. Claude Farrere has also turned to socioscientific fiction; his novel *The Condemned,* however, is considerably less successful than his usual exotic works.

Germany and Austria, which have gone through revolutions, provide a far more fruitful soil for the growth of fantastic literature than other countries, which are still resting on their old foundations. The postrevolutionary years in these two countries have yielded the richest harvest of fantastic novels: *The Third Road* by Colerus, Brehmer's *The Andromeda Nebula*, Roland Betsch's *Messiah*, Scheff's *Flaming Sea*, Eichacker's *Panic*, Hans Christoph's *Journey into the Future: A Novel of Relativity*, Madelung's *Circus Man*, and the remarkable philosophic-fantastic novel of the Czech writer, Karel Čapek, *The Absolute at Large*.

The petrified life of the old, prerevolutionary Russia produced almost no examples of social fantasies or science fiction, as indeed it could not. Perhaps the only representatives of this genre in the recent history of our literature are Kuprin, with his story "The Liquid Sun," and Bogdanov, with his novel *Red Star*, which has more journalistic than literary value. And, if we look further back, Odoyevsky and Senkovsky (Baron Brambeus). But postrevolutionary Russia, which has become the most fantastic country in modern Europe, will undoubtedly reflect this period with literary fantasy. And the beginning has already been made: A. N. Tolstoy's *Aelita* and *The Hyperboloid of the Engineer Garin*, *We*, by the author of this essay, and I. Ehrenburg's novels *Julio Jurenito* and *Trust D. E.*

1922

O. HENRY

Advertisements shout; varicolored lights blink, in windows, on walls, in the sky; trains clatter somewhere in the air overhead; floors madly climb on floors, each on the other's shoulders—the tenth, the fifteenth, the twentieth. It is London, Paris, Berlin, wound up ten times more feverishly: it is America.

At top speed, by telephone, by telegraph, one must make millions, swallow something on the run in a bar, and then—a ten minute rest over a book in a flying coach. Ten minutes, no more, and in those ten minutes one must have something complete, whole, something that will fly as fast as the one-hundred-mile-an-hour train, that will make one forget the train, the clatter, the whistles, everything.

This demand was met by O. Henry (William Sidney Porter, 1862–1911). His short, sharp, quick stories hold a condensed America. Jack London is the American steppe, its snowy plains, its oceans and tropical islands; O. Henry is the American city. It does not matter that London wrote *Martin Eden* and urban stories; and it does not matter that O. Henry wrote a book of the steppes, *The Heart of the West,* and a novel, *Cabbages and Kings,* depicting the life of some South American province. Jack London is still, first and foremost, the Klondike, and O. Henry is New York.

It is wrong to say that the cinema was invented by Edison: the cinema was invented by Edison and O. Henry. In the cinema, the most important thing is motion, motion at any cost. And in O. Henry's stories the most important thing is dynamics, motion; hence his faults and his virtues.

The reader who finds himself in O. Henry's cinema will come out of it refreshed by laughter: O. Henry is invariably witty, amusing, youthfully gay—like A. Chekhonte who had not yet grown into Anton Chekhov. But occasionally his comic effects are overdrawn, far-fetched, somewhat crude. The feelings of the movie public must be touched sometimes: O. Henry stages charming four-page dramas for it. Once in a while these dramas are sentimental and cinematically edifying. But this happens seldom. O. Henry may wax emotional for a second, but immediately he rushes on again, mocking, laughing, light. A quick tongue, a quick wit, quick feelings—every muscle is in motion, very much as in the case of another American national favorite, Charlie Chaplin.

What does Charlie Chaplin believe in? What is Charlie Chaplin's philosophy? Probably nothing; probably none: there is no time. And the same is true of O. Henry, and of millions of New Yorkers. O. Henry begins one of his stories, "The Higher Pragmatism," punning and playing with the sound of the words: "The ancients are discredited; Plato is boiler-plate; Aristotle is tottering; Marcus Aurelius is reeling; . . . Solomon is too solemn; you couldn't get anything out of Epictetus with a pick." And this is, perhaps, one of the few occasions when O. Henry speaks seriously. As a rule, when he is not afflicted with sentimentality, he laughs and jests. Even through his makeup, we occasionally catch a glimpse of the inimitable Charlie Chaplin. Smiling, he starves; smiling, he goes to prison; and he probably dies with a smile. Perhaps his only philosophy is that life must be conquered with a smile. O. Henry is one of those Anglo-Saxons who sang hymns on the *Titanic* as it was slowly sinking. He probably understood, or, at least, sensed remotely, that the huge, comfortable *Titanic* of nineteenth-century civilization had struck an iceberg and was majestically sinking to the bottom. But O. Henry was at home on his ship; he would not abandon it. With jests on his lips— sometimes frivolous, sometimes tinged with bitterness—he would die courageously, like Spengler's "Faustian" man.

This ineradicable, resilient vitality had been bred into O. Henry by his whole life: the hammer tempers the steel. He himself had lived in the shabby furnished rooms where he often brings his reader. He himself spent nights on park benches. He is the New York bohemian, the romantic American tramp. His biography would probably make an excellent motion picture: O. Henry the salesman in a tobacco shop; O. Henry the clerk behind a drug-store counter; O. Henry over a ledger in a business office; O. Henry the member of a gang of railway thieves in South America; O. Henry in prison for three years. And, after prison, not the "Ballad of Reading Gaol," but gay, light stories, splashed with laughter. The blow that broke the pampered, delicate Wilde struck the first creative spark from O. Henry.

Want, and the fever of the huge American city, drove him, whipped him on. He wrote too much—some years as many as fifty or sixty stories. This is why his work is uneven. True, even among his weakest lines there will be an occasional glint of true O. Henry gold. But then, the same carbon produces both coal and graphite and diamonds. At any rate, O. Henry has produced diamonds, and this brings him into the vicinity of such masters of the short story as Chekhov and Maupassant. And it must be said that O. Henry's technique—at least in his best works—is sharper, bolder, and more modern than that of many short-story writers who have already assumed their place as classics.

A pungent language, glittering with an eccentric and unex-pected symbolism, is the first thing that captures the attention of O. Henry's reader. And this is not the dead, mechanical eccen-tricity found in the symbols of the Imagists. In O. Henry the image is always *internally* linked to the basic tonality of his char-acter, incident, or entire story. This is why all his epithets or images, even when seemingly incongruous or far-fetched, are convincing and hypnotic. The housekeeper of a rooming house (in the story "The Furnished Room") has a "throat lined with fur." At first the image is difficult to assimilate; but as the story proceeds, it is varied, becoming sharpened with each variation. Now it is simply a "furry throat," or "she said in her furriest tones"—and the cloying figure of the housekeeper, never de-scribed in detail as it would have been by the old narrative method, is etched in the imagination of the reader.

O. Henry achieves especially striking effects by employing the device which can most accurately be described as that of the *integrating image* (in analyzing literary prose we are compelled to create our terminology afresh). Thus, in the story "The De-feat of the City," Miss Alicia Van Der Pool is "cool, white and inaccessible as the Matterhorn." The Matterhorn—the basic image—is developed as the story goes on; it becomes ramified and embraces almost the entire story broadly and integrally: "The social Alps that ranged about her . . . reached only to her knees." And Robert Walmsley attains this Matterhorn. But, even if he has found that the traveler who reaches the mountaintop finds the highest peaks swathed in a thick veil of cloud and snow, he manages to conceal his chills. "Robert Walmsley was proud of his wife; although while one of his hands shook his guests' the other held tightly to his alpenstock and thermometer."

Similarly, the story "Squaring the Circle" is permeated with the integrating image: nature is a circle, the city a square. In "A Comedy in Rubber," the image is of the rubbernecks as a special tribe, and so on.

O. Henry's kind of story approaches most closely the *skaz* form (to this day, one of the favorite forms in the Russian short story): the free, spontaneous language of speech, digressions, purely American coinages of the street variety, which cannot be found in any dictionary. His, however, is not that ultimate, complete *skaz* form from which the author is absent, in which the author is but another character, and even the author's comments are given in a language close to that of the milieu depicted.

But all these are the static aspects of a work of art. The urban reader, who grew up in the mad whirl of the modern city, cannot be satisfied with only the static elements; he demands the dynamics of plot. Hence all that yellow sea of criminal and detective literature, usually crude and unartistic verbally. In O. Henry, brilliant language is usually combined with dynamic plot. His favorite compositional device is the surprise ending. Sometimes the effect of surprise is achieved by the author with the aid of what may be called the *false denouement:* in the plot syllogism, the reader is deliberately led to the wrong conclusion, and then, somewhere at the end, there is a sudden sharp turn, and an altogether different denouement reveals itself (in the stories, "The Rathskeller and the Rose," "Squaring the Circle," "The Hiding of Black Bill"). Very complex and subtle compositional methods may be found in O. Henry's novel, *Cabbages and Kings.*

Unfortunately, the composition of O. Henry's stories, especially in the endings, suffers from sameness. The chronic surprise loses its point; the surprise is expected, and the exception becomes the rule. The reader has much the same feeling as he experiences under Wilde's shower of paradoxes: in the end he sees that each paradox is but a truism turned inside out.

However, Tolstoy's Nekhludov did not love Katyusha Maslova a whit less because her eyes were just a little crossed. And his faults did not prevent O. Henry from becoming one of the most beloved writers of America and England.

1923

ANATOLE FRANCE:
An Obituary

If someone were to watch the progress of our earthly culture from a neighboring planet, he would—across a distance of hundreds of millions of miles—see only the highest peaks. And if he were to draw an atlas of our culture for the past quarter of a century, the highest summit on the map of Russia would, of course, be Lev Tolstoy, and the highest summit on the map of France would be Anatole France. These two names represent not only the spiritual poles of two nations, but also the poles of two cultures: one which casts off into the unknown from the shore called European civilization, and another which remains, to destroy and to build, on this shore. And these two lofty names throw their shadow on everything below. Tolstoy is the absolute, emotion, faith (even if it refracts in the form of faith in reason); France is all relativism, irony, skepticism.

In spite of their polarity, the same energy flows through both positive and negative electrons. And the same energy of revolution animates these two poles, Tolstoy and France. Both are great heretics. Many of their works have won the highest honor a writer can expect, a listing in the catalog of proscribed books.

Nevertheless, the polarity remains. Our efforts to assimilate France are merely testimony to the natural, lusty appetite of youth, which is sometimes tempted by the indigestible. The touchstone which demonstrated to me with particular force the polarity of France in relation to us was Blok's response to him. Blok said that he could not accept France: "He is somehow unreal, he is all irony." France was "unreal" to Blok because France was a real European, through and through; because, of the two possible solutions of the problem of life, Blok, Russia, chose the tragic, with hatred and with love that stopped at nothing, while France chose the ironic, with its relativism and skepticism—also stopping at nothing.

"It takes extraordinary spiritual strength to be an atheist," says Monsieur Larive-du-Mont in France's story, "The Shirt," when the conversation turns to how difficult it is to die. Monsieur du-Mont is right. But we must add that it takes even greater strength of spirit to be an atheist, a skeptic, a relativist—and yet live fully and love life. Anatole France passed this ordeal by fire—indeed, not even by fire, but by something still more terrible, by cold. Remaining a skeptic to the very end, he loved life with a young and tender love to the very end. "The irony that I invoke," said France, "is not cruel. It does not mock either love or beauty. It teaches us to laugh at evil men and fools, whom, without it, we might be weak enough to hate."

France died in deep old age. But he died very young. Just recently, when he was over seventy, he gave world literature a gift of the most characteristically Francian, the most French, the gayest, the most merciless, and the wisest of his works—*The Revolt of the Angels*. And therefore we experience his death not as the natural end of an artist who had completed his earthly journey, but as a violation, as something unnatural—as we experience the death of the young.

1924

Евгений Замятин

LETTER OF RESIGNATION FROM THE SOVIET WRITERS' UNION

When I returned to Moscow after a summer journey, the entire affair concerning my novel *We* was already finished: it had been decided that the publication of excerpts from *We* in the Prague journal *Volya Rossii* was my act, and all the appropriate resolutions in regard to this "act" had already been passed.

But facts are stubborn, they are more stubborn than resolutions. Every fact can be confirmed by documents or people. And I want to make these facts known to my readers. They consist of the following:

1. The novel *We* was written in 1920. In 1921 the manuscript of the novel was sent (by the simplest method—by registered mail through the Petrograd Post Office) to the Grzhebin Publishing House in Berlin. This publishing house had branches at that time in Berlin, Moscow, and Petrograd, and I was bound to it by contracts.

2. At the end of 1923 a copy of this manuscript was made available by the publisher for translation into English (this translation appeared only in 1925), and later into Czech. I made public mention of the appearance of *We* in translation several times (in my bibliographies and autobiographies—see *Vestnik literatury, Literaturnaya Rossiya,* etc.); there were also items about it in Soviet newspapers. Up to now, I have not heard any protests in connection with the appearance of these translations.

3. In 1924 it became clear that, owing to difficulties with the censorship, my novel *We* could not be published in Soviet Russia. In view of this, I declined all offers to publish *We* in Russian

abroad. These offers came from the publisher Grzhebin and, later, from Petropolis (the latest offer came in 1929).

4. In the spring of 1927 fragments of the novel appeared in the Prague journal *Volya Rossii*. I. G. Ehrenburg was comradely enough to inform me of this in a letter from Paris. This was how I first learned about my "act."

5. Soon after that, in the summer of 1927, Ehrenburg wrote at my request to the editors of *Volya Rossii,* demanding in my name that they discontinue publication of fragments from *We.* A similar demand was sent to *Volya Rossii* in my name by another Soviet writer who was then abroad. *Volya Rossii* chose to ignore my demands.

6. From Ehrenburg I learned one more thing: the fragments from *We* published in *Volya Rossii* were supplied with a preface, informing the reader that the novel was being published in translation from Czech into Russian. I have not seen *Volya Rossii* and do not know what came of this translation of a Russian novel from a foreign language back into Russian. But whatever the results, the most modest logic should make it clear that such an operation on a work of art could not take place with the knowledge and consent of the author.

This, then, is my "act." Does it resemble what has been said about it in the press? (Such as the direct assertion, for example, in the *Leningrad pravda* where I read several days ago [September 22, 1929] that "Yevg. Zamyatin has given *Volya Rossii* carte blanche for the publication of his novel *We.*"

The literary campaign against me was launched by an article by Volin in number 19 of the *Literary Gazette.* In his article Volin forgot to say that he remembered my novel *We* nine years late (as I have said, the novel was written in 1920).

In his article, Volin also forgot to say that he remembered the publication of fragments from *We* in *Volya Rossii* two and a half years late (these fragments, as I have said, were published in the spring of 1927).

And, finally, Volin forgot to mention the editorial preface of *Volya Rossii,* from which it is clear that the fragments of the novel were printed without my knowledge or consent.

This is Volin's act. Whether his omissions were deliberate or accidental, I do not know, but they resulted in the subsequent presentation of the case in a false light.

The matter was discussed in the executive committee of the Federation of Soviet Writers' Unions. The executive committee's resolution was published in number 21 of the *Literary Gazette*. In paragraph 2 the committee "decisively condemns the acts of the above-named writers," Pilnyak[1] and Zamyatin. And in paragraph 4 of the same resolution, the executive committee recommends that the Leningrad branch of the Federation of Soviet Writers' Unions "make an immediate investigation into the circumstances of the publication abroad of Zamyatin's novel *We*."

Thus, we have first—condemnation, and after that—investigation. No court in the world, I believe, has ever heard of such a procedure. That is the act of the writers' federation.

To go on: the question of the publication of the novel *We* in *Volya Rossii* was taken up at the general meeting of the Moscow branch of the All-Russian Writers' Union, and after that, at the general meeting of the Leningrad branch.

The general meeting in Moscow, without waiting for my explanations, without even expressing a desire to hear them, adopted a resolution condemning my "act." The members of the Moscow branch also took the occasion to express their protest against the contents of the novel, written nine years ago and unknown to the majority of them. In our times nine years are, in essence, nine centuries. I have no intention here to defend a novel that is nine centuries old. I merely think that it would have been far more timely if the Moscow members of the union had protested against the novel *We* six years ago, when it was read at one of the union's literary evenings.

The general meeting of the Leningrad branch of the union was held on September 22, and I know of its results only from a newspaper report (in *Vechern. krasnaya* of September 23). From this report it may be seen that in Leningrad my explanations had already been read and that opinion at the meeting was divided. A number of the writers, after reading my explanations, considered the incident closed. Nevertheless, the majority found it more prudent to condemn my "act."

Such is the act of the All-Russian Writers' Union. And from this act I draw my own conclusion: I find it impossible to belong

---

[1] Pilnyak and Zamyatin were among the first victims of the RAPP when it became virtual dictator of the Soviet literary scene in the late 1920s. Pilnyak recanted of his "sins"; Zamyatin refused to submit.

to a literary organization which, even if only indirectly, takes part in the persecution of a fellow member, and I hereby announce my resignation from the All-Russian Writers' Union.

Yevg. Zamyatin

Moscow
24 September 1929

LETTER TO STALIN

DEAR YOSIF VISSARIONOVICH,

The author of the present letter, condemned to the highest penalty, appeals to you with a request to change this penalty to another.

My name is probably known to you. To me as a writer, being deprived of the opportunity to write is nothing less than a death sentence. Yet the situation that has come about is such that I cannot continue my work, because no creative activity is possible in an atmosphere of systematic persecution that increases in intensity from year to year.

I have no intention of presenting myself as a picture of injured innocence. I know that among the works I wrote during the first three or four years after the Revolution there were some that might provide a pretext for attacks. I know that I have a highly inconvenient habit of speaking what I consider to be the truth rather than saying what may be expedient at the moment. Specifically, I have never concealed my attitude toward literary servility, fawning, and chameleon changes of color: I have felt—and I still feel—that this is equally degrading both to the writer and to the Revolution. I raised this problem in one of my articles (published in the journal *Dom iskusstv,* no. 1, 1920[1]) in a form that many people found to be sharp and offensive, and this served

---

"Letter to Stalin" is reprinted from *The Dragon: Fifteen Stories by Yevgeny Zamyatin* (translated by Mirra Ginsburg), by permission of the publisher. © copyright, 1966, 1967, by Random House, Inc.

[1] The reference is to "I Am Afraid" published in *Dom iskusstv* no. 1, which bore the year 1920 on its cover, but appeared in Jan. 1921.

as a signal at the time for the launching of a newspaper and magazine campaign against me.

This campaign has continued, on different pretexts, to this day, and it has finally resulted in a situation that I would describe as a sort of fetishism. Just as the Christians created the devil as a convenient personification of all evil, so the critics have transformed me into the devil of Soviet literature. Spitting at the devil is regarded as a good deed, and everyone spat to the best of his ability. In each of my published works, these critics have inevitably discovered some diabolical intent. To seek it out, they have even gone to the length of investing me with prophetic gifts: thus, in one of my tales ("God"), published in the journal *Letopis* in 1916, one critic has managed to find "a travesty of the revolution in connection with the transition to the NEP; in the story, "The Healing of the Novice Erasmus," written in 1920, another critic (Mashbits-Verov) has discerned "a parable about leaders who had grown wiser after the NEP." Regardless of the content of the given work, the very fact of my signature has become a sufficient reason for declaring the work criminal. Last March, the Leningrad *Oblit* [Regional Literary Office] took steps to eliminate any remaining doubts of this. I had edited Sheridan's comedy *The School for Scandal* and written an article about his life and work for the Academy Publishing House. Needless to say, there was nothing of a scandalous nature that I said or could have said in this article. Nevertheless, the *Oblit* not only banned the article, but even forbade the publisher to mention my name as editor of the translation. It was only after I complained to Moscow, and after the *Glavlit* [Chief Literary Office] had evidently suggested that such naïvely overt actions are, after all, inadmissible, that permission was granted to publish the article and even my criminal name.

I have cited this fact because it shows the attitude toward me in a completely exposed, so to speak, chemically pure form. Of a long array of similar facts, I shall mention only one more, involving not a chance article, but a full-length play that I have worked on for almost three years. I felt confident that this play —the tragedy *Attila*—would finally silence those who were intent on turning me into some sort of an obscurantist. I seemed to have every reason for such confidence. My play had been read at a meeting of the Artistic Council of the Leningrad Bolshoi Dra-

matic Theater. Among those present at this meeting were representatives of eighteen Leningrad factories. Here are excerpts
from their comments (taken from the minutes of the meeting of
May 15, 1928).

The representative of the Volodarsky Plant said: "This is a
play by a contemporary author, treating the subject of the class
struggle in ancient times, which was analogous to that of our
own era. . . . Ideologically, the play is quite acceptable. . . . It
creates a strong impression and eliminates the reproach that contemporary playwrights do not produce good plays."

The representative of the Lenin Factory noted the revolutionary character of the play and said that "in its artistic level, the
play reminds us of Shakespeare's works. . . . It is tragic, full of
action, and will capture the viewer's attention."

The representative of the Hydro-Mechanical Plant found
"every moment in the play strong and absorbing," and recom-
mended its opening on the theater's anniversary.

Let us say that the comrade workers overdid it in regard to
Shakespeare. Nevertheless, Maxim Gorky has written that he
considers the play "highly valuable both in a literary and social
sense," and that "its heroic tone and heroic plot are most useful
for our time." The play was accepted for production by the theater; it was passed by *Glavrepertkom* [Chief Repertory Com-
mittee]; and after that— Was it shown to the audience of workers who had rated it so highly? No. After that, the play, already
half-rehearsed by the theater, already announced in posters, was
banned at the insistence of the Leningrad *Oblit.*

The death of my tragedy *Attila* was a genuine tragedy to me.
It made entirely clear to me the futility of any attempt to alter
my situation, especially in view of the well-known affair involving my novel *We* and Pilnyak's *Mahogany,* which followed soon
after. Of course, any falsification is permissible in fighting the
devil. And so the novel, written nine years earlier, in 1920, was
set side by side with *Mahogany* and treated as my latest, newest
work. The manhunt organized at the time was unprecedented
in Soviet literature and even drew notice in the foreign press.
Everything possible was done to close to me all avenues for further work. I became an object of fear to my former friends, publishing houses and theaters. My books were banned from the
libraries. My play *The Flea,* presented with invariable success

by the Second Studio of the Moscow Art Theater for four seasons, was withdrawn from the repertory. The publication of my collected works by the Federatsiya Publishing House was halted. Every publishing house which attempted to issue my works was immediately placed under fire; this happened to Federatsiya, Zemlya i Fabrika, and particularly to the Publishing House of Leningrad Writers. The latter took the risk of retaining me on its editorial board for another year and ventured to make use of my literary experience by entrusting me with the stylistic editing of works by young writers, including Communists. Last spring, the Leningrad branch of the RAPP succeeded in forcing me off the board and putting an end to this work. The *Literary Gazette* triumphantly announced this accomplishment, adding quite unequivocally: "The publishing house must be preserved, but not for the Zamyatins." The last door to the reader was closed to Zamyatin. The writer's death sentence was pronounced and published.

In the Soviet criminal code, the penalty second to death is deportation of the criminal from the country. If I am in truth a criminal deserving punishment, I nevertheless do not think that I merit so grave a penalty as literary death. I therefore ask that this sentence be changed to deportation from the USSR and that my wife be allowed to accompany me. If, however, I am not a criminal, I beg to be permitted to go abroad with my wife temporarily, for at least one year, with the right to return as soon as it becomes possible in our country to serve great ideas in literature without cringing before little men, as soon as there is at least a partial change in the prevailing view concerning the role of the literary artist. And I am confident that this time is near, for the creation of the material base will inevitably be followed by the need to build the superstructure—an art and a literature truly worthy of the Revolution.

I know that life abroad will be extremely difficult for me, as I cannot become a part of the reactionary camp there; this is sufficiently attested by my past (membership in the Russian Social Democratic [Bolshevik] party in tsarist days, imprisonment, two deportations, trial in wartime for an antimilitarist novella). I know that, while I have been proclaimed a right-winger here because of my habit of writing according to my conscience rather than according to command, I shall sooner or later probably be declared a Bolshevik for the same reason abroad. But even under the most difficult conditions there, I shall not be condemned to silence; I shall be able to write and to publish, even, if need be, in a language other than Russian. If circumstances should make it impossible (temporarily, I hope) for me to be a Russian writer, perhaps I shall be able, like the Pole Joseph Conrad, to become for a time an English writer, especially since I have already written about England in Russian (the satirical novella *The Islanders* and others), and since it is not much more difficult for me to write in English than it is in Russian. Ilya Ehrenburg, while remaining a Soviet writer, has long been working chiefly for European literature—for translation into foreign languages. Why, then, should I not be permitted to do what Ehrenburg has been permitted to do? And here I may mention yet another name— that of Boris Pilnyak. He has shared the role of devil with me in full measure; he has been the major target of the critics; yet he has been allowed to go abroad to take a rest from this persecution. Why should I not be granted what has been granted to Pilnyak?

I might have tried to motivate my request for permission to go abroad by other reasons as well—more usual, though equally valid. To free myself of an old chronic illness (colitis), I have to go abroad for a cure; my personal presence is needed abroad to help stage two of my plays, translated into English and Italian (*The Flea* and *The Society of Honorary Bell Ringers,* already produced in Soviet theaters); moreover, the planned production of these plays will make it possible for me not to burden the People's Commissariat of Finances with the request for foreign exchange. All these motives exist. But I do not wish to conceal that the basic reason for my request for permission to go abroad with my wife is my hopeless position here as a writer, the death sentence that has been pronounced upon me as a writer here at home.

The extraordinary consideration which you have given other writers who appealed to you leads me to hope that my request will also be granted.

June 1931

SOURCES

Part 1

"Autobiography"—*Vestnik literatury*, nos. 2/3 (1922).

"Autobiography"—*Pisateli*, ed. V. Lidin (Moscow: Sovremennye Problemy, 1926).

"Autobiography"—*Uyezdnoye* (Moscow: Federatsiya, 1929).

Part 2

"Sirin"—*Yezhemesyachny zhurnal*, no. 4 (April 1914).

"Scythians?"—"Skify li?" *Mysl*, no. 1 (Petrograd: Revolutsion-naya Mysl, 1918). Signed with the pseudonym Mikh. Platonov.

"Contemporary Russian Literature"—"Sovremennaya russkaya literatura," a public lecture delivered 8 September 1918 at the People's University in Lebedyan. The Russian text first appeared in *Grani*, no. 32 (October–December 1956), published by Posev Verlag, Frankfurt am Main.

"Tomorrow"—"Zavtra," in *Litsa* (New York: Chekhov Publishing House, 1955). Originally appeared in the collection *V zashchitu cheloveka* (Petrograd, 1919).

"I Am Afraid"—"Ya boyus," in *Litsa*. Originally published in *Dom iskusstv*, no. 1 (1921).

"Paradise"—"Rai," *Dom iskusstv*, no. 2 (1921). Signed Mikh. Platonov.

"Gryadushchaya Rossiya"—Dom iskusstv, no. 2 (1921). Signed Mikh. Platonov.

310

"The Serapion Brethren"—"Serapionovy bratya," *Literaturnye zapiski*, no. 1 (May 1922).

"On Synthetism"—"O sintetizme," in *Litsa*. Originally published in *Portrety*, by Yury Annenkov (Petrograd: Petropolis, 1922).

"The New Russian Prose"—"Novaya russkaya proza," in *Litsa*. Originally published in *Russkoye iskusstvo*, nos. 2/3 (1923).

"On Literature, Revolution, Entropy, and Other Matters"—"O literature, revolutsii, entropii, i prochem," in *Litsa*. Originally published in *Pisateli ob iskusstve i o sebe* (Moscow: Krug, 1924).

"The Day and the Age"—"O segodnyashnem i sovremennom," in *Litsa*. Originally published in *Russky sovremennik*, no. 2 (1924).

"The Goal"—"Tsel," in *Litsa*. Date of writing unknown, probably 1926.

"A Piece for an Anthology on Books"—"Dlya sbornika o knige," in *Litsa*. Written 23 December 1928.

"Moscow-Petersburg"—"Moskva-Peterburg," *Novy zhurnal*, no. 72 (June 1963), published in New York. Written in Paris for a French journal in 1933.

Part 3

"The Psychology of Creative Work"—"Psikhologiya tvorchestva," *Grani*, no. 32 (October–December 1956). Originally prepared as a lecture in the course on the craft of fiction given at the House of the Arts in 1920–21.

"Theme and Plot"—"O syuzhete i fabule," *Novy zhurnal*, no. 75 (March 1964). Originally a lecture (see above).

"On Language"—"O yazyke," *Novy zhurnal*, no. 77 (September 1964). Originally a lecture, as above.

"Backstage"—Appeared untitled in the collection *Kak my pishem* (Leningrad: Izd. Pisateley, 1930). The title "Zakulisy [Backstage]" was given the essay when it was reprinted, somewhat abridged, in *Litsa*.

Part 4

"Alexander Blok"—*Litsa*. Originally published as "Vospominaniya o Bloke," *Russky sovremennik*, no. 3 (1924).

"Fyodor Sologub"—*Litsa*. Originally published as "Belaya Lyubov," in the collection *Sovremennaya literatura* (Leningrad: Mysl, 1925).

"Chekhov"—*Litsa*. Originally a speech given at an evening in memory of Chekhov organized by the Moscow Art Theater in February 1925.

"Meetings with Kustodiev"—"Vstrechi s Kustodievym," in *Litsa*. Originally published in *Novy zhurnal*, no. 26 (1951). Written in 1928.

"Andrey Bely"—*Litsa*. Written in Paris, 1934.

"Maxim Gorky"—*Litsa*. Written in Paris, 1936.

"H. G. Wells"—*Litsa*. Originally published as *Gerbert Uells* (Petrograd: Epokha, 1922).

"O. Henry"—*Litsa*. Originally published as a preface to O. Genri, *Rasskazy* (Petrograd: Vsemirnaya Literatura, 1923).

"Anatole France"—*Litsa*. Originally published in *Sovremenny zapad*, no. 2 (1924).

Part 5

"Letter of Resignation from the Writers' Union"—"Pismo v redaktsiyu," *Literaturnaya gazeta*, no. 25 (7 October 1929).

"Letter to Stalin"—"Pismo Stalinu," in *Litsa*. Written June 1931.

INDEX